Benjamin Bennet

Discourses on the credibility of the Scriptures

In Which the Truth, Inspiration, and Usefulness of the Scriptures are Asserted and

Proved

Benjamin Bennet

Discourses on the credibility of the Scriptures
In Which the Truth, Inspiration, and Usefulness of the Scriptures are Asserted and Proved

ISBN/EAN: 9783337184391

Printed in Europe, USA, Canada, Australia, Japan

Cover: Foto ©Lupo / pixelio.de

More available books at **www.hansebooks.com**

CREDIBILITY

OF THE

CRIPTURES:

WHICH THE TRUTH, INSPIRATION, AND
USEFULNESS OF THE SCRIPTURES
ARE ASSERTED AND
PROVED.

By the late Reverend BENJAMIN BENNET. .

NEW-BRUNSWICK:
RINTED BY ABRAHAM BLAUVELT. 1795.

READER.

SOLOMON *observes that many are the devices of a man's heart, but the counsel of the Lord, that shall stand. Many have been the devices of men's hearts and heads, against christianity. From its youth up have they fought against it; but it is the counsel of the Lord, and therefore has hitherto stood, and if there be any truth in the divine promises, it will forever maintain its ground. This is an age when the love and practice of true religion is greatly on the decline, when iniquity abounds, and when infidelity raises her infernal head, and refuses to be ashamed. There are many who boldly profess their disbelief of a divine revelation, and employ all their wit and ingenuity in order to exhibit the most important doctrines of our holy religion in a ridiculous point of view. Persons of such depraved minds, examine the Scriptures as it were with a microscope, which confines them to some single point, but does not enable them to contemplate the beauty and consistency of the whole, or to perceive the relation which each part has to another. Nay, some of our modern infidels are so daring and presumptuous* as to condemn the whole *system* of divine revelation as a cunningly devised *foble*, declaring at the same time, that the Bible is a book with which they are very little acquainted. But every good man can say from his own experience, that the more he examines the Scriptures, with an humble, an honest, and unprejudiced mind, and with a sincere desire to attain the knowledge of the truth, the more he will admire them. For they are like those persons whom an intimate acquaintance endears more and more, whatever prejudices we might at first sight have conceived against them. He will find that they afford as much light as our present condition stands in need of, and much more than we could possibly attain, by the exercise of our unassisted faculties. The Bible is a book which takes in a vast extent of time. It begins with the creation of the world, and the formation of man, and ends in eternity, with the last judgment and the consummation of all things. And yet, through all this variety of dispensations there is one chain, and regular series of well connected events. And is it not highly proper, that christians should be firmly established in the faith of these important truths, and be able to give a good reason for the hope that is in them: especially at a period when the emissaries of Satan are employing every engine to undermine the grounds of our holy religion. But from what source does infidelity spring? The answer is obvious; it proceeds from the depravity of the human heart. When our hearts are deceitful, when our lives are immoral, we wish to banish from our minds the idea of the righteous judge of all the earth, who will render unto every one according to his works. And it is not very difficult for us to persuade ourselves into the belief of what we earnestly wish to be true. And it has been frequently observed, that the more vicious the age, the more has infidelity gained ground. This was the case in ancient Greece and Rome, when the senseless system of Epicurus was patronised by many of much greater and more eminent abilities, than any that now espouse infidelity. This was also the case in Judea, when the sect of the Sadducees prevailed. But perhaps some may be ready to say, that the great number of deistical books, which have been lately written in this country, and also imported from Europe, has occasioned the great degeneracy of the present age. But the truth is, it is the almost total depravity of sentiment in matters of religion, to which bad writers will be always ready to accommodate themselves, which has occasioned those infidel writings, which are so carefully circulated and so eagerly read by those who deny the Lord Jesus Christ. And is it not high time for the friends of Jesus to exert themselves in his service, and to employ every mean in their power, for the support of his religion. And is not this the time, when men of piety, and learning, and abilities, ought to employ their talents, in the defence of that gospel, upon which our everlasting all depends. Many publications have appeared in the present age, which seem to be very properly calculated to answer this purpose. Some of these, however valuable in themselves are but little known. This is the case with the volume which is now offered to the public, and it is hoped that it will be peculiarly seasonable at this time, when our modern deists are so exceedingly zealous in supporting and propagating the unhappy cause they have the misfortune to espouse. If these sermons are read with an unbiassed mind, I doubt not but they will be read with great advantage, which will certainly be the most effectual way of praising and recommending them. The Almighty who is wonderful in counsel, and excellent in working, can easily bring good out of evil. We seem to be sunk into a fatal indolence and insensibility with regard to the great objects of religion, and some signal judgments, some extraordinary manifestations of the divine displeasure, perhaps may be necessary, to purge the inhabitants of this country, of their dross, and to rouse us to a serious attention to religion, as when the sky is full of noxious and pestilential vapours, some violent hurricane, some dreadful bursts of thunder, are necessary to disperse them, to clear the infected air, and to restore it to its former serenity. That these awful calamities may be prevented, may the Lord Jesus Christ, the great king and head of the church, by his blessed spirit, render these discourses effectual for rebuke, for correction, and for instruction in righteousness.

The insufficiency of Natural Light,

AND

The necessity of a Supernatural Revelation.

2 TIM. iii. 16.

All scripture is given by inspiration of God, and is profitable for doctrine, for reproof, for correction, for instruction in righteousness.

THERE has been a mighty controversy in the world about fundamentals in religion, points absolutely necessary to be believed by all christians; how many such there are, and which they are. Now without entering into that debate, I take it for granted the subject before us, (the divine original of the Bible) must be reckoned in the number of fundamentals. It is certainly a thing of the last importance to be well instructed in this matter. I have therefore thought fit to give you a few discourses upon the inspiration, and great usefulness of the scriptures. I have heretofore treated upon this subject; but finding that several of you desire a fuller account of these things, I have determined to resume the point, and en- the plan and scheme; that I may take in the

the establishing and vindicating the authority of the Bible: which I reckon the more seasonable in regard of the peculiar opposition it meets with at this time. To this purpose, I shall consider the words I have read, *All scripture is given by inspiration of God, and is profitable for doctrine, for reproof, for correction, for instruction in righteousness.* Where we have two things observable.

1. We have here asserted the divine original and authority of the scriptures. *All scripture is given by inspiration of God.* That the apostle refers immediately to the scriptures of the *Old Testament* cannot be questioned. For, not to say the *New Testament* was not (all of it) then written, he speaks of the scriptures that *Timothy* had been educated in the knowledge of, *from a child thou hast known the holy scriptures*, which could be no other than the scriptures of the *Old Testament.* But whereas he affirms, that *all scriptures were given by inspiration of God*; and it is probable several books of the *New Testament* might then be written, these must be included in the general expression. Besides, when he mentions *Timothy's* knowledge of the holy scriptures, and takes notice of their sufficiency *to make wise to salvation*, he adds, *through faith in Christ Jesus*; which seems to lead us to the *gospel*, where we have the fullest and clearest revelation of him.

And indeed, whatever evidence the *Jews* had of their canons being divine and given by inspiration, we have the same, and greater, for the divinity of ours. If the scriptures of the *Old Testament* were *by inspiration of God*, those of the *New Testament* are certainly no less so; and consequently, we may retain the apostle's general term, including the whole canon or all the books of the Old and New Testament, and say, that *all Scripture is given by inspiration of God.*

2. We have the usefulness of these inspired writings asserted here. They *are profitable*, says the text, *for doctrine, for reproof, for correction, for instruction in righteousness*. The meaning of these several phrases I shall enquire into afterwards, and shew how the scripture is useful for all these purposes.

In the mean while, two propositions very naturally offer themselves from hence; which I shall lay down as the foundation of what I design upon this subject, viz.

(1.) That *all scripture*, or all the writings of the Old and New Testament, *were given by inspiration of God*. And

(2.) That the scriptures, or the several books and parts of the *Bible*, are of great use and service to the church. Particularly, they *are profitable for doctrine, for reproof, for correction, for instruction in righteousness*.

I shall begin with the first of these, namely, that the scriptures, all the books of the *Old* and *New Testament, were given by inspiration of God*. This is a point of great consequence, among the fundamentals of the christian religion, as I said before; and therefore I shall now take occasion to consider it pretty fully. To most of you, I doubt not, what will be said will be wholly new, and others may find advantage in a review of the subject, as it tends to refresh their memories, confirm their faith, and improve their joy.

In speaking to this observation, I shall, (1.) give some account of the inspiration of the holy scriptures. (2.) Shew how it must be understood, that *all scripture is given by inspiration of God*. And then, (3.) prove the divine inspiration of the scriptures, or, as we commonly express it, that the Bible or scriptures of the *Old* and *New Testament*, are the word of God.

B

DISCOURSE I.

I. I shall give some short account of the inspiration of the holy scriptures: the subject is too *copious*, and it may be too *curious*, to be handled largely here, and is fitter for the *press* than the *pulpit*. However, I shall mention a few particulars for explaining it, as far as such a discourse will allow.

1. I suppose divine revelation lay in some extraordinary, immediate, sensible intercourse that the inspiring spirit, from whence the afflatus or inspiration proceeded, had with the minds of those that were inspired: in making impression or motion on the imagination, and thereby conveying such and such things to the mind of the person concerned. When we converse with one another by words, a vibration or peculiar kind of motion is made in the air, which strikes the ear of the person, and occasions a motion in the brain, whereby thoughts and ideas are excited, or our thoughts transmitted to the mind of him we speak to: now when God inspires any he makes such impressions upon, or motions in the brain immediately, and so transmits his mind and will to the person he inspires. Indeed this is not easily apprehended by us; nor is it easy to apprehend how my speaking to you, conveys such or such ideas to your minds. But as we are sure this is possible and fact, the other certainly may be allowed equally possible.

2. Those that were inspired knew as certainly that they were so and that it was from God that they received the impressions, as you know that I am now speaking to you. I grant this is not easy to be conceived or explained by others, (as I have already said.) But those concerned in it had such a sensible assurance that it was God who spake to them, as left them free from all suspicion of imposture. This is manifest in the case of *Abraham*. He heard a voice from Heaven, which bid him *take his son, his only son, whom he loved, and get him into*

the land of Moriah *and there offer him up for a burnt-offering.* A command so surprising and startling, in regard to the matter of it, that had he not had the utmost assurance it was from God, he would have abhorred the motion. There was something in the manner of the inspiration, that carried its own evidence along with it.

3. The inspired were not only assured themselves of their own inspiration, but were enabled to give satisfaction to others concerning that matter. They felt, and certainly knew, they were inspired; and could evidence it to others. How the ancient prophets proved their commission, authority and inspiration, I must not now enquire; only I would hint in short, that there were three ways, among others, of proving this, viz. by working of miracles, by foretelling things to come, things that came to pass afterwards, and by the testimony of known allowed prophets. When God sent any to make a new revelation, they did not expect men should believe them upon the authority of their own mere word, but they produced their credentials, *the works they did testified concerning* them, as Christ speaks in his own case. Thus we read that God *bore Witness* to the apostles *with signs, wonders and diverse miracles, and gifts of the Holy Ghost.* This testimony often attended the doctrine of inspired persons, and always it may be, when they delivered a new doctrine to the world. In other cases, when they were only sent to inculcate a doctrine already revealed, and call men to the observation of a known law, miracles or predictions might not be necessary. But then such persons had the testimony of known and approved prophets; were received by the school of the prophets, or by some or other of the prophetic character, whose authority had been sufficiently sealed from heaven. And then,

4. The inspiring spirit did not act and influence all that were inspired in one and the same manner, but variously. This the apostle hints at *Heb.* i. 1. *God who at sundry times and in diverse manners spake in times past unto the fathers by the prophets, hath in these last days spoken unto us by his son.* He spake by the prophets in *diverse manners.* Some had revelations made to them by vision in the day, others by dreams in the night: some by a voice formed in the air, (called a voice from heaven) and others by a more immediate secret suggestion. In short, God sometimes spake to their outward senses when awake, and sometimes to their more inward senses, as I may say, in dreams and extacies, the mind being still informed concerning the meaning of such representations in both cases. Again,

5. As the spirit communicated himself to them in different ways, so there was a difference in the kind or degree of inspiration. And here to pass over other less material distinctions, I shall take notice of that common and well known one, into an inspiration of suggestion, and an inspiration of direction.

There was an inspiration of suggestion; which was, when the whole matter that this or that inspired person was to publish to the world, whether by word or writing, was revealed to him *de Novo,* and entirely communicated to him from above. Many of the writers of the Holy Scripture had such an inspiration as I now refer to, an inspiration of suggestion. The ancient prophets had it in such of their prophecies as contained predictions concerning the future state of the church; as the coming of the Messiah, his life, death, and the like. They had it also in their prophecies concerning the rise and fall of the four monarchies, and in foretelling many other events relating to the church and the world; and no doubt in describing many past events. So Moses, in giving the history of the creation, may well be supposed to have had the whole matter, the entire process of that great work laid before him, and communicated to him, by the spirit of God. This was also the case of the *New Testament* writers in many instances; as in their prophecies concerning the destruction of *Jerusalem*, the spreading the gospel, &c. and it is certain *John* must have this kind of inspiration in delivering his visions mentioned in the *Revelations*. He paints there a scene of things which extends through every age of the church, to the end of the world; which he could not have done without that sort of inspiration I am speaking of, or with any less degree of it. The apostles had a like degree of inspiration in publishing to the world such things as are termed *mysteries*; as the calling of the *Gentiles*, Eph. iii. 2, 3, 4, 5; the conversion and calling of the *Jews* into the christian church, Rom. xi. 25, 26. The resurrection of the body, 1 Cor. xv. These and the like were mysteries, things they could have no notion of, till God revealed or suggested them to them by his spirit. And I reckon they had the same inspiration in expounding many passages of the *Old Testament*, and accommodating them to the state of things under the gospel, applying them to this or that event. In these, and many other instances, the sacred writers had the inspiration of suggestion, the matter they delivered and published they had wholly and immediately from the spirit of God.

But then there was another kind, a lower degree of inspiration, namely, that of direction. And this I suppose all the sacred writers had in several cases. As for instance, when the evangelists relate that *Judas* betrayed his master, and that *Peter* denied him, they need not herein be inspired in the former sense, need not have these points of history suggested to them, as if they had known nothing of the matter, which observation may be applied to most of the other historical narrations contained in the scriptures. Where the penmen knew the things they recorded, it is reasonable to conclude they had no more than the inspiration of direction : the spirit of God first stirring them up to write, directing them to make a fit choice what to write, and what not to write ; and then guiding them in the performance. Further,

6. All the penmen of the holy Scripture had that degree of inspiration, that divine *afflatus* or assistance that effectually secured them from errors and mistakes. Some had the higher measures thereof, the whole matter, and it may be the very words and syllables suggested to them, while others had only direction and conduct in delivering what they were intrusted with. Yet all of them were infallible, they delivered nothing but what is true, and what may be depended upon as true. I might add,

7. That the holy spirit when he inspired the persons who penned the Scriptures, not only left them possessed of their natural faculties, but to the free exercise and use of them. They were not like a trumpet that a man speaks through, nor like the *Pagan Oracles*, mere passive instruments in delivering their messages and doctrines. But they had their reason, memory, understanding, and all their rational powers, which they made use of and employed : And in many instances were even allowed to indulge their own fancies and phrases.

Thus I have briefly touched and explained the inspiration of the Bible ; in the next place.

II. I am to hint how it must be understood, that *all Scripture is given by inspiration of God*. For so says the text, and this is what we are taught to believe that the whole Bible is of divine original,

DISCOURSE I.

the word of God. The question is, How we must understand this? Now certainly it is not meant, that God himself spake immediately all the things contained in the Scripture; sometimes indeed he is introduced and represented as speaking immediately, as to *Job* out of a whirlwind, *Job* xxxviii. 1. and at the giving of the law on *Mount Sinai, Exod.* xx. Though some passages in the *New Testament* make it probable, that he used the ministry of angels on that occasion, particularly, *Heb.* ii. 2. *If the word spoken by angels, was stedfast, &c.* The matter seems to have been thus; the *Schechinah* appearing on the *Mount* with the usual guard of attending angels, made use of their ministry in delivering the law to the people of *Israel*.

Nor must we suppose that all those who are brought in speaking in the Scripture, speak from God. The *Old Testament* contains a great many histories of the words and actions of bad men. The book of *Job* relates the words of the Devil himself, and the mistaken speeches of *Job's* friends. The evangelists give you the words of the *Scribes, Pharisees*, and other avowed enemies of Christ and his gospel: as likewise doth *Luke* in his history of the acts of the apostles.

So that when the apostle here says, *All Scripture is given by inspiration of God,* we are to take it thus, that all the writers of the sacred Scripture were by the spirit of God infallibly assisted to write those things that are contained in the Bible for the use of the church. In some things they had an inspiration in the fullest, highest sense, receiving their doctrine wholly from God. In other things they had only infallible conduct. So that all contained in the Bible is either a divine doctrine, or a true history. There are several wicked speeches of bad men, several mistaken speeches of good men, there recorded. But the history is faithful and true.

Nothing is here faid to be done, which was not done; nothing is here feigned; nothing falfely reprefented. The whole of it, as it is written for our ufe, fo it is one way or other *profitable for doctrine, for reproof, for correction for inftruction in righteoufnefs.* But to infift no longer on this fubject, I now proceed to the main thing intended, which is,

III. To prove the divine authority of the Scriptures; that *all Scripture is given by infpiration of God,* or that the whole canon thereof is of divine original, the Bible the word of God. Here I fhall,

1. Premife fome particulars to prepare my way for the proof of the point.

2. Offer arguments for that purpofe. And,

3. Anfwer the moft material objections aga'nft the divine authority of the Scriptures.

I. I fhall premife fome particulars to prepare my way for what I intend to fuggeft for the proof of the point. And

1. Let me premife that the queftion, Whether the Scripture be the word of God? is not to be taken for granted, nor the refolution of it expected from the immediate teftimony of the holy fpirit. But it is capable of folid evidence, and may and ought to be fubmitted to a rational enquiry and trial.

It is not to be taken for granted as a firft principle. Such principles there are (firft principles we call them), generally allowed and received: feif-evident maxims agreeable to the reafon of mankind; and thefe are not to be difputed and proved; but are the mediums by which we prove other things. But that the Scripture is the word of God, is not a principle of this kind. Indeed among chriftians it is a principle allowed and received on all fides. But when we have to do with unbelievers, or when we are eftablifhing the ground and foundation of our faith, we propose it to examination. And I am satisfied we may stand the trial here, and submit it to the most critical enquiry that will proceed without prejudice and partiality. In short, this proposition, that our Bible is an inspired book, is not to be believed without rational evidence, not to be admitted purely because others have told us so, because it is received in the country where we live, or because it pretends to be a revelation from God : for as much may be said of the *Alcoran*. But it is to be proved ; and upon evidence to be received and believed. The *Christian* pretends his *Bible* is a revelation from heaven, the *Mussulman*, or disciple of *Mahomet*, pretends his *Alcoran* is so. Now, I say, in order to determine that question, reasons are to be offered on both sides ; and if the *Mahometan* can produce better reasons in behalf of the *Alcoran*, than can be produced in behalf of our Bible, the *Alcoran* ought to be preferred.

Nor must we depend on the testimony of the spirit for the resolution of this question, Whether the Scriptures be the word of God. Indeed the divine veracity, or authority of God speaking in his word, is the reason into which our faith is ultimately resolved. *Whatsoever God says, is true ;* this is a first principle and maxim. I therefore believe all things contained in the Scripture, and what God has revealed, because God is true, and cannot deceive me ; here the faith of a christian rests. But if it be asked, How do I know that God has spoke these things, or that the Bible is a revelation from God ? I must here seek for rational evidence (as I said before) ; and not rely purely on God's testimony, as it is recorded in the word, or expect an immediate testimony from the spirit, a secret whisper, an inward suggestion, that the

C

Scripture is the word of God. For this is to resolve faith into private inspiration, and make one inspiration a reason of receiving another, which opens the way to dangerous delusion.

2. Though the Scripture is to be proved by rational arguments, and received upon proper evidence; yet the testimony of God's spirit, rightly understood, is of great use and necessity to us, in order to the discerning the evidence of Scripture, and resting in it as a divine revelation. By the testimony of the spirit, I do not mean a particular inspiration to this or that particular person, but the inlightening sanctifying work of the holy spirit in the hearts of believers. And concerning this, let me note two or three things. As, that the testimony of the spirit doth not produce the evidence of the divinity of the Scriptures, but helps us to discern it. It doth not give, but show the evidence, and prepares us to receive it. Thus when God opened the heart of *Lydia*, that she attended to the apostle, *Acts* xvi. 14. she became better disposed to inquire into and receive the christian revelation, and to take in the evidence of the truth of it. God writes his law in the hearts of believers, impresses their minds with it, sanctifies them by his word, produces affections and inward frames agreeable thereto; and hereby he gives testimony to his word in their hearts. *The entrance of thy word giveth light,* faith the *Psalmist,* Psal. xix. That *it converts the soul, maketh wise the simple,* &c. He intimates that this was the ground and reason of that high value that he and other devout persons had for it. *Thy testimonies are more to be desired than gold, yea, than much fine gold: sweeter also than the honey, and the honey-comb,* Psal. xix. 10. So Psal. cxix. 140. *Thy word is very pure, therefore thy servant loveth it.* Now when good men find the great usefulness and excellency of the word of

God, that it converts, quickens, conducts, comforts them; when they find an inward correspondence with it, that it describes their various cases, conflicts and frames, affords relief and consolation in all their difficulties, is their light, their monitor and comforter; as they cannot but love it, so they are better prepared to believe it on this account. And this, I reckon is that testimony of God's spirit, which helps believers to receive the word of God, *as it is indeed the word of God*. It has taken fast hold of them, they feel the power of the word, and taste its consolation. God has given them his spirit, and they know of the doctrine that it is of God. But it must be considered, this is not the evidence of Scripture; but a help to receive that evidence, it removes prejudices, makes us attentive, recommends the Scripture to the mind; but it doth not exclude other reasons of believing, though it enforces them.

Further, I would note, that this testimony of the spirit of God did (it is likely) generally attend the preaching of the gospel in the first ages of christianity, together with miracles, and other extraordinary works. There was some extraordinary supernatural assistance indeed accompanying the ministry of the word. Thus *Peter's* sermon we read converted three thousand at once, *Acts* ii. 41. And besides the numerous and speedy conversions remarkable at that time, the christian religion appeared to have an uncommon wonderful efficacy and power among those that recieved it. Hence, Lactantius says, " Shew me a person that is wrath-
" ful and furious, by a few words of the gospel,
" I will render him as meek as a lamb; shew me
" a person that is intemperate, unclean, the christi-
" an religion shall render him sober and chaste."
And the like he says in other instances. It pleased God at the first planting of the gospel, and

in order to it, to arm his word with power. There was a glorious effusion of the divine spirit, which subdued the hearts of men to the belief and obedience of the Scriptures, and wrought a general reformation, even to the aftonishment of the world. Now where any experienced this divine energy of the spirit, going along with the word and bearing testimony to it, they could never question the doctrine itself. They found *the word of God quick and powerful*, and consequently, could not but believe it was the word of God.

I might add, the same testimony in one or other degree of it, is still necessary to the saving belief of the Scriptures. We may give a general assent to this proposition, that the Scripture is the word of God; may be convinced by clear rational arguments, that it is so. But we shall not believe it, so as to mind it, relish it, delight in it, and comport with the design of it, (without which we do not indeed believe it, and receive it as a revelation from God) we shall not do this, I say, without the spirit influences on our minds, enlightening the eyes, opening the heart, removing prejudices, and casting down lofty imaginations.

Though still let me repeat it, that whatsoever the spirit of God doth here, signifies not so much to give evidence, as to discover evidence. His testimony doth not prove the Scripture to be the word of God, but helps us to see the proof of it. It may indeed tend to satisfy us in particular concerning the proof; but the proof is distinct from the testimony; at least, this testimony is but one part of the proof, and cannot be pleaded with others, of whatever use it may be privately to ourselves. But these things I know require a great deal more discourse to explain them, and set them in a full light, than at present I have room for. To proceed to another proposition.

3. The revelation contained in the Scripture, is not inconfiftent with, or oppofite to natural religion, (or the dictates of right reafon and natural light;) nor, properly fpeaking, diftinct from it, but includes it, and perfects it. I reckon the firft law or covenant innocent man was under, was made known in nature, the will of God concerning duty and rewards was vifibly therein. Man in his integrity could not but difcern his obligations to his maker, not to fay, that he had the whole law and all his duty written upon his heart, and found a propenfity and inclination thereto. There was no darknefs in his mind, or depravity in his affections, but it was natural for him to love God, to converfe with, and obey him in every inftance; and likewife a principle of love, juftice, and benignity to his neighbor was implanted in him. This, which may be called, the law of nature, was the firft law, antecedent to any fupernatural revelation. This was the covenant of innocency, or works revealed in nature; and I reckon that the pofitive command not to eat of the tree of knowledge of good and evil, *Gen.* ii. 17. was not the covenant itfelf, or firft law, but added as a teft and trial of man's obedience, and as a mark of God's fovereignty.

Now this law, founded on the nature of things, and on the relation man ftands in to God, his creator, preferver, and fovereign, is immutable, cannot be changed, and never ceafes. Accordingly it runs through every difpenfation of religion. The patriarchs and *Jews* were under the obligation of it. And it ftill remains as a branch of the gofpel-difpenfation. It was fummed up in the *Decalogue* given to the *Jews* of old. Chrift makes it in part the fubject of his fermon on the mount, where he illuftrates and comments upon it; and it is explained through all the writings of the *New Teftament*. So that fhould any afk, Whether the *Bible*, or the law of nature, be a revelation from God? The anſwer muſt be, that theſe two are not oppoſed. The *Bible* comprehends all the laws of nature. Whatever is agreeable to reaſon, and that reaſon could diſcover as matter of duty towards God, our neighbor and ourſelves, this the *Bible* takes in and eſtabliſhes. In a word, the *Bible* contains the moſt excellent ſyſtem of morals in the world. There is nothing valuable in all the writings of the philoſophers, but it is to be found in the *Bible;* all the laws of juſtice, charity, meekneſs, gratitude, patience, &c. that they have recommended in their books, are not only ſet in a better light, but more ſtrongly inforced in the *Bible*. Not but that the *Bible* contains a great deal more than this; but I thought fit here to remark, that it contains this; and conſequently, that our modern *deiſts*, that talk ſo much of natural religion, have no reaſon to object againſt the *Bible*, as being defective in that point. If they are for natural religion, they may find it there, and (as I ſhall ſhew by and by) with unſpeakable advantage, compared with what they can learn and attain without the help thereof.

4. Had mankind preſerved their integrity, the light and purity of their minds, I do ſuppoſe, they would have underſtood their duty in the whole compaſs and latitude of it, without any ſupernatural revelation. All the precepts of divine morality, all man's obligations and debts towards God, his neighbor and himſelf, would have laid open to him. He would have ſeen them clearly and diſtinctly, and been convinced of the equity and reaſonableneſs of them without teaching and argument.

Not but that God might, even in that ſtate have given poſitive laws by ſpecial and ſupernatural revelation. He gave one ſuch, you know, to *Adam* in innocency, concerning the tree of knowledge; and you read, *Gen.* iii. 8. that *they heard the voice of* the Lord God, *walking in the garden, in the cool of the day*: intimating, that they had been used to converse with him in a sensible manner, and therefore immediately knew his voice. There would have been a constant intercourse, no question, between God and man, had not man apostatized, and it is probable some occasional revelations, especially with reference to positive duties. But here, I grant, I am talking in the dark, and can only conjecture. But what I chiefly assert, is, that had not man fallen and lost his original light and rectitude, all the duties of natural religion (as we call it) had been obvious and self-evident, and there would have needed no supernatural revelation, either to discover, or inculcate and inforce them. I add,

5. Such is the state of mankind, having apostatized and fallen from God, such the weakness and blindness of his mind, and so general the depravity and corruption of his nature; that a supernatural revelation is now become exceeding necessary. This I might prove, (I think I might call it demonstrate) at large. But that I may not be tedious, I shall satisfy myself with just touching a few heads of arguments. And,

1. Let it be considered, that the law of nature with the rules and maxims of moral good and evil, however certain in themselves and obvious at first, are now become less legible to us. Such is the weakness and darkness of the human mind, so many our prejudices, lusts and passions, that we cannot easily read the law of nature, nor apprehend the demands of it. Some have magnified that representation and description, the great philosopher *Tully* gives us of this matter, *(Tusc. Quest.* lib. iii,) part of which I shall here recite, *If we had come into the world in such circumstances as that we could clearly and distinctly have discerned nature herself, and been able in the course of our lives to have follow-*

ed her true and uncorrupted directions; this alone might have been sufficient, and there would have been little need of teaching and instruction. But now nature has given us only some small sparks of right reason, which we soon extinguish with corrupt opinions and evil practices, that the true light of nature no where appears. As soon as we are brought into the world, immediately we dwell in the midst of all wickedness. And then he goes on to shew the influence that our senses and evil examples have upon us, and concludes, that hereby our very natures are transformed as it were into corrupt sentiments. Now this being so, the voice of nature or of right reason, is not heard without extraordinary attention, and such as the most of mankind are unacquainted with. And indeed what we now call the law of nature, is of so nice a consideration, and requires so much nice abstract reasoning, that none but men of parts, liberal education, and great study, are capable of deducing the doctrines of it from their first principles, and of representing them with proper light and evidence. So that considering the universal depravity of men's minds, and considering the circumstances of the bulk of mankind, it may I think be asserted, that the law and light of nature, would have been a very insufficient rule, and comparatively of little use to us. We that have the *Bible* to direct us, and the labours of learned men, who have lighted their torch at that sun, can talk finely of the law of nature; but without that help, very few, I am persuaded, would have had any tolerable notions of it. Which will appear more evidently, if we consider,

2. That the greatest proficients in study, the most profound philosophers, were at a loss, and at great uncertainty as to some of the most important doctrines in religion. To represent this would require a discourse by itself, and therefore you can

expect only a few hints. They were grossly in the dark as to the foundation of all religion, the being and perfections of God; as appears from their notions of these matters, and particularly from this, that they allowed a plurality of gods, which is in effect to undermine and destroy all true divinity, and really leave no God. They *worshipped creatures*, besides, and instead of *the creator*, as the apostle charges them, *Rom.* i. 25. and *did service to them which by nature are no Gods, Gal.* iv. 8. What a rabble of deities they had brought into the world, and honored with sacrifices, and all sorts of religious rites, I shall not now stand to shew: only take notice, that though some great men among them laughed at these superstitions, and contemned in their hearts the base and vile deities of the vulgar; yet it was a principle allowed by them, and according to which they themselves practised, that all were to comply with the rites established in the country where they lived, and worship the gods according to the law. So that natural religion as taught by the philosophers, and universally established in the heathen world, failed in this fundamental article, the unity of the Godhead, the owning and acknowledging one only living and true God.

Further, they were ignorant of the origin of the world, and maintained opinions on this head utterly inconsistent with religion. It was their common maxim, that nothing could be made out of nothing; and consequently, they held that matter was 'uncreated,' and the world self-existent. Some of them thought the world was not made at all, but from eternity, either with or without a deity, and so was God itself, or with a deity, being co-existent with God, and a sort of necessary emanation from him; which is said to be the opinion of *Aristotle*, and his followers. Others afcribe it to chance, or a fortuitous concourfe of atoms, as the *Epicureans*.

They were equally bewildered in their notions of providence: a numerous fect of the philofophers, the *Epicureans*, denied all providence: others, as *Aristotle*, and his fchool, confined it to heaven, leaving all human affairs without any fuperintendency of God: others acknowledged a general providence, but denied it extended to particular perfons and their concernment. And even the *Stoicks*, the moſt zealous affertors of divine providence, confined it to the more important affairs of mankind. Now it would be eafy to fhew, that fuch a doctrine as this, fuch principles as generally, and almoſt univerfally, obtained among them on this head, tended not only to leffen, but deftroy every thing that deferves the name of religion. For why fhould we love, fear, truſt, pray to, or worfhip a God that concerns not himfelf about us, on whom we do not depend, and who neither doth us good nor evil.

They were equally at a lofs about the *Summum Bonum*, the great end and happinefs of man. They knew not wherein happinefs confifted, and confequently, muft rove in uncertainties, act and live without any particular aim. Some of them placed happinefs in one thing, others in a different; and fo ſtrangely were they divided here, that *Varro* reckoned up no lefs than two hundred eighty-eight opinions about it.

Nor were they at any certainty about the immortality of the foul and a future ſtate. The greateſt part of them were downright *infidels* as to thefe points; and the beſt of them, after their utmoſt refearches, fluctuated, lived and died in fufpence. *Socrates*, though he feemed to incline to believe and hope for another world, fpeaks doubtfully: and so does *Cicero*, he owns, he could but guess; and plainly says, which of the two opinions (that the soul is mortal, or is immortal) is true, God only knows: and again, which is most probable, is a very great question.

Now, if the great men among the *Pagans*, whose business it was to study the book of nature, and who had carried their inquiries to the highest, fell into such errors and mistakes, and at best were at such uncertainties; one may easily infer, the case of the ignorant vulgar would be very deplorable, and that religion among them would be in a most wretched state. I may add,

3. As those that cultivated natural religion, and made the greatest improvements in the study of it, thus blundered and run into errors in matters of the highest consequence; so natural light, in its utmost extent, was defective. Supposing the law of nature had been understood better by those that studied it, it is not sufficient to direct men in all the concernments of religion. In two points particularly it falls short, viz. *The right manner of worshipping God, and the terms upon which sinners may assuredly be accepted with him.* Neither of these two things, which yet are of the utmost moment to us, doth it discover with any satisfaction.

As to the first of these, *the right manner of worshipping God;* the light of nature could not of itself be a sufficient direction. I do not ground my argument or proof of this upon the absurd, cruel, and filthy manner in which generally they worshipped. For, I grant, natural reason would condemn that; and we find the wiser among the philosophers, exclaiming against such fooleries very freely; however, they fell in with them in practice. *What a frenzy is it to imagine,* (says Seneca) *that the Gods can be delighted with such cruelties, that even the worst of men would scruple to authorise or commit.* One out of zeal mutilates himself, another lances and cuts himself; he adds, *if this be the way to please the Gods, what should a man do if he had a mind to anger them?* and again, *if this be the way to please them, they deserve not to be worshipped, or pleased at all.* Reason would vote against many of the follies of their worship, and their wise men were generally ashamed of them. Nor do I deny, but the philosophers spake many grave and good things concerning the worship of God. The love of him, and obedience to him, they concluded was the most acceptable service, and that a pure heart was infinitely better than all their hecatombs or most costly oblations. But then, as to the particular manner and form of external worship, they knew not, neither could the reason and light of their minds herein direct them. They could not tell, what mode of external service would be acceptable to God. And hence, even the greatest of them thought it best to comply with established customs, which they did so, as to involve themselves in the guilt of the most vile and stupid idolatry.

And then, as to the other point, the terms upon which they might hope for, and have assurance of acceptance with God, and of being received into favor: reason, or the light of nature could afford them very little satisfaction. Here their oracle was silent, and the light of nature utterly failed.

It is considerable to my purpose, that the light of nature could not discover the origin of evil, *whence this evil*, was the great puzzle of their divinity; and it would be no great difficulty, to infer hence, that it could not sufficiently direct how to get it removed; at least, those that had nothing but nature for their direction, were at a mighty loss as to both these particulars. Some of them attributed evil to antipathy, a certain quarrelsome principle, which they knew not what to make of. Others to the necessary perversity of matter. Others to a certain malignant spirit. Though the most common opinion was, that there were two Gods, the one the author of all good, and the other, the author of all evil. Now such confusion as this, I dare say, must leave them in the dark, to whom, and how to apply for the removal of evil, the pardon of it, &c. should they apply to God, the living and true God, as I grant reason would direct; yet they could not be assured, that he would be propitious to them, and pass by their offences. They might indeed infer something encouraging from the mercy and goodness of God; might build some probable hope upon the methods of his providence, the kindness, and forbearance discovered in the constant course thereof. But yet, there are insuperable difficulties remaining here, in which natural reason cannot relieve us. For instance, as we are sinners, as all men must own themselves to be, and the heathens universally did acknowledge it. We stand exposed to the justice of God, deserve punishment, and God has a right to punish us; and I think natural reason cannot assure us, he will depart from his right. If it be said he is merciful, and this reason discovers; I answer, it also discovers, that he is just and righteous; and how can we be assured that he will exercise mercy against the demands of justice. Should it be suggested, that reason may satisfy the sinner, that if he repent, so good and gracious a being, as all men believe God to be, will forgive sin. I answer, reason cannot give any assurance of this. Repentance we see does not satisfy human governors, who, as concerned for the honor of their laws and government, often punish criminals, notwithstanding their repentance, and for ought reason can tell us, the righteous governor of the world may do so too.

Further, reason cannot assure us, how often God will pardon; whether he will pardon all sin; whether he will not only pardon, but receive into favor; how he will pardon, whether absolutely, or upon what terms. That the heathens were at a loss as to all these things, is evident from the shifts they were put to, when under apprehension of the divine displeasure. Witness their numerous sacrifices, and superstitious rites, their offering the *fruit of their body for the sin of their soul*, and the like; which were the means they devised for appeasing the anger of the Deity, and rendering him propitious. In short, the utmost length that natural light could carry any in this matter, we have I think exemplified in the case of the Ninevites, *Who can tell if God will repent, and turn away from his fierce anger, that we perish not?*

Upon the whole, they were in so much darkness about the nature of God, about sin, about repentance, and the methods of applying to God; they had so much to increase their fears, as well as encourage their hopes; that in these respects it must be owned, that natural religion, had they attended to its utmost light, was lame and defective.

It is too soon to infer from hence, the necessity of a supernatural revelation; that I shall do with more advantage from all the particulars when I have finished them. Only let me observe as I pass on, how great a blessing we have in the Bible on this account as well as many others. This clearly shews us our disease and points out our remedy. This tells us, that *God made man upright*, but that *he sought out many inventions;* and that *God is in Christ reconciling the world to himself.* We now know that he will forgive sin, having published an act of grace and indemnity from heaven, declaring that if we repent, *our sins shall be blotted out*, that he *will be merciful to our iniquities, and our sins he will remember no more.* This our Bible is full of. We cannot doubt of it, but have a sure foundation for our faith and hope to rest upon, and are not left to fluctuate in uncertainties, as the Gentiles did that knew not God, nor were acquainted with the discoveries of the gospel. The Son of God came from heaven to procure this favor, and he left stated officers in commission to proclaim it to the world; for so we read that he commanded, that *repentance, and remission of sins should be preached in his name among all nations, beginning at* Jerusalem, Luke xxiv. 47. We have reason therefore to be thankful for the Bible, and value it exceedingly. But this will further appear in the progress of my discourse on this subject. In the mean time to proceed,

4. As it might be probably concluded from the foregoing particulars, that there would be great disorder, darkness and corruption among mankind that wanted a supernatural revelation; so it is evident this was the case. The heathen world as they were the regions of darkness, the dark places of the earth, so among them were the habitations of cruelty. Their minds were wofully depraved, their principles corrupt, and their manners vile and abominable. A short view of the state of heathenism, which you will consider, as the state of those that wanted the advantage of the Bible, will convince you of this. And as it may be of use to my present argument, you will not I hope think it unworthy of your attention.

I have said something already concerning their principles with reference to religion; by which it appears how defective their notions were. They were ignorant of some of the greatest and most important doctrines; others they so much depraved by a mixture of their own fancies, and in all were at such uncertainties, that their principles could be of little use, either as to practice or comfort.

To shew this, let me briefly compare their faith with that of christians, as we have the latter summed up in an ancient creed, which we call the apostles, containing the chief doctrines of christianity. They were so far from believing aright in God the Father Almighty, that the generality of them run into the absurdity of polytheism, believing there were many Gods. And few of them had any tolerable notion of the Supreme Being, the one true God. They were so far from owning him as maker of heaven and earth, that many of them thought that heaven and earth had no maker. And for the rest of their belief, there is an entire chasm and defect. It is all blank in their creed. They knew nothing of Jesus Christ, his only Son our Lord; of his birth, death, resurrection, ascension; nothing of the Holy Ghost; the holy catholic church; had no solid principles on which they could ground the hope of forgiveness of sin; without which even the best of them must live in continual suspicion and fear. As for the resurrection of the body, that great article of the christian faith and hope, their philosophers could not reach it, but rejected it as absurd and ridiculous when proposed to them. Nor had they any steady belief of the concluding article, the life everlasting. Some hoped there might be another state after this; others laughed at the notion as weak and groundless, possessing men with needless apprehensions; and the best of them were in suspence between hope and fear. So that, it is evident, if we had wanted our Bible, we had wanted our creed, wanted these great articles of religion, on which a christian founds his faith and comfort, and which have so constant and powerful an influence on practice: we had known little of God, nothing of Christ, little of heaven, or the way to it.

DISCOURSE I.

And as their faith, so their worship, was sadly defective, and depraved, as would appear upon a short view of it, even to amazement. They were mistaken as to the object of religious worship. For as they had deified in their own imaginations the vilest creatures, and things, and distributed the divinity among a multitude of fictitious deities; accordingly, to these they paid their honors, doing *service to them that by nature were no gods.* The apostle tells us, they had *gods many, and lords many.* They had, indeed, multiplied them to a prodigious number, and divided them into various classes; as celestial, aerial, terrestial, infernal, hurtful gods, and kind beneficent gods. The sun, moon, and stars, were their most ancient deities, to which they had added a vast many more, deifying almost every thing they thought, they had cause either to love or fear. Their kings and emperors were usually brought into the class, and received divine honors. Not to take notice, how much lower the superstition of the vulgar carried them, worshipping the vilest things. *

E

---

* *Worshipping the vilest things*] As a Cat, or a Plant. For we are told, that the Egyptians in particular worshipped such things, and the best apology or excuse, that can be made for them, is to say, it was only a civil and political worship or regard they paid to these objects, and had very little of sacred or religious in it, even among the vulgar. Husbandry being the chief employment and way of living among that people, they declared by a law, that all those creatures which were of eminent service in agriculture, destroyers of vermin, or upon some other account in peculiar esteem with them, should be holy, sacred, and inviolable; so that it was death to destroy any of them, either designedly, or by accident. For considering them as instruments of divine providence towards the support of human life, they treated them as things set apart and sacred to that particular use and purpose, nor did they consecrate any thing without such a view, as Cicero tells us, *Ægyptii nullam belluam, nisi ob aliquam utilitatem quam ex ea caperent, consecraverunt.* De Nat. Deor. 1.

Hence Juvenal ridicules them, as making the produce of their gardens, a fort of gods.

O fanctas gentes quibus haec nafcuntur in hortis numina——

Thus vain were they become in their imagination. Let me only obferve here, that as they worfhipped this confufed medley of gods, the devil took the advantage of their folly, played upon them and abufed them by his impoftures, and really drew them to the worfhip of himfelf. This the apoftle exprefsly charges upon them, *The things which the gentiles facrifice, they facrifice to devils, and not to God.* They had various images and altars erected to this or that deity, before thefe they worfhipped, thefe they confulted as oracles; and in doing fo, they really worfhipped devils, who poffeffed themfelves of their idols, fpake in them, and received the homage of thefe wretched people.

And, as this was the common cafe of the gentile world, it was the cafe of the ancient Britons in particular, as hiftory informs us, " They were foul " idolaters, faith a learned writer, * who mifapply- " ing that great truth, that God is in every thing, " made every thing God, as trees, rivers, hills, " mountains." He adds, " they worfhipped devils, " whofe pictures remained in the days of *Gildas*, " within and without the decayed walls of their " cities, drawn with deformed and ugly faces," as no doubt they fometimes appeared. Their great goddefs was *Diana*, the goddefs of the game. They thought their bufinefs was mainly with that deity, becaufe hunting was not their recreation but their life; and venifon the chief of their food. And we are told, that there is a place near St. Paul's

* *Fuller's* Church Hiftory; p. 1.

DISCOURSE I.

in London, called in old records *Diana's Chamber*, where in king Edward the firſt's time, thouſands of the heads of oxen were dug up, which had been offered in ſacrifice to *Diana*.

Thus were our anceſtors *carried away to dumb idols, as they were led*, 1 Cor. xii. 2. And this had been our caſe, had we not been viſited with the light of the goſpel, and had the Bible put into our hands ; we had been ſacrificing our ſheep, and our oxen, and our children to *Diana*, *Apollo*, and a hundred more deities ; *i. e.* to devils, under diſferent names and appearances. The conſideration of which ſhews us plainly how much we needed a revelation, and at the ſame time ſhould excite our gratitude for it. But to proceed,

As the objeƈt of their worſhip was wrong, the manner of it was no leſs ſo. To inſtance only in two things, *viz.* the cruelty, and filthineſs of their worſhip. The cruelty of it, as cutting, lancing and maiming themſelves ; which was frequently their praƈtice in religious worſhip, and thought to be an acceptable ſervice to their gods ; to which I may add human ſacrifices, * very common among them, and becauſe they thought, the more dear to them and valuable the ſacrifice was, of greater account

---

* *Human Sacrifices.*] There is a curious account of two contradiƈtory diſſertations upon the ſubjeƈt of human ſacrifices in *l' Hiſtoire de l' Academie Royale des Inſcriptions and Belles Lettres*. The Abbot de Boiſſi produces abundance of teſtimonies both from greek and latin authors to prove that they were in uſe among the moſt polite, as well as barbarous nations. That the Phænicians, Egyptians, Canaanites, Tyrians, Carthagenians, Athenians, Lacedemonians, Iconians, and all the Grecians, both of the continent and the iſlands ; Romans, Scythians, Germans, Britons, Spaniards, Gauls, &c. were equally involved in that ſuperſtition, which he, with many more, concludes was derived from an imperfeƈt tradition, of Abraham's intended ſacrifice of his ſon ; the attempt of that patriarch leading the neighboring people really to ſacrifce their children. On the other hand ; M. Morin, out of a concern and zeal for the honor of mankind, endeavors to vindicate and clear them,

it would be, and the more effectual; to appease their gods, they were wont to sacrifice their own children: some that had no children, used to purchase them of the poor for this purpose. And it is likely, this practice was taken up by others out of tenderness to their own off-spring. Hence *Diodorus Siculus* tells us, the *Carthagenians* apprehending *Saturn* might be angry with them, because they formerly sacrificed the best of their own sons, but of late had sacrificed such as they bought; they therefore chose out two hundred of the prime of their children and publicly sacrificed them.

For the other instance, the filthiness, the obscene rites of their worship, it would be indecent to mention them. Their *Floralia* and *Bachanalia* were celebrated with the utmost vileness, debauchery, and lewdness. But I shall not enter into so horrid a subject. The apostle seems to give us a caution here, when he says, refering it may be to their behaviour on these occasions, *It is a shame even to speak of those things which were done of them in secret.* I shall only remark, that as abominable as these ceremonies were, they placed a great deal of religion in them, and held it as an opinion, that to be initiated and entered into such mysteries, was a means of purging them from their other sins, and of procuring them a place in their *Elysium*, the region of happiness. If it be said, their wise men and philosophers laughed at, and despised such fol-

---

from the guilt of so odious, shameful, and inhuman a practice. To this end, he either rejects, or labors to weaken, the numerous authorities alledged to prove the fact, saying many plausible things on his side of the question; from whence he would infer, that if the pagans ever offered human sacrifices at all, they never sacrificed any but prisoners of war, or criminals condemned to die. But, I believe, few will think his reasons satisfactory; especially since, if travellers may be credited, the practice obtains among many uncivilized nations, even at this day.

lies; I anſwer, it is true. But it muſt be conſidered, they were the eſtabliſhed rites reverenced by the bulk of the people, and even thoſe that knew better, gave them countenance by maintaining, that the gods were to be worſhipped according to the cuſtom and law of every country.

What their morals would be conſequent upon ſuch principles, and ſuch a manner of worſhip, it is eaſy to conjecture; and I ſhall leave it very much to be inferred without deducing the particulars. Try them upon the decalogue, and you will find them living down all the duties of it, and deſtroying both tables in their avowed practices. I have hinted how ill they can ſtand examination upon the firſt table, and might ſhew the ſame with reference to the ſecond.

They groſsly violated the ſixth commandment, by authoriſing murders in their gladiatory exerciſes, by procuring the abortion of children, by expoſing new-born infants, and by laying violent hands on themſelves, which they plead for as matter of honor on ſeveral occaſions. They as boldly condemned the ſeventh commandment by adultery, inceſt, ſodomy, which they allowed, and even brought into their religion as ſacred rites. *Tully* in a public oration pleads for fornication. They tranſgreſſed the eighth commandment by theft, which many nations gloried in, rather than accounted it a fault. And the ninth by lying, which their philoſophers recommended as lawful, whenever it might be profitable.

Thus vile and immoral were the heathens, too generally as is evident from their own books and hiſtorians. And I need not tell you, that the *New Teſtament* conſtantly repreſents them in characters agreeable hereunto. See the apoſtle's deſcription of them in *Rom.* i. from *ver.* 21, to the end of the chapter. He tells us, *God gave them up to unclean-*

nefs, and to vile affections, and a reprobate mind; the confequence of which was, that they *were filled with all unrighteoufnefs, fornication, wickednefs, covetoufnefs, malicioufnefs, envy, murder, debate, deceit, malignity,* with many other defilements of flefh and fpirit, there fpecified; and in the fame manner the Scripture every where paints them. I fhall only mention one paffage thereof more, *Eph.* iv. 18, 19. where, fpeaking of the Gentiles, he fays, *their underftandings were darkened, being alienated from the life of God;* he adds, *who being paft feeling, have given themfelves over unto lafciviousnefs, to work all uncleannefs with greedinefs.* This was the general character of the heathen world. They had corrupted their notions of God and religion, their underftandings were darkened, hearts hardened, and confcience utterly laid wafte. So that their lives were ftained with the worft abominations. In a word, it is in them that defcription we have, *Rom.* iii. 11, 12. is moft literally fulfilled and anfwered, *there is none that underftandeth, there is none that feeketh after God; they are all gone out of the way, they are altogether become unprofitable; there is none that does good; no not one:* and again, ver. 6. *deftruction and mifery are in their ways.*

Now from hence, I think, I may conclude, the propofition I am upon ftands good, *viz.* That a fpecial revelation from heaven, was become neceffary. You have feen the infufficiency of natural light; have heard fome of the blunders and errors of thofe that cultivated it, the defects in principle, and univerfal depravation of worfhip and manners that overfpread the heathen world: the confequence from which is exceeding clear, that there needed help and light from heaven to retrieve matters, and to reftore the knowledge and worfhip of the true God.

But here it may be objected, that there were excellent men among the philosophers, who taught divine and noble doctrines, sufficient to reform the world, and heal the distempers of it, had they been attended to. Christian divines often borrow from them, embellish their discourses with their sayings, quoting their writings with great applause. In answer to this, I grant there were. *Socrates*, for instance, seems to be preserved, like *Noah* in the old world, in the midst of a deluge of immorality. Some such there were, but few, here and there one in an age, that overcame vulgar prejudices, and gave themselves up to the conduct of nature's light, without suffering themselves to be biassed with their passions. A *Socrates* in one age, a *Tully* in another, a *Seneca* or an *Antonine* in another. But as these were over-numbered by libertine philosophers and poets, who spread the poison among the people; so the notions, principles, and religion of the country was against them. *Socrates* lost his life for standing up for that fundamental point of all religion, the unity of the godhead. Besides, even these few great men labored under the defects, I before-mentioned. They could not attain to any true scheme of divinity. They were at an uncertainty, as to some of the more important articles of faith, the immortality of the soul, a future state of rewards and punishments, *&c.* And even their morality was far from being complete. They have not so much as a name for the great christian grace of humility: what we call so, passed with them for abjectness, lowness and littleness of mind. And their purest morals had a dangerous mixture: self-sufficience, pride, and revenge, were not only allowed, but accounted, a sort of virtue with them. There were great blemishes in the lives of their best men. *Socrates* had his *Nævi*: he did not wholly abstain from idolatry, nor from a regard to the heathen oracles.

I will only add, that how great and excellent foever thefe men were, and how excellent foever their writings; they wanted authority, they were too few to be much heard, too weak to ftem the tide. This they themfelves faw, and fome of them are faid to have declared their apprehenfions, that without a divine and fupernatural affiftance, no confiderable reformation was ever like to be wrought in the world; that their reafonings and philofophy would not do, unlefs God appeared from heaven, and in a divine manner influenced the hearts of men. The general prevailing notions were exceeding corrupt: idolatry was eftablifhed; the public rites of their religious worfhip were fcandalous and lewd; and they found by experience, that their philofophy was too feeble to fubdue finful paffions and headftrong lufts, to perfuade men to renounce their falfe gods, and falfe worfhip, and purfue the maxims of reafon and virtue. This they themfelves were convinced of, (fome few among them I mean) wherein they owned a great truth that ought always to be in reputation with chriftians, *viz,* that fupernatural help, or what we call grace, is neceffary to change the hearts and reform the manners of men.

It may further be objected, that many of thofe that receive and profefs the chriftian religion, are as bad as the poor Pagans: that as the Jews of old were exceeding vicious, notwithftanding they enjoyed a revelation from heaven, fo there are multitudes even among chriftians themfelves, as fcandalous in their practice, as the heathens were. I muft confefs this is an objection that may be urged too plaufibly, and give occafion to take up the apoftle's complaint in his days, *The name of God is blafphemed among the Gentiles, through you, as it is written.* But notwithftanding, there is no force in the argument, if it be offered to prove, that a divine revelation is not neceffary, or that it is of no ufe; that the world needs it not, or has been no better for it. For as to the Jews, it is utterly falfe, that they were generally as bad as their heathen neighbors. It is granted they often apoftatized, and were feverely punifhed on that account. Yet I think it highly probable, that they knew more of God, and practiced more of religion, than all the world befides. Even when things were worft with them, they had many eminent and great men, among the lower fort, that preferved their veneration for God and religion. But, as the objection more peculiarly concerns chriftians, feveral things might be faid to it: as, that there are great numbers that ufurp the name of chriftians, and live in the chriftian church, who yet really are no chriftians, can fcarce be faid to receive the Bible. If they have a Bible in their houfe they feldom look into it, and make no other ufe of it, than to cavil at a few paffages that fall in their way. And no wonder, that fuch are not reformed and bettered by divine revelation, when they have fo little regard to it. But then, as the chriftian church juftly difowns them, at leaft the head of it doth, and will do fo at laft, their behaviour ought not to be turned to the reproach of the chriftian profeffion. *He is not a Jew that is one outwardly:* every man that was baptifed, by the care and procurement of his parents, is not therefore a chriftian, he might as well be called a Mahometan, a Pagan, did he not live in a chriftian country. I anfwer further, that where the chriftian revelation is received to purpofe, it has glorious effects; enlightening, transforming, and making a beautiful change in the ftate of things, which was feen eminently in the firft ages of chriftianity. The reformation the gofpel wrought in the lives of its profeffors was fo remarkable, that their heathen neighbors ftood amazed at it. Once more, confider the christian church under all its disadvantages from the infirmities of good men, and the scandals given by hypocrites, and there is no comparison between that and the Pagan world. Not, but there are some called christians, as vile and every way as bad, as any of the heathens were, but the main body of christians are another sort of persons, they have not only better principles but they practise better; the bad among them are not so bad, do not run to the same excess of riot, and the good among them are far better.

So that, I think, I may still adhere to the proposition I laid down, that the state of mankind required a supernatural revelation; that this was necessary to relieve them amidst their prevailing darkness and depravity. Nor can it be said, that it hath not this tendency, or where it is truly received, has not this effect, in some measure. I go on now to another proposition, which I shall insist upon but briefly.

6. That it is reasonable to expect God should give such a revelation. How much this was wanted you have heard; and that we might expect it may be proved. I shall only offer two things for this purpose.

1. It may be argued, with some probability, from the attributes of God. His mercy is such as would incline him to pity his creatures in their deplorable circumstances, groaping after him in the dark, and led captive by the devil. His wisdom also encourages the expectation. By the fall, man was so disabled, and by a course of sin, the world was become so degenerate, a mere mass of darkness and corruption; that had not God interposed, I cannot see but this part of the creation must have been lost to all the purposes of religion : all intercourse between God and man must have been cut

off, at least, in a great measure; God must have abandoned man, and man must have lived without God in the world. Now God's gracious purpose of redemption being supposed, it seems reasonable to expect there should be a revelation from him, enabling man to answer the ends of his creation, to teach him his duty, fit him to fill his place among the creatures, and prepare him to receive the blessings intended through a redeemer. And accordingly,

2. Some of the wisest and greatest men among the heathens had such an expectation. Thus *Socrates* is brought in by *Plato*, expressing his sense that they wanted a divine revelation; and therefore, having taken notice of the uncertainty they were at, as to some things, after their utmost inquiries, he tells his disciples, that he thought it best to wait patiently till such a time, as they should learn certainly, how they ought to behave themselves towards God and towards man; and then, after some discourse upon the subject, he intimates his apprehension, that a divine person will appear and take the mist from before their eyes. This is mentioned by some,* and I think justly, as a most wonderful passage, and what looks like a hint, to that celebrated philosopher, of the gospel revelation. All the use I make of it is this, that as the world exceedingly needed a revelation; so it is evident hence, that one of their greatest men, the greatest and wisest among them, had a conviction that they needed it. He saw they were plunged in difficulties, and could not find the way to extricate themselves, could not attain to a clearness and certainty in things; and therefore, as he found the necessity of it, so he had a presage in his own mind, I do not know but it might be from heaven, that God would

* *Clark* of natural and revealed religion, *p.* 203.

one time or other, in an extraordinary manner relieve them.

Thus I have advanced pretty far towards the main point defigned, and fhall only fubjoin here one propofition more.

7. Suppofing it reafonable to expect a revelation from God, and that there is fuch a thing in the world, I think it certain our Bible muft be that revelation. Two confiderations will fupport this propofition, *viz.*

1. That there is no other book that pretends to be a revelation from God, that can have an equal claim to be fo, or that fo well deferves to be received as fuch. As to the books of nature, or natural law, I have already faid the Bible doth not exclude that. The Scriptures contain nothing contrary to natural religion, but comprife it, explain, and improve it; they take in all that is valuable and truly deduced from the principles of reafon, among the philofophers. So that there needs be no oppofition between the one and the other. If philofophy be fet up as a competitor with the Bible, you have heard how very defective it is, and enough I think has been faid to difgrace its pretences.

As to the books of Mofes, they are a part of Scripture revelation. There remains therefore, but one book more of any account in the world, that can be called a competitor, and that is the *Alcoran*, the Bible or pretended revelation of *Mahomet* and his followers. And if the queftion be, whether that, or the chriftian Bible, be truly a revelation from heaven? we need but compare them together, and it will be eafy to make a judgment. Concerning the *Alcoran*, let me remark a few things without enlargement: as that what is valuable in it, is generally taken from our Bible; and then it is, for the greateft part of it, fuch a jargon, a mixture of incoherent nonfenfe as renders it unworthy of a wife man, much more of the infinitely wife God. Besides, there are a great many direct contradictions in it, one revelation inconsistent with another, laws given, and then revoked, just as occasion required; which show, it could not be by divine inspiration. Further, it proposes an heaven of sensual delights, which it neither becomes man to expect, nor God to promise. And in short, all its success and progress in the world, is owing to the sword and outward violence; which certainly are characters that sufficiently disparage it. It follows therefore, either that the Bible is a revelation from God, or there is no such thing in the world. To which let me add,

2. That the Bible is a revelation, every way worthy of God; such as we might expect, supposing God should afford mankind so great a favor as a supernatural revelation. My time is gone, and I have, it may be, staid long enough on these things; or I might let you see the several general characters of this revelation, which would make it at least probable that it is from God. Let me only just mention such as these.

It comprehends, as I said before, all that is excellent in the books of the moral philosophers. They have indeed their enlargements, their fine sayings, and ornaments, which are not to be found in the same form in the Bible. But there is no moral law or duty, no necessary rule of life and practice, in any of them, but the Bible takes it in. Not to say, that as it delivers all with greater authority, so it enforces all with higher motives and arguments.

It corrects the mistakes of the philosophers, blots out their errata. It delivers the precepts of universal benevolence and love, without restraining that affection as they did to friends only. It recommends justice and charity, without admitting revenge. In a word, it contains the law of right reason in a more correct edition than is to be found elsewhere.

Again, it supplies the defects of natural religion, and particularly, as it is delivered to us in the books of the professed students thereof, the philosophers. And here, as a conclusion to this discourse, I shall just mention some points of no small consequence, wherein the philosophers of the heathen world were at a loss, and in which our Bible gives us abundant satisfaction.

It makes known the great object of all religious worship; assures us there is a God, and that there is but one God.

It gives us just notions of this God, sets him forth in the several perfections of his nature; as a spirit of infinite power, wisdom, goodness, every where present, unchangeable, and eternal. Now as some of the heathens were grossly ignorant of both these points, so others knew them but very imperfectly; and yet all acceptable worship, all true religion, depends on them.

The Bible gives us a clear, satisfying discovery of the origin of the world, and of all things in it. The first verse of the Bible tells us more than we can learn from all the writings of Plato and Aristotle, and the other wise men of old: *In the beginning God created the Heavens and the Earth.*

It asserts the doctrine of divine providence in the full extent of it, and lets us know that the same power and wisdom that made the world, constantly upholds and governs it; watching over all creatures, and superintending their affairs.

It informs us of the rise of evil in the world, which was the great problem of heathen divinity, that about which they could never come to any certainty; acquainting us, that the first man sinning against God, corrupted the human nature, and hence the fountain being defiled, the streams that issue from it are defiled also.

It reveals the great design of God, and the scheme for the restoration and recovery of guilty, lost man. It sets forth a saviour, and proclaims reconciliation in his blood: a point of the highest use and comfort to mankind; and yet not one word of it in nature, or in the books of the philosophers.

It provides supernatural help for us in the discharge of all our duties. This it doth by the promise of the holy spirit. The heathens, as I have hinted, were convinced of their wants and necessity here, but knew nothing of a remedy.

It calls men up to a divine, spiritual intercourse and converse with God, as the life and comfort of their minds. Indeed here lies the true secret of religion; for which all moral duties and acts of worship fit us, and thereby prepare us for heaven. And how little the heathens knew of this by the light of nature, I need not say.

The Bible is full of glorious promises suited to a christian in all the varieties of his case. And I add to all the rest, it gives him assurance of a future state of immortality and blessedness.

Now as these are points of the utmost importance to us, and of the highest consolation; points in which natural religion, and the writings of the philosophers, leave us in the dark, and at a loss; but wherein our Bible gives us full certainty; they should, methinks, serve to recommend it to us as most likely to be a revelation from God. I do not say, they absolutely prove it to be so; but they may prepare us for the belief of this truth, which is all I intend by them, making it manifest, that it is such a revelation as we wanted, and had reason to expect.

All Scripture is given by inspiration of God, and is profitable for doctrine, for reproof, for correction, for instruction in righteousness.

HAVING prepared my way to what I design from this subject, shewn you how much we need a revelation from heaven, what reason there is to expect one, and that if there be such a thing in the world our Bible must be it: I now proceed directly to prove that it actually contains such a divine revelation. And that I may do this the more effectually and distinctly, I shall consider three things of very great importance in the present argument, and all tending to establish the authority and divinity of the Scriptures.

I. I shall prove that the Bible is true, or that the facts there related are so.

II. That it is inspired. And,

III. That our Bible, or the books of the *Old* and *New-Testament*, are the books that were originally inspired.

I. I shall prove that the Bible is true, or that the facts therein related are true, and truly related. And here let me propose the following arguments.

1. That our Bible is of equal credit with any other

G

ancient history; and consequently, if it be not true, we have no sufficient reason to receive and believe any ancient book in the world. 2. That our Bible has greater marks of credibility than any other ancient book. And, 3. That the circumstances of it considered, it is morally impossible it should not be true.

1. That our Bible is of equal credit with any other ancient book; I do not say, it has not a superior credit. I shall endeavor to prove by and by that it has. But it is enough for my present purpose to claim an equal credit in behalf of the Bible. And what I assert, is, that nothing can be said for any ancient book, any history wrote before our time, (whether more or less ancient is not material) but the same may be said for the Bible; nor any thing objected against the Bible, as to the truth of it, but the same may be urged as strongly against that ancient history, whatever it is. So that if there be sufficient reason to receive and believe any ancient history; for instance, *Thucydides*, *Plutarch*, *Livy*, or *Tacitus*: to believe that these books were wrote by the persons whose names they bear, and to whom they are ascribed, and to believe the facts they relate; there is as good reason to receive the Bible, to believe the several books of it were wrote by such and such persons who pass for the writers of them, and to believe the account of things they give, to be genuine and true. This I dare undertake to prove; and consequently, that no man can reject the Bible under pretence that it wants evidence; but he must at the same time reject all other ancient Books, and turn a perfect *Sceptic* and unbeliever with respect to all history.

That this may appear, let us examine upon what evidence, what principles and motives, we receive and believe any ancient books or histories. And you will allow me to suggest here something in the negative, to hint what is not neceſſary in the evidence, and what cannot be thought an objection againſt them: as

1. It is not neceſſary that we ourſelves ſaw the things done which we are to believe. In this caſe, there would be no proper believing; for faith or believing, is, an aſſent upon the teſtimony; and what a man ſees, he does not receive upon the teſtimony of another, but he knows it by means of his own ſenſes. Nor could we believe any thing that was tranſacted before our own time, or at which we were not preſent.

Nor is it neceſſary that we ſhould ſee the hiſtorian write his book, and put his own name to it. For if this was requiſite, there are few or no hiſtories in the world, not to ſay of ancient times, but even of our own, that we could be capable of believing.

I the rather mention this to ſtrike at an objection, that I am afraid is lurking in the minds of many, and is at the bottom of their infidelity, though they may not ſpeak out. They never ſaw *Moſes, Chriſt*, nor the apoſtle *Paul*, for inſtance, how do they know there were ſuch perſons? and that they did or wrote ſuch things? but I aſk, did you ever ſee *Alexander, Julius Cæſar, Pompey*, or *Henry* VIII of *England?* and yet do you not believe that there were ſuch perſons? he that doth not believe there were ſuch perſons becauſe he never ſaw them, has ſo far laid aſide the nature of man, that he is not capable of being dealt with in a reaſonable way. But if he doth believe, though he never ſaw them, then the not ſeeing *Moſes* and *Chriſt* can be no reaſon againſt the believing the Scripture account of them, that there were ſuch perſons, and did ſuch things.

2. Nor ſhould it be any objection againſt believing an ancient hiſtory, that there have been, and

are some false histories in the world. There are cheats and impostors we know; but it doth not thence follow, that there are no honest men. There is a great deal of trick and juggle, a great deal of falshood and knavery in the world; but I hope notwithstanding, that there is some sincerity and truth; otherwise, all mutual confidence and trust would be destroyed, there would be no conversing together, society must disband and break up and mankind either live separate, or put themselves into a state of war; look upon every body as an enemy, and arm for self-defence.

In short, as bad as the world is, there always have been, and will be some upright, honest men. While God continues the human race and his government over mankind, he will preserve some degree of justice, fidelity, and truth so necessary to the being and order of society. The pretence therefore, that there have been false histories, only bids us be cautious what histories we receive, but not that we receive none, according to the apostle's admonition in another case, *Beloved, believe not every spirit, but try the spirits whether they are of God; because many false prophets are gone out into the world.* There are many false histories and false men: we should therefore try them before we believe them. But as this does not prove there are no true histories, and no honest men on whom we may with safety depend; so it is no argument against giving credit to such. Nor.

3. Is it necessary in order to believe an ancient history or ancient book to be true, that it should be impossible for it to be false. To expect this is the most unreasonable thing in the world. We do not go upon such evidence in other matters, but believe and trust without such high security. All trade and commerce proceeds upon probabilities, and what we call moral certainty. The merchant

believes there are such and such places in the East and West-Indies. It is not impossible but he may be mistaken. But the concurring testimony of so many persons, gives so strong a moral evidence, that he cannot reasonably question it. Men depend on their servants, on their fidelity and honesty, and often they themselves, and all they have in the world, are in their power. They put their lives in the hands of their physician, and even of their barber. There is no impossibility in it but they may be undone in all these dependencies; and yet that is no argument against such trusts, or for being uneasy therein. It is possible any morsel of meat you take may poison you: but we do not abstain from eating for all that; it is enough that there is a great deal of wholesome food, and we have no reason to suspect what we take, though it is possible it may be pernicious. In a word, as it is the part of a prudent man not to believe a thing purely because it is possible to be true, so it is equally his part not to reject any thing because it is possible it may be false. We are to consider the probabilities of things, the evidences they have, what evidences are to be expected, what they are capable of, and should be thought sufficient: For as it is folly and rashness to believe without proper and sufficient evidence, so it is unreasonable not to believe with it, or when we have it. It is possible this or that book or history may be false, that any book or history may be so; but then I say, if we will exercise no faith, no trust, no dependence but where it is absolutely impossible we should be mistaken; we must believe nothing, trust no body, we must converse with mankind no more; but withdraw from the world, or at least live in continual jealousy and fear.

I would not have this thought impertinent or a digression. I apprehend it to be full to my purpose: nor would it appear any great difficulty to prove that most of the objections of our deists and cavillers at Scripture turn upon this. I do not say they make this a formal objection; but I am persuaded, if they would examine their own minds, and inquire what it is that sticks with them, it would be found this is all that remains to keep their infidelity in countenance. They may have learned to flourish a little upon other topics of raillery; but push them home and this will be their last resort. They cannot pretend to prove the Bible is false, or that they can demonstrate it to be so, nor pretend that they have less evidence of it, than of other books which yet they believe. But their evasion is this, these things were done a great while ago, we neither saw nor knew any thing of them; they may be so, but they may be otherwise; and we ought to have good proof before we give our faith to we know not what. I fear this is the case of a great many among us, that call in question the Bible. But how unreasonable their cavil is, appears from what has been said. The question concerning the Bible, or any other book, is not, whether it is possible it may be false, but whether we have sufficient reason to believe it is true. If so, certainly our unbelievers must be highly faulty, who so boldly reject it; especially considering the weight and consequence of the things it proposes. And they are the more inexcusable here because they do it upon a pretence that will destroy the credit of all history in the world, turn mankind into *Sceptics*, make them distrust one another, and distrust themselves too in every thing.

But to go back to my point, my argument is, that we have equal evidence that the Bible is true, as that there is any true history in the world; or that any other ancient book or history is true. And that this may appear, I told you we must inquire upon what evidence we receive an ancient history, what evidence is sufficient to make it pass, and actually doth make it pass current, as a true and good history.

And I reckon the credit of ancient books depends upon such things as these,

1. That the persons, who wrote them, had sufficient knowledge of the things they wrote.

2. That they were men of integrity. The former shows they were not deceived, and this that they would not deceive.

3. That they wrote at the very time when the facts, they relate, are said to be done, and might be known, publicly known, to be done.

4. That their account of things be confirmed by the co-temporary writers of good credit, by persons that lived at the same time and had sufficient opportunity to know the facts recorded in the history. I add,

5. Any ancient book or history receives a mighty confirmation if it treats of subjects of great importance, in which the interests of mankind are highly concerned or at least of a part of mankind: so that as it would be carefully examined by others, it was not contradicted by any, but in the main facts of it owned and acknowledged by all.

Were it proper to enlarge on the subject in this place, I could show that these are the characters and principles upon which the credit of all our ancient books stands. But as this would carry me into a long discourse, which many of you would account unprofitable speculation, of how great importance soever it may be, I shall at present omit it and instead of that shall immediately apply myself to the point before us, shall illustrate the several particulars I have mentioned, in the instances of the Bible; show that they all belong to it, and consequently, that we have reason to receive it, as a true history, a faithful record of things; which is all I am at present contending for. And,

1. The Bible was wrote, by persons that had sufficient opportunity, of being fully informed, concerning the things they report; and who could not but know them. A learned man* in a celebrated performance, has abundantly proved this, concerning *Moses*, who has given us the history of the origin of the world, the fall of man, the promise of a saviour, the beginning of a church, and the first institutes and main doctrines of religion. This is a considerable part of the Bible, and contains an history of about 2500 years, and is the foundation of all the rest. And how excellently *Moses* was qualified to write this history, the author I refer to has shown at large. His inspiration, which we christians believe, and of which we have the strongest evidence, removes all difficulties at once. But setting that aside, and consider him only as a common historian, he had a very exact intelligence of the things he relates, and such as would enable him to write of them in as authentic a manner as any other common historian in the world.

As to the four last books that go under his name, the histories of *Exodus, Leviticus, Numbers, Deuteronomy*, he himself was an actor in all, and had the chief management of affairs as lawgiver and ruler; every thing was done under his eye and cognizance. So that this part of the history, excepting the last chapter of the last book, which gives the story of his death, may be fitly called the history of Moses's life and times.

As for the first book, that of *Genesis*, he might learn the contents of it from tradition; which as the piety and interest of the first patriarchs obliged them to preserve pure and uncorrupt, so their long

---

* *Stillingfleet's* Originæ Sacræ.

lives enabled them to do it. All these facts passed but through a few hands, and could not well be misunderstood or misrepresented. For instance, can we imagine that the grand-children of *Jacob* could be ignorant of the affairs of their family, of their pedigree, and whence they came into *Egypt* ? can we imagine a thing so remarkable, which was attended with so many memorable circumstances, especially the selling of *Joseph*, should be forgotten in so little a time ? Could *Jacob*, the father of these *Israelites*, *Moses* conversed with, be ignorant of the country whence his grand-father *Abraham* came, especially when he himself married into the country, and lived so long there in *Laban*'s family ? could *Abraham*, when he was co-temporary with *Shem*, be ignorant of the truth of the flood, when *Shem* from whom he descended, was one of the persons preserved in the ark ? and can we suppose *Shem* ignorant of the transactions before the flood, when he was born near 100 years before the death of *Methuselah*, who lived a considerable part of his time with *Adam* ? So that the knowledge of these things would easily be conveyed down to *Moses*. For as *Adam* might carry it down to *Methuselah*, and *Methuselah* to *Shem*, so it is likely *Shem* lived some part of *Jacob*'s time, at least of *Isaac*'s. And how short and easy the passage of such things in the hands of such men, from *Jacob* to *Moses*, any one may collect.

Let me further remark here, that *Moses* was a person of great wisdom, judgment and experience, capable of distinguishing truth from falshood, reality from imposture. He was this way at least, as well qualified as any other writer. The *Egyptians* are famed for their learning in all ancient books. They were indeed, the great source of learning from whence other nations derived theirs. Now the Scripture gives this account of *Moses*, that as he was brought up in *Pharaoh's* court, so he was skilled and *learned in all the wisdom of the Egyptians*, Acts vii. 22. It is likely he was eminent for his natural and political knowledge. He lived and conversed with the most eminent men, it is probable, of every profession; and that he did not neglect the opportunities he had of improving himself, the text I mentioned witnesses, which says, he was *learned in all their wisdom*.

The use I would make of this consideration is, that *Moses* was not like to be easily imposed upon. If you allow him to be honest and upright, as to which I shall say something presently, there is no reason to suspect him credulous, and that he would publish any thing, the truth of which he had not reason to know or believe. For instance, had there been any thing absurd and repugnant to reason, in the history of the creation, of the fall of man, the flood, the dimensions of the ark, and the like: such a person as *Moses* would not have published them in the manner he doth. He was a wise and learned man, of far greater capacity to know and judge of these things, I do not say than the poor little cavillers of our age, but than most men ever since of any age.

So that it is evident, *Moses* who wrote one considerable part of our Bible, had this first qualification of a good historian in an extraordinary manner. He did not write of things he understood not, and of which he had not a sufficient knowledge.

It would be too tedious in such a discourse to go through the *Prophets* and the *Chetubim*, the writers of the other historical and poetical books of the *Old Testament*. Otherwise, such an account might be given of their acquaintance with the materials they published as would be satisfactory to modest, reasonable men.

DISCOURSE II.

But I pass to the writers of the *New Testament*, the apostles and evangelists, in whose writings are contained the doctrines of the christian religion; and in the historical part of them the facts upon which the whole of christianity is founded. Now though they had not the learning of *Moses*, they had the qualification I am insisting upon, as necessary in an historian, *viz.* a particular acquaintance with the things they wrote. St. *Luke* owns this in the preface to his gospel, Luke i. 1, 2, 3, 4. *Forasmuch as many have taken in hand to set forth in order, a declaration of those things which are most assuredly believed amongst us; even as they delivered them unto us, which from the beginning were eye-witnesses, and ministers of the word:* he adds, It *seemeth good to me also, having had perfect understanding of all things from the very first, to write to thee in order, most excellent Theophilus, &c.* They did not write without a perfect understanding of the things they related, as he there intimates; nor could they want this when they were eye-witnesses of all that passed. That they were so is plain, since we find it insisted upon as a necessary part of an apostle's character, that he must have conversed with Christ. *Am not I an apostle? have I not seen Jesus Christ our Lord?* says the apostle *Paul*, 1 Cor. ix. 1. he was *born out of due time*, as he tells us, had not seen Christ on earth; and therefore to supply that defect, Christ appeared to him in heaven. The apostles were not only select men, chosen of God; but were eye-witnesses of the majesty of Christ, 2 *Pet.* i. 16. *They had heard and seen, had looked upon, and their hands had handled the word of life,* The great subject of their testimony, 1 *John* i. 1. 2. This I say was of absolute necessity, and therefore when *Judas's* place was to be filled up, one must be chosen that had *accompanied with them all the time that Jesus went in and out among them,* Acts i. 21. An apostle was a witness of Christ, and that he might be assured of the matters he was to testify, it was necessary he should personally converse with Christ, hear his doctrine, see his miracles, and have a sensible evidence of the truth of all he was to bear witness of.

It would add some strength to this should I shew you, what is exceeding evident concerning them, that these persons were so far from being credulous, that they were with difficulty brought to believe several of the main articles of their doctrine and testimony. They could not tell how to be reconciled to the notion of their master's death, and could scarce be persuaded of his resurrection. Thus it is said, when he appeared to them after his resurrection *that they believed not*, Luke xxiv. 41. They believed not till he *opened their understanding, that they might understand the Scriptures*. And you read of *Thomas* in particular, one of their number; that he declared, he would not believe, unless he should *see in his hands the print of the nails, put his finger into the print of the nail, and thrust his hand into his side,* John xx. 25. An argument that these witnesses were not prepared to report any thing, but must be convinced of the things before they could believe them themselves and report them to others.

Now I think it is evident, that the apostles and evangelists, must on this account be esteemed very authentic and sufficient witnesses. It is a rule in the civil law, that testimony upon hearsay, is not valid; because, say the civilians, witnesses are to testify the truth, and not the possibility of things; which is agreeable to the law of nature, and every where received. Witnesses are to tell what they themselves have seen and heard, and not what others report. And thus did the apostles of our Lord.

So that this first and most necessary character is

found in the writers of the Bible. They had sufficient knowledge of the things they wrote.

2. As they were acquainted with the facts they published, so they were persons of integrity, and may be depended on in the account they give. The former is necessary that they might not be imposed on themselves, and this is necessary that they might not impose on others. And in how eminent a manner they possessed this character, might be shewn at large, would the time and your patience allow me to insist on the argument.

As for Moses, he has many characters of great openness, integrity, and simplicity. We find him spoken of by ancient historians with a very high encomium, as also by Stephen who represents him as exceeding fair, as learned in all the wisdom of the Egyptians, as mighty in word and deed; and yet these things he himself passes over, without any mention at all; though he takes very particular notice of his own infirmaties; as his want of eloquence, and being *slow of speech*, Exod. iv. 10; his impatience, Numb. xi. 10; his unbelief, Numb. xx. 12; his rebelling against the commandment of God, with which God was so far displeased that he excluded him the promised land, Numb. xxvii. 14; of his great anger, Exod. xi. 8; and of his being very wroth, Numb. xvi. 5. He takes notice of his declining the measures God calls him to over and over; ascribes the new modelling of the government to Jethro's advice; and not to his own wisdom and policy. In short, he neither spares his people nor himself; but sets forth their murmurings and apostacies, and his own weaknesses and frailties with all imaginable freedom. And when he came to die was so far from seeking to aggrandize his family, that he leaves them in obscurity, and devolves the government upon Joshua, a man of another tribe.

I will add one consideration more, which I think a glorious instance of Moses's integrity, and that he was fully convinced of the truth of what he wrote, and the justice of the cause he espouses, *viz.* his forsaking the honors and advantages of a court, and his turning his back on all the preferment he might have expected there. This the apostle remarks as a proof of his self-denial, that he *refused to be called the son of Pharaoh's daughter ; chusing rather to suffer affliction with the people of God, than enjoy the pleasures of sin for a season.* And I think it no less a proof of the conviction he had of the call of God, and that he engaged in the office he undertook upon principles of religion and sincerity. In a word, there is nothing that looks like ambition, vanity and a selfish design in any of the writings, or any part of the conduct of Moses ; nothing that favours of counterfeit and imposture : but a great air of simplicity, self-denial and honesty appears in all.

The same I might shew with reference to the apostles and writers of the New Testament. Give me leave to select a few instances. That they were no cheats, and did not design an imposture, and impose upon the world by fraud, is evident from a great many particulars in their character and conduct. I will but just mention three or four things.

1. They were plain illiterate men, no way qualified to manage so great and high an imposture as they were concerned in, if it must be supposed an imposture. Their education was low and mean, and some have observed their employment as fishermen, tended to flatten their spirits; for being much on the water in open boats, and in the night often, they were exposed to cold and phlegmatic air, that must naturally dull their minds and spirits. Now can we imagine that such men as these, rude and unacquainted with the world, utter strangers

to the arts of politicians, should be capable of carrying on so deep an intrigue, inventing such stories as the gospel contains, and palming them upon mankind. That they should undertake it is not reasonable to be supposed; but that they should succeed in it, as actually they did, against all the power and learning of the world, exceeds even the wildest imagination that can be formed.

2. The doctrine they preached to the world was such as shews it could not be a contrivance of their own; but that they faithfully delivered what they had received and learned from above. Had it been of their own framing, they would certainly have suited it more to the genius and gust of mankind. Whereas nothing was more contrary thereto. They lay restraints upon the darling passions of all sorts of men; the ambitious, the covetous, and the voluptuous; and call them to the ungrateful duties of mortification and self denial. Instead of falling in with the common prejudices of the world, and of their own countrymen particularly, who expected a pompous triumphant Messiah, they constantly represent him under the low and ignominious character of one crucified, than which nothing could be more offensive, being to the *Jews a stumbling block, and to the Greeks foolishness*. They insist upon the abrogation and repeal of the ceremonies of the *Jewish law*, which they knew their nation would never bear; having the highest zeal for that law, and being persuaded it must abide for ever. They declare with the greatest freedom against pagan idolatry, endeavor to demolish the altars of their gods, and pour contempt upon their sacred rites. They set themselves to oppose the traditions and customs that were held most venerable, both among Jews and Gentiles; and as was complained of them, *turned the world upside down*. Now I would ask any reasonable person, whether if they had been

impostors, had published a history and a doctrine out of their own heads, they would have laid the beginning in so unpopular a manner? certainly, had they designed to win proselytes by inventions of their own, they would have made their inventions more agreeable, more like to have gained on those they hoped to deceive.

3. There are eminent marks of sincerity in their writings. How freely do they publish their own faults? their pride, ambition, cowardice, covetousness, emulation, and the like. They tell you that one of themselves betrayed their master, that another of them denied him, that all of them forsook him and fled. They publish a shameful story of themselves, that they contended which of them should be greatest. And Matthew leaves a censure upon his former life, which Eusebius observes is mentioned by none but himself, *viz.* that he had been a *publican and sat at the receipt of custom*, a thing of very ill fame at that time. Peter, supposing that Mark wrote his gospel under his conduct, as is generally thought, sets forth his denying his master with all the aggravations of the sin, more than is to be found in the rest of the evangelists; but passes over very slightly the account of his repentance.

Now these, and the like, are such instances of simplicity, humility, and honesty, as are never to be found among impostors and writers of false history. They generally take care to secure their own reputation, and make themselves the heroes of the story, and to serve their party and their cause at any rate. But as these writers are free from such blemishes, and thus on all occasions lay open their own infirmities, it is a good argument they had no cause to serve but that of truth. I might add,

4. They could propose to themselves no worldly

advantage, but fully expected reproach, persecution, poverty, and all sorts of sufferings, as what would attend and follow the cause they had espoused. And accordingly it fell out. But yet,

5. Notwithstanding they persisted in their story even to death, and sealed their testimony with their blood. Not one of them ever recanted, or ever owned himself an impostor.

Now to suppose these men were cheats, that they did not themselves believe the truth of what they published to the world, is I think to suppose human nature in them different from what it is in all others. One must really change it into another thing in them, quite different from what we know it and feel it to be in ourselves, before he can imagine that herein they acted a part and designed to deceive. For let us suppose them cunning enough to have forged their history, and hammered the scheme of the gospel out of their own heads, which yet I think is impossible, and let us suppose them wicked enough to have undertaken it. Yet I ask, what motive could they have to do it? would they be at all this pains, and guilty of all this vileness, for no other end but to be undone in this world, and damned in the next? as they must know was their due, if they believed another state.

What has been said may let us see that the writers of the Bible were qualified to publish a true history. What follows will more fully prove that their history is certainly true; otherwise there is no true history in the world. I proceed therefore to illustrate the next particular requisite in an authentic historian.

3. They wrote at the time when the facts they relate are said to have been done; and I add, those facts are of such a nature that it could not but be publicly known, whether they were done or not.

I

Cheats generally lay the scene at a great distance, when none alive is capable of disproving them. Thus the heathen mythologists tell strange stories of things transacted many ages ago, no body knows when nor where. But the writers of the Bible report things done in their own times, and fresh in the memory of multitudes to whom they appeal.

That Moses did so, is evident to any one that peruses his history. He wrote when that generation was alive that was concerned in the main subject of his book. And he published such things that it is impossible he should have imposed them upon the people, had they been false. For instance, the ten plagues of Egypt, their deliverance out of that land, their passage through the red sea, the drowning of Pharaoh and his host therein, with the many surprising circumstances that attended that event; the feeding them in the wilderness by the constant miracle of manna, the issuing water out of the rock at Horeb upon Moses's smiting it with his rod, the defeat of Amalek, the giving the law at mount Sinai, the pillar of fire, and of a cloud, which conducted their march through the wilderness, the destruction of Corah, Dathan, and Abiram, with their company, the earth opening her mouth and swallowing them up. Now I would ask any impartial person, whether there was room for imposture here? could not this people tell whether they had seen any of the wonders in Egypt, Moses gives so particular an account of? could they not tell, whether they had passed through the sea? or had seen the Egyptians drowned therein? whether they had been fed with manna or not? and heard the thunders of Sinai, and seen the glory of the Lord there?

I might take notice, could I here expatiate, that there were several circumstances of these events, which rendered them so remarkable and notorious, that it is not possible they should be mistaken. Thus when the law was delivered at Sinai, the people were commanded to prepare themselves for it three days beforehand; and it is said that all the people saw the thundering and lightning, and beheld the mountain smoaking, which filled them with so much terror, that they stood afar off, and desired Moses might mediate between them and the Lord, and that the Lord might not speak any more least they should die. And we read, that *the cloud of the Lord was upon the tabernacle by day, and fire was upon it by night, in the sight of all the house of Israel, throughout all their journies,* Exod. xl. 38. And so great a regard had they to it, that it prescribed and determined all their marches whilst in the wilderness. *Whether it was two days or a month, or a year, that the cloud tarried upon the tabernacle, the children of Israel abode in their tents and journeyed not: but when it was taken up, they journeyed,* Numb. ix. 22. So the manna was their constant supply till the day after they had eaten of the corn of Canaan, and then it ceased, Josh. v. 12. So long also their garments lasted without any decay, Deut. xxix. 5. This Moses relates in his history. Whether it was fact or no, there were as many witnesses as there were people; their eyes, their ears, all their senses were witnesses whether these things were so. Had not they been true, or had they been otherwise than is related, thousands might have stood forth and discredited the whole story; and supposing them false, I dare defy any unbeliever in the world to give a reasonable account why they did not.

Let me observe further, as what very much strengthens the argument, that we find Moses himself making a solemn appeal to them concerning these facts. Consult the passage, *Deut.* xi. from *ver.* 2, to the 8th, *And know you this day: for I speak not with your children which have not known, and which have not seen the chastisement of the Lord your God, his greatness, his mighty hand, and his stretched-out arm ; and his miracles, and his acts which he did in the midst of Egypt, unto Pharaoh the king of Egypt, and unto all his land ; and what he did unto the army of Egypt, to their horses, and to their chariots, how he made the water of the red sea overflow them ; and what he did unto you in the wilderness, until ye came to this place ; and what he did to Dathan and Abiram, how the earth opened her mouth and swallowed them up, their housholds, tents, and all the substance in their possession in the midst of all Israel. But your eyes have seen all the great acts of the Lord, which he did,* You see he appeals to the people themselves as witnesses, eye-witnesses of what he saith, and what he records; which he could never have done, had he acted the impostor, and designed to have imposed upon them a narrative of strange things, without any foundation.

But it may be objected, that the people were not witnesses of all the history he relates ; that in Genesis particularly. They knew nothing of the creation, the flood, and affairs of the patriarchs. These things were at a great distance, and Moses might here impose on their credulity.

I answer, that beside the extraordinary character of Moses's fidelity, he gave such proofs of his divine inspiration, (of which hereafter) that he could not be suspected. But more directly to the objection, I say, that it was scarce possible for Moses to forge this part of his history, and make the people believe it. These things passed through but a few hands, as remarked before, and the memory of them was easily preserved. Granting there were above two thousand years from the creation to Moses, yet if Adam, Methuselah and Shem, lived the far greatest part of them, they ought to be esteemed no more than three generations. And therefore, allowing for the length of men's lives at that time, the distance from the flood to Moses, cannot be computed so much as from the reformation to the present year. Now is it possible that such things as Moses's history contains, should be invented by an historian at this time, and the nation made to believe them? could any man in his senses be made to believe that Henry VIII, was the first king of England, that there was a deluge in his time that took off all the inhabitants of the island, except seven or eight persons, or that at the revolution, the Thames was diverted from its proper channel, and the prince of Orange passed over with his army on dry land. And yet this, as absurd as it appears, might as easily be believed among us, as what Moses says of the deluge, and of the children of Israel's deliverance out of Egypt, by the people of his time, had it not been true. Several hundred years were no more, by a just computation, considering how much longer men lived than they do now, than one hundred years is with us, a thousand years, not much more than a hundred now, in one part of the period, and but about equal to two hundred in another part of the period. And upon this principle, I do affirm, it was no more possible for Moses to invent the things of an earlier date in his history, and bring the people of his age to believe them, than it would be for a cunning sophister to contrive a legend of prodigious things done at, or since the reformation, and make them pass current among us.

Some may farther object, that the history we ascribe to Moses, might not be wrote at the time that is pretended, but might be the invention of later times. But that there is not the least probability of this, I think I could demonstrate, was the pulpit the proper place for such an argument, and the auditory prepared to attend to it. I will only mention a few things, that would admit of greater enlargement.

1. That Moses was universally owned as the lawgiver of the Jews. That people themselves universally believed this, and have in all ages paid the utmost veneration to his memory. Nor did any of the most ancient heathen writers pretend to deny, there was such a person as Moses, or question, whether he gave laws to the Jewish nation.

2. The objector cannot give any account when, or by whom, this history, and these facts related in the five books we ascribe to Moses, were forged. He cannot tell us the name of this imaginary historian that personated Moses; tell us when he lived, nor produce any authentic vouchers of the thing he supposes. So that in reason, the objection ought to be looked upon a mere cavil, and such as might be made against any other book in the world.

3. It is most absurd to imagine these things should be the invention of later times, or of any time. For,

1. The whole polity and government of the Jews was founded upon their laws. Not only their religion, but civil rites depended upon them, their courts of justice, their private privileges, their several properties, their inheritances, all depended upon, and were regulated by the laws said to be given by the ministry of Moses. Now let any one consider, whether it be possible for any impostor to contrive a body of laws, and when he has done, impose them upon a whole nation, and persuade them to submit all their rights, claims and privileges, to the decision of those laws. He that supposes this in the case of the Jews, supposes a thing altogether singular, and what never came to pass in any other nation in the world.

2. Many of their laws were of that nature, that one cannot with the least reason, think they would have received them, had they not been assured they were divine. How burthensome a rite was that of

DISCOURSE II. 65

circumcision? how costly and troublesome their sacrifices, with all the numerous precepts about eating, uncleanness, purgation, washing and the like. These things made their law a yoke, as the apostle calls it, *which they were not able to bear.* Their weekly sabbath, was a very great confinement and restraint, which they never would have come under upon the motion of a private man, that enjoins such things without authority. And to add only one particular more, their sabbatical year I reckon a law of such a nature, that it would never have been established among them upon the credit of an impostor. The law in short was, that every seventh year their land was to rest. They were neither to sow their ground, prune their vineyards, nor to gather any corn or fruits that grew spontaneously that year, Exod. xxiii. 10, 11. This was a statute that their lawgiver, whoever he was, obliged them to. The observation of which would have exposed them to the greatest misery and distress, without the special interposition and blessing of heaven for their relief. That they might justly apprehend this, is intimated, Lev. xxv. 20, 21, 22. *And if ye shall say, what shall we eat the seventh year? behold we shall not sow nor gather in our increase.* It follows by way of answer, *Then will I command my blessing upon you in the sixth year, and it shall bring forth fruit for three years, and ye shall sow the eighth year and eat yet of old fruit until the ninth year, until her fruits come in ye shall eat of the old store.* Here was you see, a law that cast them entirely upon an extraordinary providence, for two years. The sixth year was to afford provision for three years. Now I ask any considerate person, whether he can reasonably suppose they would have embraced such a law from an impostor? or if they had not thought it to be from heaven? I ask further, if they did receive it, as it is certain they did, was this security given them, of an extraordinary bleffing the fixth year, made good or not? If not, that of itfelf would have difcovered the cheat. If it was made good, it is a full evidence the law was divine,

So that confidering the nature of thefe laws, I think it a demonftration, they could not be the contrivance of any, but were given by Mofes, and that by the fpecial appointment of heaven, as he affirms. The reafon is, they would not otherwife have received them. They were fo much againft their eafe and their prefent interefts, had not God made up all to them by a peculiar providence, they had fo much of burden in them, that no lefs authority, than that by which Mofes acted, and which they knew he was invefted with, could have inforced them upon them. Their heathen neighbors laughed at them as a foolifh people, for throwing away a feventh part of their time; becaufe they kept the weekly fabbath, and would they have yielded not only to this, but to a fabbatical year, and to many other cumberfome obfervances, if they had not had a full conviction of Mofes's commiffion, and of the divine authority of their laws.

3. The methods taken to inftruct the people, both in the law from the firft promulgation of it, and in matters of fact from the time that they happened; were fuch as leaves no room for impofture. They were all of them obliged to the moft careful ftudy of the law, and to propagate the knowledge of it in their families: *Thefe words which I command thee this day*, (fays their legiflator) *fhall be in thine heart, and thou fhalt teach them diligently unto thy children, and fhall talk of them when thou fitteft in thine houfe, when thou walkeft by the way, when thou lieft down, and when thou rifeft up.* Add to that, every feventh year, at the end of the year, the book of the law was brought forth and read in the audience of all the people, men, women, children, and ftran-

gers, *Deut.* xxxi. 10. The autograph or original book of Moses, as some think, was then produced that the people might hear their law recited in the words in which Moses left it.

Now it must be remembered, that this book contained not only their decalogue, their ordinances of worship, sacrifices and ceremonies, their appointments of festivals, and the like; but also the history of God's providence towards them, the judgments he had wrought among them, and the deliverances he had wrought for them. These they often heard read, these they read themselves, and were so well acquainted with, that Josephus tells us, they knew them as perfect as their own names. And this being the state of that people, of the main body of them at least, I would demand, could it be possible for any man after Moses's time to invent such a book, and persuade people to receive it? to invent a narrative of such facts, and prevail with a whole nation to own them as facts, though they knew nothing of them, and though they could not but know they were false?

The books were in their hands, and in their hearts, as you have heard. Now there must be a time when these books were first read. If it was a long time after the facts were done, could not the people tell, whether they had ever heard of such things before, as the plagues in Egypt, the dividing the red sea, the delivering the law at mount Sinai, and the miracles in the wilderness? and if they knew all these things, the point is granted I am pleading for, the book was wrote, when we say it was wrote, in Moses's time, and when a great part of the generation remained, that had seen the transactions there described. If they knew them not, how came they to receive a book that relates such strange things, and not only so, but appeals to them-

K

selves as knowing them. He that can suppose this, is strangely prepossessed in favor of infidelity, and indeed prepared to believe any thing, but the Bible.

Let me add, they had public memorials of many of their great events. To say nothing of the names of persons, and places, which were given at the time of this or that event, and designed to perpetuate the memory of it; some of their festivals were of this nature. Their passover was a monument raised up to preserve the memory of their deliverance from Egypt, and of the slaying the first-born there. The feast of tabernacles was a memorial of their dwelling in booths in the wilderness. Aaron's rod, the pot of manna, the golden censor, the brasen serpent; these and the like were standing records of great and eminent providences towards that nation.

And two things I infer from them, *viz.* that as they were monuments, public records of ancient facts expounded to the people and well understood by them, they could not be ignorant of these facts. The feast of the passover was a constant memorial of what happened in Egypt, and whilst it was yearly repeated among them, they could not forget that great salvation. And further, as these memorials took rise, and were instituted immediately, upon such events to which they refer, the history of these facts could not be the forgery of after times.

And thus I have sufficiently proved, that Moses's history was wrote at the time when the facts they relate are said to be done, and that it could not be an invention of a later date. You will excuse me for insisting on such things. I am sensible they will be less acceptable to those, that never had their thoughts employed about subjects of this nature. But as I am persuaded of their importance, so, I hope, in the progress of these discourses, to make you sensible of their usefulness.

DISCOURSE II. 69

Some may alk probably, though we allow the hiftory to be as ancient as is defired, how doth it appear that Mofes was the writer of it? I anfwer, it was conftantly believed by the Jews themfelves: other places of Scripture afcribe it to him; it was owned by the moft ancient writers among the Pagans, at leaft he was owned by them as the Jewifh lawgiver. As for the objections of Spinofa, Hobbs, and father Simon, I apprehend it would be thought tedious, fhould I go about to confider them diftinctly. They all amount to little more than this, that fome paffages in the Pentateuch could not be written by Mofes; and, I muft declare, I know no inconvenience in allowing they might be inferted by fome after-writer; as, for inftance, by Ezra; though I am fatisfied moft of thofe they infift on, may fairly be accounted for, without any fuch conceffion.

I next proceed to confider the *New Teftament*. And what I have here to affert and maintain is, that the facts there recorded were publicly done, and the hiftory wrote at the very time when it might be known, whether they were done or not.

As to the firft of thefe, I think, I need not difcourfe at large upon that fubject. The doctrine, the miracles of Chrift and his apoftles were none of them concealed; but all things were tranfacted in the prefence of their enemies, and expofed to their view. Hence our Lord pleads in his own defence before the high prieft, *I fpake openly to the world, I ever taught in the Synagogue, and in the temple, whither the Jews always refort; and in fecret have I faid nothing.* And both the gofpels, and the hiftory of the Acts, inform us of the miracles the apoftles wrought in the moft populous cities, at Jerufalem, Samaria, Antioch, and other places. How eminent an event was the effufion of the Holy Ghoft upon the apoftles on the day of Pentecost; and how visible and public the effects of it. They were enabled to work miracles, and to speak with all sorts of tongues, which they did in the presence of a multitude of people from all parts of the world. At that great festival, Jerusalem was filled not only with the natives of Judea, but with the Jews of the dispersion. They came from the east as far as Persia and Media; from the west, as far as Rome and Lybia; from the south, as far as Arabia; and from the north, as far as Parthia, and many provinces of Asia the less. Now in this convention, in the midst of such an assembly, and in the most public manner, the apostles and preachers of Christ gave a specimen of the extraordinary power with which they were indued from on high, and spake all kinds of languages they had never learned: an astonishing thing! at which the auditory were all amazed: *Are not these Gallileans?* say they, *and how hear we every man in our own tongue, wherein we were born?*

Further, as the facts recorded in the New Testament, were done in the face of the world, so the history was published in that age, and whilst the witnesses were alive. That it was thus early published is evident, since it mentions the temple and nation of the Jews as still subsisting: so that consequently, it must be written before the destruction of Jerusalem. The Acts of the Apostles, were wrote by St. Luke, soon after St. Paul's going to Rome, an account of which he gives at the close of that history. Now this was but about twenty years, after our Lord's resurrection. And you find he there mentions his gospel, as wrote before that time. But I need not stand to prove what none of the enemies of christianity dare take upon them to deny. Hobbs himself owns, that the writers of the New Testament lived all in less than an age after Christ's ascension, and had seen our Lord, or been his disciples.

The purpose I bring this for, is, to shew that the history of the New Testament, must be unquestionably true; otherwise, the writers of it would never have published it to the world, and in the midst of their enemies of all sorts, when so many thousands were living that could have detected the falshood. The books they wrote, were immediately dispersed, read in all christian assemblies, as Justin Martyr assures us, And the apostles and first preachers, wherever they came, always insisted upon the great facts of them, the death and resurrection of Christ, and the miracles that were wrought, *God still working with them, confirming their words with signs following.* To which may be added, that the next christians, * in the age after Christ and his apostles, constantly professed an assurance of the facts recorded in the New Testament.

Now I appeal to any reasonable person, whether this looks like imposture, or whether there be any instance in the whole world, of an imposture that

---

* *The next christians in the age after the apostles.*] Remarkable to this purpose, is that of Quadratus, who as Eusebius assures us, dedicated and presented an apology for the christian religion to the emperor Adrian, about the year 120: in which were these words, *The works of our Saviour were always conspicuous, for they were true. Those that were healed, such as were raised from the dead, did not only appear after they were healed, and raised, but also were afterwards seen of all, and that not only whilst our saviour was conversant upon earth, but also after he was gone; they continued alive a great while, insomuch that some of them survived even to our times.* Eusebius declares in the same place, that this book of Quadratus was extant among many of the brethren in his time, and that he himself had it, Eccles. Hist. L. iv. c. 3. And we have another observable passage to the same effect in the epistle of Irenæus to Florinus, where that father, who flourished before the year 170, speaks of his being with Polycarp in his youth, whose person and discourses he perfectly remembered, the conversation, he used to say, he had with St John, and others, that had seen the Lord: and what Polycarp had received concerning our Saviour, his doctrine and miracles, from those who had been the eye-witnesses, all exactly agreeing with the scriptures. Euseb. Hist. Eccl. L. iii.

comes up to it? Would the apostles have taken this method, and have exposed themselves to the contempt of mankind, had they not been conscious of their own integrity, and assured that none of their enemies could contradict what they say? They report to the world that their master rose again, that the Jews sealed the sepulchre, that they craved a watch of Pilate to guard it, that the guard run away, and that the chief priests, and others, hired the soldiers to say, while they slept, his disciples came and stole him away. They affirmed, that a person born lame, and known to all the inhabitants of Jerusalem, by begging daily at a gate of the temple, was cured by Peter, only with invocating the name of Jesus, Acts iii. 6.

These and the like things, they report and write, and you will consider, that they do not write in a remote country and age, but at the very time when, and in the very place where, the matters were transacted: which I think so strong an argument of the truth of their history, that all the cavils of infidelity can never shake it.

But perhaps some may object, that in all this argument, we appeal to the history itself, and are taking that for granted, which is the question. We suppose that there were such persons as Moses, as Christ and the apostles; that they did such things, and that their history was wrote at such times. But this, saith the unbeliever, wants to be proved. I answer, that it is certain these histories are now in the world, and I dare say, the objector will not pretend they were wrote either this or the last century. I demand therefore, when they were wrote? who wrote them? who invented the stories of Moses and Christ, and when they were invented. It is but reasonable to expect from them, that they should fix upon something as certain, in opposition to the account we give; which yet, I am confident, they will not pretend to; and consequently, this objection must pass for a cavil.

However, I shall more directly consider it, and remove the difficulty that it seems to throw in our way, which will bring me to the next head, viz. That we do not depend purely on the authority of the historians of the Bible, but have the chief facts confirmed by very ancient, and some of them cotemporary writers. Now this, as it fully answers the objection I just mentioned, so it tends very much to confirm the truth of the scripture history. But as the subject is too copious to be brought into this discourse, and too important to be passed over superficially, I shall take leave to resume it on another occasion. At present, let me make a reflection or two upon what has been said.

1. If the Bible be true, as I am proving it is; how weighty and important a thing is religion? the doctrines and concerns of which have been handed down to us in the way mentioned there, by such a train of wonderful providences, such surprising miracles, such labors and sufferings of holy men; and which eclipses all the rest, of the Son of God himself. The Bible gives that account of these things, and makes all subservient to the great ends of religion: that one cannot but infer, it must be the most important thing in the world. The interest of the church, divine worship, God's covenant and promises, his favor and eternal life, &c. These must certainly be the most momentous affairs. They must be so if the Bible be true; otherwise, they had never been so much the care of heaven, had never employed the council of God so much as they have, if we may believe the Bible.

2. If the Bible be true, it deserves our most diligent and serious study, its subject is so great, its tendency so divine, and we have so mighty an interest in the discoveries it makes, and encourage-

ments it proposes, that to neglect it, must argue great stupidity. And indeed, it is to revive and increase our veneration for the Bible, and to assist you in understanding and improving it, that I have undertaken these discourses, and the exercises that may follow. Did we believe the Bible more, converse with it, and study it more, it would tend to give us a distaste of many of those little things that fill our time and thoughts. Nor do I ever expect to see religion recover its lustre, till the Bible recovers its reputation among us. I do not mean, only rescued from the contempt of such low triflers as prefer a play book to it; but from the neglect and carelessness with which most christians treat it. Were our tempers and frames right, we should only divert and turn aside to the things of this world, when, and so far as the necessity of our affairs, and duties of our places obliged us. But the study of the Bible, and the practice of the great things it directs to, would be the main business to which our minds stood bent. And happy will it be for us, if we find a strong and prevailing bias this way! I have good authority for it, when I say, *Blessed is the man whose delight is in the law of the Lord, and therein doth meditate day and night.*

DISCOURSE III.

The Truth and Credibility of the Scripture.

2 Tim. iii. 16.

All Scripture is given by inspiration of God, and is profitable for doctrine, for reproof, for correction, for instruction in righteousness.

I AM endeavoring to prove the Bible is true, and particularly, that it is of equal credit with any other history in the world. To which purpose I have shewn,

I. That the persons who wrote it, had sufficient opportunities of knowing the things they published.

II. That they were persons of integrity, who, as they were not deceived themselves, would not deceive others.

III. That they wrote at the time when the facts they relate, are said to be done, and might be known to be done. I now add,

IV. The account the writers of the Bible give of things. The particulars of their history is confirmed by co-temporary, or at least, very ancient writers, that had an opportunity of knowing the facts published there, and could not be supposed to be biassed in favor of those that published them.

What can one expect more in an historian, than that he knows his subject, whether the things he publishes be true or false; that he be a person of unblemished honesty; that he writes at the very time of action, and when the things he relates were done; and that persons of the same age, who have an opportunity also of knowing the same things, do not deny, but confirm his account. If these characters be not sufficient to make an ancient historian authentic, there is none in the world to be depended on. Now the writers of the Bible have them all in a degree above any others. I have proved this with reference to the three former particulars, and am now to do it in relation to the last.

As to the first part of the Bible, the history of Moses, there may seem a defect and want of vouchers. And it must be granted, we cannot find cotemporary writers to confirm Moses's history. The reason is, there are no such, Moses being the most ancient historian in the world. And yet something we have to alledge in confirmation of the sacred history, and indeed as much as can reasonably be expected, in the first ages of the world. Now this being a point of great nicety, and yet of great necessity in the present argument, allow me to make a few observations; in which, I shall not only let you see what footsteps we have of Moses's history among the most ancient writers, but also why we have no more, nor more early vouchers among them. And,

1. Let me observe that the sacred history, that of Moses, is properly the history of the church. After the dispersion of the sons of Noah, when the world was relapsed into idolatry, God was pleased to single out Abraham and erect a church in his family, to give them a covenant of peculiarity, distinguishing them by many special favors and privileges. Thus he tells them, *Deut.* xiv. 2. *Thou art an holy people unto the Lord thy God; and the Lord hath chosen thee to be a peculiar people unto himself, above all the nations that are upon the earth.*

DISCOURSE III. 77

They were a separate peculiar people, had peculiar laws; *he shewed his word unto Jacob, his statutes and judgments unto Israel. He hath not dealt so with any nation; and as for his judgments they have not known them,* Psal. cxlvii. 19, 20. The apostle takes notice of this, *Rom.* ix. 4. *To them pertaineth the adoption, and the glory, and the covenants, and the giving of the law, and the service of God, and the promises.* God was pleased to inclose and incorporate this people, for the special purposes of religion, to set them apart for himself; among them was his tabernacle and shechinah, the seat of his worship, his special presence, the displays of his grace, and theatre of his wonderful works. Now it must be considered, that the history of the Old Testament, particularly of Moses, is an history of facts that more especially concerned this people; of revelations made to them, and of things done among them and for them, that is, of things done within the inclosure.

2. The circumstances of the rest of the world were such, that no very authentic memoirs, no particular history, especially of the affairs of this people, could be expected from them. They were left out of the pale of the church, and could have but a very imperfect knowledge of what was transacted within it. It was the posterity of Abraham, the children of his grandson Jacob, that went down into Egypt and sojourned there, they and their descendants for some hundreds of years; who were the persons that saw the miracles in Egypt, and at the red sea. These were they that received the law at Sinai, and were entertained with that surprising scene of wonders in the wilderness, for forty years. The rest of the nations as they bore no part in these things, so all the knowledge they could have of them must be by distant reports. They never saw Moses by his rod turn the waters of Egypt into blood,

and afterwards divide the red sea, never saw the flaming mount, on which the divine law was delivered; the mysterious cloud that descended, and conducted God's people for so long a time. All these strange phœnomena were among the Israelites, and part of that glory and distinction God put upon his peculiar people.

And besides, it must be considered, that the nations of the world were involved in gross ignorance, over-run with idolatry, and sunk into barbarism. Upon the confusion of tongues at Babel, and the defeat of that impious attempt thereby; the knowledge of God, and of the true religion, began to decline in the world, and in a few generations was very much lost. I cannot better represent this, than in the words of a learned man. * " The sons of " Noah, after their several dispersions and planta- " tions of several countries, did gradually degene- " rate into ignorance and barbarity; for upon their " first settling into any country, they found it em- " ployment enough to cultivate the land, and pro- " vide themselves habitations and food" He adds, " They were often put to remove from one place to " another, which Thucydides speaks of as the case " of the ancient Grecians, and it was a great while " before they came to embody in towns and cities, " and from thence to spread themselves into pro- " vinces, and to settle the bounds of their territories.

This being the state of most nations in the first ages after their plantation, there was no likelihood of any great improvement in knowledge; so far from it, that there would probably be a great decay of that knowledge, which had been conveyed down to them; their necessities keeping them in continual employment. It was a considerable time before they were settled under regular and formed govern-

---

* *Stillingfleet* Originæ Sacræ. p. 11.

ments: and till then, they had no opportunities to pursue arts and sciences, or write history. And that this was the case is past question, with respect to most of them, they had so far lost knowledge of themselves, and their ancestors, that they could give no tolerable account of their own original, but generally thought themselves to have sprung out of the earth, where they inhabited. From which opinion, Thucydides tells us, the Athenians used to wear their golden grasshoppers.

There were two other causes, besides what I have just mentioned, of the ignorance, and particularly of the defect of records and history, among the heathens, namely, the want of necessary means and helps to preserve the memory of things. The Grecians, that most of all others glory in their antiquity, had not the use of letters till Cadmus * taught them the same; who, carry his antiquity the highest, was but co-temporary with Joshua, and many think him only co-temporary with Samuel. And as they wanted means, so also an inclination to such work.

---

* *Had not the use of letters till* Cadmus.] Some learned men indeed have imagined the Greeks had the knowledge and use of letters before his time, having learned them from Cecrops the first king of Athens, who led a colony out of Egypt, where learning and letters had long flourished, fixed in Greece, built that city, and taught the use of letters to that people. But this conjecture, how probable soever it may appear, is not supported by so many and good arguments, as the opinion of those, who make Cadmus the first author of the Greek letters. It is very certain if Cecrops did introduce any, there are no monuments of his characters remaining, nor were they known to the most ancient writers of that nation, whose works are come down to us. The oldest we have any memoirs of being those taught by Cadmus, and his followers, that seem at first to have been the same with the Phænician, as Herodotus tells us they were, and as may be concluded from the most ancient Greek inscriptions, that we have copies of, particularly the Sigæan, given us by Dr. Chishul; whence it is easy to observe a very great affinity between the old Greek letters, and those now called Samaritan, thought by many to have been originally the Hebrew and Phænician characters.

They had not learning sufficient, to record things concerning themselves, much less any inclination to interest themselves in the affairs of other nations. The great events of the Bible were done among another sort of people; as those barbarians knew little of them, so they had little zeal about them.

Add to this, as what may reasonably be supposed, that after God had confounded their language at Babel, and scattered them abroad upon the face of the earth; he in a great measure took his holy spirit from them. And as they had not the special revelation from heaven, that the family of Abraham enjoyed, nor that intercourse with God; they gradually fell into a forgetfulness of him; lost the knowledge of the true God, set up idolatry, and run into those horrid superstitions, that in process of time, were the disgrace and reproach of human nature.

Now that a people in these circumstances; thus abandoned of God, *a people sitting in darkness, and in the regions of the shadow of death;* destitute of arts and sciences, in a great degree, and for a long time of letters; that knew little of their own affairs, had few or no memorials of their ancestors; and seldom extended their view beyond their own times and concerns; that these should not be historians, and especially historians of the church is no wonder.

3. As there are no histories among them, but what fall much below the time of Moses, so when they began to write the history of their respective nations, and of others, they mix it with fables to that degree, that little dependance can be had on the accounts they give.

Thucidides owns, they have no records of Greece before the Peloponnesian war. All that he could discover in the ancient state of that country, was a great deal of confusion, as he tells us, unquiet stations, frequent removals, continual piracies, and no settled form of government. So that before that period, according to this writer, who is justly celebrated as the most impartial of all the greek historians, there was nothing certain among them, but all was mere chaos and confusion. Indeed, the Phœnician history by Sanconiatho, is acknowledged to be of more antiquity.* And yet his greatest advocate, Porphyry, is forced to grant he was younger than Moses; Bochart makes him co-temporary with Gideon; though others think him much later.

I hinted, as their histories are of less antiquity than the sacred history, so they are very much disguised with fables. This might be shewn at large, was it proper here to stand upon it. They found themselves at a loss for materials for true history, wanting ancient monuments, and therefore made use of inventions to supply the defect. Hence the famous distinction by Varo, of time into unknown, fabulous, and historical; accounting all time, either absolutely unknown, or fabulous, till the first Olympiad, which was when the world was three

---

* The Phœnician history by Sanchoniatho is acknowledged to be of more antiquity.] It is so by the generality of learned men, as to say nothing of Eusebius and others anciently, by Grotious, Bochart, Stillingfleet, Cumberland, and many more among the moderns: not to mention Kircher, who pretended he had seen Sanchoniatho's original history; but there are several others, both of the last and the present age, who have called it into question, and even rejected it as spurious. That great antiquary Mr. Dodwell offered divers arguments to prove it to be so, and to shew it was a forgery, if not of Porphyry himself, yet of Philo Biblius the translator; and an ingenious writer has of late expressed his suspicions concerning the genuineness and antiquity thereof, in some dissertations published in the present state of the republic of letters, with a view of confuting bishop Cumberland's system of mythology in his learned treatise upon Sanchoniatho's Phœnician history, in order to defend and establish the chronology of the incomparable Sir Isaac Newton. However, without entering into that dispute, and admitting the book under consideration to be genuine, and as old as it can be supposed to be, there are several things therein that are a surprising confirmation of the Mosaic history.

thousand years old. If it be asked, what purpose this serves? I answer, it affords a satisfactory reason why we should not expect the records of the Bible among heathen historians.* You see they were out of the church, that Goshen of the world, the land of light, and spot where God displayed himself in the wonders of his providence. They can give no tolerable account of themselves, their own original and affairs, for want of sufficient authentic records. And we need not think it strange that they say so little of a people separated from them, and confined within such an inclosure as the Jews were.

And then, what has been said may also serve to promote our veneration for the Bible. We had known little of the origin of the world, the maker of it, or of those glorious acts of providence on which our religion is founded; had it not been for Moses's history. So that however our modern deists despise the Bible, and insult Moses, as they sometimes do with an impious freedom, they are

---

* It is no wonder we find so little in heathen authors concerning the Jews, their religion and affairs. As for the Romans their writers are comparatively of a late date. And for the Greeks they were not only very ignorant in antiquity, but so full of themselves as to despise all other people, and esteem them barbarians; not excepting even the Romans, whom they appear to have known little of, till they were brought into subjection to them. Add to this, that it seems highly probable, if not certain, that many of their authors designedly omitted speaking of the Jews, and their concerns, out of envy and hatred to them as Jesephus observes, and indeed proves by a remarkable instance. Besides, it is not to be doubted, but several of their works are now lost, wherein we might have met with accounts of that nation that would have confirmed the sacred history. This we know to be actually the case with Hecatæus's book relating to the Jews, and we may be sure it is so in regard of many other Greek authors. Though after all, there are not a few of the old heathen writers, whose works are come down to our hands, that make mention of them, and some particulars of their affairs agreeably to the sacred records, as Herodotus, Strabo, Diodorus Siculus, Trogus, Pompeius, and others.

beholden to the sacred writings for all that is valuable in their knowledge of ancient things; the creation of the world, the fall of man, God's purpose of grace towards fallen mankind, the manifestation of his power and providence in the government of the world for some thousands of years; the knowledge of these things we derive from the Bible, and entirely depend on divine revelation for. The most ancient profane historians here give but very little satisfaction; they do not begin soon enough, their discourse is dark, obscure, broken, and disguised; the reason of which has been sufficiently intimated. So that not only our faith, as christians, is established, but our curiosity, as men, gratified by the Bible. But,

4. Notwithstanding the great disadvantages the heathens lay under, and the manifest defects of their histories; it may reasonably be expected, that there should be preserved among them some memory of the great events recorded in the Bible. I ground this chiefly upon a fact, which with me admits of no dispute, *viz.* That all mankind proceeded from the same stock, and had originally the same parents. What cavils are advanced against this, I shall not at present take notice of; nor can I find the least weight in any of them. The Scripture is so plain in this matter, that I apprehend none can make a question of it that believes the sacred writings. The apostle tells us Adam was the first man. And our Lord, speaking of Adam and Eve, says, that at the *beginning of the creation God made them male and female.* And the apostle more directly to our purpose, *God hath made of one blood all nations of men, to dwell on the face of the earth;* some Greek copies followed herein by the Arabic, vulgar Latin, and others, read " of one," that is, of one man, leaving out " blood ;" but there is no need of the criticism; blood signifies,

as is common in the best Greek authors, the stock out of which mankind springs. Add to this, that Adam expressly calls his wife, the mother of all living, making that the reason of her name Eve. So that I need not call this a postulatum, and desire it may be granted by those that receive the Bible: It is a certain truth, fully revealed there, that from this pair, Adam and Eve, all mankind derived, and the whole world was peopled.

I am only to observe further, that after the destruction of the world by the deluge, Noah and his sons were the heads and parents of a new world. For this, at present, I appeal to the Scriptures; you have it in express words, *Gen.* x. 32. after an account of the descendants from Japhet, Ham, and Shem, it is added, *these are the families of the sons of Noah, after their generations, in their nations, and by these were the nations divided in the earth after the flood.*

Now to apply this to my present purpose, since all mankind had a common original, first, from Adam, and then from Noah and his sons, it is most reasonable to think they should have among them some memory of the chief facts in the Mosaic history, that were of common concernment; as the creation of the world, with the manner of it; the name of the first man, the first institutions or ordinances of religious worship, the general flood, and the like. It is not accountable that all these things should be utterly lost, and no footsteps of them continue in the heathen nations, since they had the same original. So that what remains here to be done, is to enquire, what traditions we find of the sacred history among the heathen writers. Your attention I know would not accompany me, should I enlarge upon this head: and therefore, though I have taken some pains to collect what I can meet with relating to the subject, and which I am sensible is of use for confirming our belief of the Bible. I shall pass it over with some short and general hints.

Let me observe, that the most ancient and celebrated historian among the pagans, Sanchoniatho, has a great many instances of the scripture history, and of the stories related by Moses: as concerning the creation, the original of idolatry, the invention of arts, the foundation of cities, the calling of Abraham, and the like; in so much, that Porphyry, an ancient philosopher and a great enemy to christianity, endeavors to establish the credit of his history, from its agreement with that of Moses.

I must not descend to particulars, and trace all the passages that occur to our purpose. The fullest account that is given, by any one author, is in that learned book of Grotius, *Of the truth of the christian religion*, an abridgment of which I shall offer, as I find it prepared to my hands by an ingenious writer.* " The manner of the formation of the earth
" out of a chaos is mentioned by the ancient Phæ-
" nician, Egyptian, Indian and Greek authors: the
" name of Adam and Eve by Sanchoniatho and
" others: the longevity of the antedeluvians by
" Berosus, Manetho, &c. The ark of Noah by Be-
" rosus: many particulars of the flood by Ovid and
" others. The family of Noah, and two of every
" kind of animals, entering into the ark with him,
" are mentioned by Lucan, as a tradition of the
" ancient Grecians: the dove which Noah sent out
" of the ark, by Abydenus: the burning of Sodom
" by Diodorus Siculus, Strabo, Tacitus and others.
" Several particulars of the history of Abraham,
" and the rest of the patriarchs, by Berosus and ma-
" ny more. Many particulars of Moses's life, by
" Berosus and others. The eminent piety of the
" most ancient Jews, by Strabo and Justin. Divers

* Dr. Clark's evidence of natural and revealed religion, p. 259.

"actions of David and Solomon in the Phœnician
"annals. Some of the actions of Elijah by Menan-
"der, and confessed by Julian himself. The history
"of Jonah under the name of Hercules, by Lyco-
"phron and Æneus Gazæus; and the history of
"the following times by a multitude of authors." *

To this I might subjoin, that a great deal of scripture history was disguised in the heathen mithology, as the names of God, Jehovah, Elohim, and the like; the names of Adam and others of the patriarchs, the name of Noah under that of Saturn;

---

* It would be easy to add a great many other particulars to these; as, the attempt to build the tower of Babel was not only sung by the poets, but recorded by Berosus, Abydenus, Eupolemus and others. The confusion and division of languages upon that occasion was generally apprehended and acknowledged by the heathens, who owned that originally there was but one language in the world, as Josephus, Eusebius, and St. Cyril informs us from Abydenus, and other of their writers. Many things concerning Joseph, his character, conduct and management in Egypt are mentioned by Justin. Several particulars relating to the Israelites of old occur in their authors; as their going into Egypt, and their coming out of it again, attested by Manetho, Berosus, Strabo, Justin, and others; the dividing the red sea for a passage to them, by Artapanus, and Diodorus Siculus; their travelling in the desarts of Arabia and coming to mount Sinai by Justin; their being fed with manna in the wilderness by Artapanus, who says, they lived there upon a certain snow which God rained from heaven. As to Moses himself, his story is witnessed to, and recorded by Egyptian, Phœnician, Chaldæan and Grecian writers. Besides, what is afterwards taken notice of by the author, there is a particular and remarkable account of him given by Artapanus and Numenius, as of his being taken out of the water, brought up at court, working miracles, and being opposed before the king by certain magicians, called Jannes and Jambres, who attempted to do the like, &c. There are divers other facts related in the Old Testament the memory whereof seems to have been preserved among the heathens, and which were probably referred to in their fables, as the story of Jephtha's daughter under the name of Iphigenia; Abraham's attempt to sacrifice Isaac his only son by Sarah, in the fable of Saturn's sacrificing his only son Jeoud, whom he had by the nymph Anobret, and the like. But these are sufficient for a specimen, and may serve to attest the truth of the Scripture history.

Bochart shews no less than fourteen instances of a parallel between the one and the other. The flood of Noah, as it could not escape them, nor the memory of it be lost, upon the principles I have mentioned, so it is taken notice of by many of them, and generally under the name of *Deucalions*,* with such particular circumstances, as shew their account must be borrowed from scripture; or if it depends upon traditions preserved among them, that very much confirms the scripture story. Change the name of Deucalion for Noah, and Lucian's representation of this matter is almost parallel to that of Moses; he tells you the first generation of men were destroyed, and Deucalion was the progenitor of a second generation: he ascribes their destruction to their wickedness, and makes the means of it to be a flood of water; that Deucalion and his family only were saved, and that in

* Berosus the Chaldæan historian, Abydenus and Alexander Polyhistor describe it under the name of Xisuthrus's flood, and mention a great many particulars concerning it, that have a surprising co-incidence with the account given by Moses. As, that he was forewarned of it beforehand, was directed to build a sort of a ship for the preservation of himself and his kindred, eight persons in all, to take provision with him for their subsistence, together with beasts and fowls; that accordingly he did so, and when the flood abated sent out some birds which returned to the ship twice but the third time came back no more, whereby he understood that the earth began to appear, upon which taking off the cover he found the ship rested upon a mountain, and after some time he went out and offered sacrifices. And no doubt Ogyges flood spoken of by other ancient writers, was only a corrupt tradition of the same event, that of Noah. Lucian says, that all creatures went into the ark by couples. Plutarch mentions the very time when Noah (under the name of Deucalion) entered into the ark, and of his sending forth the dove to discover the state of the waters, whether they were decreased or no: and he adds, that it returned into the ark again. Indeed there was hardly any nation that had not some notion remaining of the deluge. If Martinius may be credited, there is a tradition of it among the Chinese, and we are even told, that the Americans of Peru, Mexico, &c. have still the like tradition among them.

a great cheſt, into which he came with his children, and with ſeveral animals; and that the deluge of water ſunk into a great hiatus, or gap in the earth. Theſe, and a great many more particulars of ſcripture hiſtory, are commemorated among them, though changed and mangled in their fables. But any one, that has the Bible in his hands, may trace them in the ſtories they tell.

I will only hint at two things more here, namely, that Moſes was univerſally owned among them, and celebrated as a lawgiver. Longinus mentions him as no ordinary man. Strabo ſpeaks of him with great commendation, and Diodorus Siculus places him among the chief lawgivers, Trogus Pompeius takes notice of his beauty and wiſdom, agreeably to the character Stephen gives of him in Acts vii. Farther, they had among them a great many religious rites, which I think is evident, they derived from the Jews; as circumciſion, ſo famous among the Iſhmaelites in Arabia. So their weekly ſabbath, new moons, and above all, the conſtant cuſtom of ſacrificing. Theſe things were notorious among the heathen nations, and I look upon them as ſo many footſteps of the original laws given to the patriarchs and Jews, and atteſtations to the ſacred hiſtory.

And from the whole, without further reaſoning, I think I may infer with good evidence, that the hiſtory of Moſes is true. That they ſpeak of them ſo fully as they do, and that there is ſuch a general concurrence and agreement among them upon the main heads of the ſacred hiſtory, I think can never be accounted for, but upon ſuppoſition that the hiſtory is genuine and authentic. Whence ſhould all the world have theſe notions of a chaos, of a creation out of it, of the flood, of Abraham and the patriarchs, of Jewiſh rites? and whence ſhould they take up the practice of ſacrificing, which univerſally obtained among them, had not God appointed it, and had it not come to them from the patriarchs and Jews? That the reason of mankind should agree in such a rite of worship for appeasing God, and recommending themselves to his favor, is not imaginable. For how should they conclude, that the deity would be pleased with the destruction and blood of any of his creatures. So that I think their opinions and sentiments, the scattered fragments of the sacred history, that occur in the pagan writers, and their religious observances, are so strong a testimony to the history of Moses, that no reasonable man can question it, unless at the same time he will question all history, and destroy all the monuments of ancient facts, both sacred and profane.

If any ask, whence had the gentiles their account of these things? I answer, in short, some of them might be had by tradition from the ancient patriarchs, from Noah and his sons. Several things they might learn from the Israelites during their stay in Egypt. And they might get intelligence of some other particulars from the Jews themselves, after their settlement in Canaan, and from their sacred Scriptures, * as might be made appear highly probable, but that I must not enlarge upon these things.

---

* The heathens may reasonably be supposed to have had their knowledge of these matters some or all of the ways here hinted at. For mankind descending from one common father Noah, who we may be sure carefully instructed all his children in the history of the world, the creation, fall, deluge, &c. It is by no means likely, that the more remarkable passages concerning these great events should soon be totally forgotten among any of his posterity. Certainly they would be handed down from age to age, and some kind of tradition be preserved of them a considerable while, though indeed it is natural to imagine, it would by degrees be so broken and altered, as exceedingly to disguise the truth. Besides, one cannot but conclude, that during the long residence of the Israelites in Egypt they would communicate many things to the Egyptians, and others, who frequently corresponded with them. Without question Joseph, and other good men, would improve the opportunity they had of spreading the knowledge of those

I muſt yet beg your patience whilſt I touch the other part of the hiſtory of the Bible, that of the New Teſtament, as recorded by the four evangeliſts, and in the acts of the apoſtles. I have here a noble ſubject, and ſufficient matter had I time to launch out. The facts related there were done openly in the face of the ſun, and expoſed to the view of the world: not done in a corner but publicly. And when the hiſtory of theſe things was formed, it was not concealed, but proclaimed and divulged to all, and therein a challenge and appeal made both to friends and enemies.

As to particulars, I muſt be forced to take the ſame method as before, give you an abſtract from the ſame learned author,* which he takes from Grotius. His words are, that a little " before the coming of
" our Saviour there was a general expectation
" ſpread over all the eaſtern nations, that out of
" Judea ſhould ariſe a perſon who ſhould be go-
" vernor of the world, is expreſsly affirmed by the
" Roman hiſtorians, Suetonius and Tacitus: that
" there lived in Judea at the time which the goſpel

* Dr. Clark's evidence of natural and revealed religion p. 271.

truths, which had been faithfully tranſmitted down to them from their excellent anceſtors the Patriarchs, and would take care to leave ſome laſting memorials of them among a people they had ſo much converſation with. And then the Gentiles undoubtedly derived a great many of their notions from the ſacred oracles afterwards, both in Judea, whither ſeveral of them travelled for inſtruction, and in Egypt, where a multitude of the Jews, occaſionally at leaſt, reſided, and whence, the beſt records we have of thoſe times inform us, moſt of the famous ſages and philoſophers of old fetched their learning, as Solon, Thales, Pherecydes Syrus, Pythagoras, Plato, &c. That this was really the caſe, we have the teſtimony of the ancient Jews, chriſtians and heathens, as has been ſhewn at large, and the matter of fact atteſted, and clearly proved, by abundance of our moſt learned modern writers, ſuch as Scaliger, Grotius, Bochart, Voſſius, Selden, Huetius, Stillingfleet, Gale, and many others.

" relates such a person as Jesus of Nazareth, is ac-
" knowledged by all authors, both Jewish and Pa-
" gan, who have written ever since that time. The
" star that appeared at his birth, is mentioned by
" Chalcidious the Platonist; as is also the journey
" of the Chaldæan wise men. Herod's causing all
" the children in Bethlehem," and among the rest
his own son " under two years old to be slain, and
" a reflection made thereupon by the emperor Au-
" gustus, that it was better to be Herod's swine than
" his son ; is related by Macrobius. Many of the
" miracles that Jesus wrought, as his healing the
" lame, the blind, and casting out devils, are owned
" by the most implacable enemies of christianity,
" by Celsus and Julian, and the authors of the Jew-
" ish Talmud. That the power of the heathen
" gods ceased after the coming of Christ," of which
I may say more afterwards, " is acknowledged by
" Porphyry. Many particulars of the collateral
" history concerning John the baptist, Herod and
" Pilate, are largely recorded by Josephus: the
" crucifixion of Christ under Pontius Pilate, is
" related by Tacitus ; and divers of the most re-
" markable circumstances attending it, such as the
" earthquake and miraculous darkness, was record-
" ed in the Roman registers, and are in a very
" particular manner attested by Phlegon."*

N

* That the most considerable facts mentioned in the New Testament are confirmed by the concurrent attestation of Jewish and
heathen authors, might be made appear, by a much larger induc-
tion of particulars; but I chose to refer the inquisitive reader to
Mr. Lardner's credibility of the gospel history, where he will
meet with full satisfaction upon this head; and instead of thinking
it strange, that we have no more and plainer corroborating testimonies from those writers to the matters of fact recorded in the
gospels, I am persuaded, he will rather admire that we have
so many, and such clear ones, as we have. Especially considering, how seldom it was to their purpose to take notice of

I might add to these testimonies the acts of Pilate, which though questioned by some, have I think a great probability in them. The case was this: it was usual for the Roman deputies, or governors of provinces, to give an account of the chief things, during their administration, to the emperor: accordingly, Pilate gave an account to Tiberius of what had happened in his time concerning Jesus of Nazareth; an account of his miracles, death, crucifixion and resurrection: upon which, it is said, that emperor proposed it to the senate, that he should be admitted into the number of their gods; and decreed, that none should be accused for being a christian during his reign. Two things I may remark with reference to this matter, namely, that Pilate's account was enrolled in the public records at Rome: and, that the fathers, as Justin Martyr, and Tertullian afterwards appealed to the emperor and senate upon the head, in their apologies for the christian religion. Which we cannot imagine they would have done, had they not been well assured of the fact, that such things were re-

these things, how unacquainted they must be supposed to have been with them for the most part, and how little they believed them, having never impartially examined into their truth. In short, nothing seems to me more unreasonable than to urge the want of plainer and fuller testimonies from heathens and Jews, to the facts on which the belief of the christian religion is grounded, as an argument against it, when the very plainness and fulness of a testimony of this sort, is by many thought a sufficient reason to suspect it to be spurious and counterfeit, the forgery of some over officious christian. This is the case with reference to that famous controverted passage in Josephus, the best argument that I know of produced against the genuineness of which is, that it contains an higher character of our saviour than it is likely an unbelieving Jew would give. And as I doubt not the case would have been the same in other instances, it must needs be very unfair to make the paucity of such testimonies an objection against christianity. So that upon the whole, I think it manifest, that we have as many and just such as we could in reason look for and expect.

gistered, and that their enemies had nothing to alledge in opposition to it.

Now this was a testimony of a public nature. Pilate, you know, was the judge before whom our Lord was tried, and by whom he was condemned. The thing was of so great consequence, and made such a noise in the world, that one cannot think he would pass it over in silence, and take no notice of it to the emperor. The fact is considered, the matter laid before the senate, and committed to their records; and thereupon a decree made in favor of the christians. That this is likely to be true, may be argued from the circumstances of the case. The emperors expected from their deputies, an account of any notable event that happened where they were. And can we imagine, that Pilate either would or durst conceal so great an event, as that concerning Jesus Christ, about which all Judea was in an uproar, and in which he himself had so great a share. From hence then, we may infer the probability of the story; and, I think, conclude its certainty from the apologies I mentioned of Justin Martyr and Tertullian. They were both learned men, lived in the next century, and I cannot think it consistent with their character to appeal, as we find they do, to the head of the Roman empire, and to so august a body as the Roman senate, concerning this fact had it been in the least doubtful.

So that here you see, we have the testimony of all sorts of authors in behalf of our point, of those that lived in the time, and nearest to the time, when the things mentioned in the New Testament history were done. The testimony of enemies, of Jews, of Pagans, of the emperor and senate, of Pilate, the very man that judged and condemned our Lord. All these own there was such a person as Jesus Christ, that he lived at the time the gospel relates, that he wrought miracles, that he was put to death by crucifixion, that he had many disciples and followers, of whose affairs several of them speak. And it deserves observation, that the most spiteful adversaries of the christian religion, and such as attacked it formerly with the greatest sharpness, as Julian, Porphyry, and Celsus, do not dare to deny the facts; they own what is said of Jesus Christ; and that he wrought miracles; only they pretend he did it by the power of magic, the Jews say by the Tetragrammaton, just like the absurd cavil of his enemies in the days of his flesh, that he cast out devils by Beelzebub, the prince of the devils.

You will allow me, I hope, to say now, that so far I have made good what I undertook, and have shewn you, that the characters of authentic historians belong to the writers of the Bible; they have, you see, the testimony of other ancient writers, even of their very enemies to confirm their history. The Old Testament has as much of this as could be expected, and the New Testament more plain, direct, and early vouchers. So that I think I need not scruple hence to conclude, that the Bible is certainly true. But I have not yet given you all the evidence of its truth. I proceed therefore to the next particular, which I shall dispatch in a few words, *viz.*

5. That the writers of the Old and New Testament treat of subjects of great importance, in which the interests of men are very much concerned: in consequence of which, we may conclude their relations of things would be examined by all sorts of persons: and yet none of the most critical examiners are able to disprove them, or pretend they were false. If any ancient history be a trifle, contains things of no moment to the world, mankind will not think themselves obliged to look very narrowly into it. Be it true or false it is all one to them. When this is the case, as it often is, no won-

DISCOURSE III.

der they let it pass, even though the greatest part of it be fiction and romance.

But when a history comes forth full of great and surprising events, especially of new laws and revelations, in which the highest interests of men are nearly concerned; we cannot imagine, it should be admitted without trial and sufficient evidence. And of this nature is the history of the Bible. There is no history of equal weight with it, as may be shewn with respect to both those parts of it, I have already more than once touched upon.

The history of Moses, that contains the memoirs of the creation, the fall of man, the promise of a redeemer to recover lost sinners, the apostacy and destruction of the old world, the preservation of Noah and his family, as heads of a new race, the laws and covenant of God, and the wonders of his providence towards the church, has something in it not only great and august, but of consequence to the world above any other history. And though I grant the Jews being distinguished and separate from the rest of the world, their law was not of general and universal concernment; yet even their history, as well as that of the patriarchs, was such as would excite the attention of mankind; particularly, as so many things are related in it that give them a preference to the rest of the nations, the miracles God wrought for them, the triumphs of his providence over their enemies, and in their behalf, in Egypt, in the wilderness, and afterwards in Canaan. Their neighbors and enemies could not be ignorant of many of these things, and had they been false, would loudly have remonstrated against them. Would not the Egyptians have borne testimony against what Moses says of the destruction of their monarch, and disgrace of their country by so strange a series and train of judgments, had there been any room to contradict his report? And yet we find nothing of this, no counter history, but, as has been observed, have evident footsteps of the facts recited by Moses, in their most ancient records.

I need not shew how important Moses's history was to the Jews, and that they could not have received it without examination. They would never have submitted to Moses, had he been an impostor; would never have embraced his laws, had they not known they were divine, nor believed his history, if they had not been assured it was true. When he delivers his law to them, he doth it in strains of very high authority, and signifies to them that he sets before them a blessing and a curse. *A blessing if they obeyed, and a curse if they would not obey.* To the same purpose he says, *I have set before thee this day, life and good, and death and evil.* And again, *I call heaven and earth to record this day against you, that I have set before you, life and death, blessing and cursing.* He tells them, that *if they walked in the statutes and judgments of God they should live and multiply, and God would bless them in the land whither they went to possess it. But if their hearts turned away and they would not hear*, he solemnly denounces to them, that *they should surely perish.* And as their law came with such an awful sanction, so the authority of it reached to all their affairs; their inheritances, civil rights, peace, health, and prosperity of every kind, depended upon it. I might add, that though the whole history of Moses tends very much to exalt the mercy and grace of God towards that people, and sets forth the wonders of his providence done among them and for them, yet it leaves them under severe censures; it represents them as a stiff-necked, rebellious, ungrateful people; gives an account of their frequent murmurings and apostacies, and of the judgments of God inflicted upon them for their sins; sets a mark of infamy and reproach upon some eminent persons and families among them, as Aaron, Miriam, Corah, Dathan, Abiram and others.

Now had not this history been true, and known to be true beyond all possibility of question, had not the laws published been from God, the censures past been just, the things related been done according to the revelation; as it had been in the power of a multitude to have confronted the deceiver and contradicted the story; they would not have failed to have done it. The account given of them was of too great consequence to the community, and too nearly touched particular persons, to pass without examination, and to be received without irresistible evidence.

As to the New Testament, every one will discern the importance of its history and of the facts it contains; the incarnation, death, and resurrection of the Son of God, were the greatest events that ever entertained the world, and could not but draw the attention of men, as we know they did. Consider the matter a little, Jesus of Nazareth an obscure person by his birth and education, assumes the character of the Messiah; declares himself sent and commissioned by God the Father; and accordingly acts as his ambassador, repeals the statutes of Moses; condemns the forms of worship that had so long obtained among the gentiles, and calls upon them to renounce their idols; reveals a new doctrine and plan of religion; works miracles and sends forth apostles to preach his doctrine, and gives them also power of miracles to confirm that doctrine. He lays down his life, rises again from the dead, promises eternal happiness to his followers, and demands of all, as ever they expect an interest in his salvation, that they believe in him, and submit to his authority.

Now these were such very important things, of so mighty consequence to all sorts of persons, that I think it was impossible they should be passed over with indolence and neglect. Here was a new state of religion introduced, the venerable rights of Moses cancelled, the superstitions of the Pagans trampled under foot, and not only so, but the reputation both of the one and the other struck at. For to say nothing of any other instances of their conduct set forth and censured in the sacred history, we find they are represented there as acting a scandalous part in the tragedy of Christ's death, the Jews persecuting and delivering him up for envy, and Pilate condemning him against the conviction of his own conscience. The former, the Jews, seem apprehensive how much their credit was touched in the matter, and therefore endeavored to silence the apostles and stifle their report, alledging they had *filled Jerusalem with their doctrine, and intended to bring this man's blood* upon them. So that had there been room for cavilling, any pretence upon which they might hope to invalidate the testimony of the sacred writers, their malice, nay, a concern for their own reputation, would have put them upon it. They were avowed enemies to Jesus Christ, nothing galled them so much as the fame of his miracles, and the spreading of his doctrine thereupon; and we may be sure as they did observe these things, they would not let them go without contradiction, but that there was no ground for it.

As for christians, the whole body of christians, they were so deeply interested in the facts recorded in the gospel, that it is certain they could not neglect them. They professed to believe the gospel history and indeed ventured their all, their present and everlasting all, upon the credit thereof. They could not be christians without believing, nor believe, ordinarily, without being martyrs. Their master made the first necessary, and their enemies the latter. Chrift would not accept them unlefs they would own him, confefs him, and be faithful to him: and if they did fo their enemies generally perfecuted them, even unto death.

This was the ftate of the facred hiftory, efpecially of the gofpel hiftory. It relates matters of the greateft importance to mankind, wherein their higheft interefts are immediately concerned; and confequently, they could not but think themfelves obliged to enquire narrowly into it, as actually they did; and after their utmoft examination, none were able to deny the facts, or deftroy the credit of the hiftory: from whence I may conclude, it is undoubtedly true.

It was not poffible to forge fuch an hiftory as that of Mofes and of Chrift, and perfuade mankind to believe the fame. The reafon is, they were too much concerned in thefe things, not to examine whether they were true or not. There are many ancient hiftories of fo little moment to any part of mankind, that no body thinks it worth his while critically to enquire into all the particulars of them; and therefore no wonder that fome fuch pafs current, whatever fictions there may be in them. But when the hiftory is of general and great moment and importance the cafe is otherwife. Should any one for inftance, pretend to give us an hiftory of our own nation, or but of the reign of one of our kings, wherein a great many facts are forged, and a great multitude of ftories told againft the intereft and reputation of any confiderable party. And fhould he moreover alter public laws, and go about to impofe a new ftatute book; I afk, whether fuch an hiftory could poffibly obtain any credit, and fuch an attempt fucceed among us? would not thoufands rife up and detect the impofture? or rather the attempt would fink and ruin itfelf by the absurdity and impudence of it. The same may be said with reference to an abuse and forgery of the records in the Bible. No man could have contrived such a book, with such laws and facts, without exposing himself to the contempt of the world, of Jews, Pagans and Christians. England may as soon be persuaded to receive a forged body of statutes never enacted in parliament, nor pleaded in any court of judicature, as the Jewish and christian church could have been persuaded to receive the laws and history of Moses and Christ, from the hands of an impostor.

And thus I have gone through the first of the three particulars I proposed to insist upon; have shown you, that the sacred history has equal credit with any ancient history, and that all the characters of credible historians belong to the writers of the Bible. They had sufficient knowledge of what they wrote; they were persons of great integrity; they wrote at the time when the facts they publish are said to be done, and when it might be known whether they were done or no; their history is confirmed by co-temporary writers, and the things, they relate, are of so much importance to mankind, that they could not but think themselves obliged to enquire into them. From whence it follows, that either the Bible is true, or we can have no evidence that there is any true history in the world.

And now to conclude this discourse with a practical remark, or inference from what has been said. If the Bible is true, then on the one hand, how sad and deplorable is the case of wicked men; of carnal, worldly, sensual sinners. The Bible is wholly against them. It censures their principles, condemns their practice, represents God as their enemy, and hell as their portion. Which, by the way, I doubt is one great reason of many persons' enmity to the Bible. It checks and controuls them in their sinful pursuits, and did they believe it, would exceedingly terrify them. Hence they hate it, as Ahab did the prophet, because it speaks evil to them. If the Bible be true, *the way of the ungodly shall perish, and the wicked shall be turned into hell.* On the other hand, we have hence matter of great joy and comfort to good men. It is so much our interest that the Bible should be true, that methinks those that are inclined to question, whether it is, or not, should yet wish it true. And indeed was that the case with the opposers of it, I do not doubt but their scruples would soon be over, and the dispute cease.

A good man would not for the world that the Bible was not true. He finds there so much satisfaction concerning God and providence, as governing all things and interesting himself in all his affairs ; so much assurance concerning another better state, so much support and comfort in this, that he justly esteems his Bible his inheritance and treasure. Rejoice then, christian, that we have such good evidence of the truth of it. There thou hast a glorious revelation, *a sure word of prophecy,* excellent rules to direct thy practice, exceeding great and precious promises to afford thee comfort, and a certain prospect of eternal life hereafter. O be thankful for the Bible ; study, love, and live the Bible ; and you shall find all true at last, and that not one iota, or tittle of the word shall pass till all be accomplished.

DISCOURSE IV.

THE TRUTH AND CREDIBILITY OF THE SCRIPTURE.

---

2 TIM. iii. 16.

All Scripture is given by inspiration of God, and is profitable for doctrine, for reproof, for correction, for instruction in righteousness.

I HAVE made it appear, I think, that our Bible is of equal credit with any other ancient history, and consequently, that if it be not true, we have no sufficient reason to receive and believe any ancient book in the world. And according to the method I proposed, I am now

II. To shew that our Bible has greater marks of credibility, stronger evidences of truth, than any other ancient book. I might argue this at large; but I shall content myself with a few observations. As,

1. The writers of the Bible seem to have excelled other historians in their moral character. They appear to have been persons of eminent integrity, goodness and virtue; and discover in all their writings, the greatest impartiality, and love of truth. Compare them in these things with most historians in the world, and it is easy to see on which side the advantage will be.

To touch only on their impartiality; how gloriously does that shine through all their narrations. Moses fully relates the evil things of his nation;

both their sins and their sufferings; their offences against God, and his judgments upon them. Nor doth he spare himself, he records several instances of his own infirmities, and tells you, that God was angry with him and Aaron, and for their sins excluded them out of the promised land. The New Testament writers represent their master under all the disadvantageous characters of a sufferer, as loaded with reproach and contempt, and at last undergoing an ignominious death. And I before took notice, they do with great freedom set forth their weaknesses; their cowardise, slowness of belief, their pride and emulations; the many rebukes they met with from their master, and their shameful forsaking him, and denying him in his last sufferings. It is left on record against the great apostle Paul, that he consented to the death of Stephen, and made havoc of the church; on which account, he calls himself the *chief of sinners, a persecutor, a blasphemer, and injurious.* And when he mentions that glorious and distinguishing instance of favor to him, his rapture into the third heaven, he doth it with such circumstances as tend to mortify him; for he tells us thereupon, *God sent a thorn in the flesh, a messenger of Satan to buffet him, lest he should be exalted above measure.* This, and the like, was the conduct of these men from first to last, as might be made out in a multitude of instances. But it is sufficient to say, there never were in the world more candid fair writers; persons that acted a more disinterested part than the writers of the Bible. Bring other writers to the test, hear and examine their characters, compare them to that of Moses and the apostles, and I am confident few can bear the trial. The common historians must fall before them, as *Dagon before the ark of God.*

What gross fables the Greek and Roman historians mixed with their histories, on purpose to aggrandife and raife the fame of their own nations, has been taken notice of; at the fame time, omitting whatfoever tended to their diminution. Among other inftances, this is remarkable, that * Porfena, in his league with the people of Rome, obliged them to make no other ufe of iron, but for the tilling the ground, none of the Roman hiftorians think fit to relate this circumftance; whereas, when the people of Ifrael were reduced to the like ftraits, their hiftorian freely owns it. And even Jofephus, the celebrated Jewifh hiftorian, paffes over in filence feveral things difhonorable to his nation; particularly, their folly in making the golden calf. But the facred writers have none of thefe blemifhes upon them, none of thefe objections lying againft them. They fought not their own glory, the honor of their own nation, their friends, their party; but appear in all they fay and do, to act from no other principle but love and zeal for the truth.

Not but there are a great many hiftories wrote by very honeft and fincere perfons, who had no defign in any particular to impofe upon the world; but as good men, the beft of men, are in all things fallible, in many things prejudiced; fo none of them could come up to the manifeft character of the writers of the Bible. Thefe have been actuated by an higher fpirit, have difcovered a purer zeal, a more fteady, uniform, divine intention in their compofures. Allow me therefore again to repeat the corrollary and confequence from hence, that if we do not admit the Bible, we muft give up all other hiftories as legend and juggle.

2. It adds to the credit of the fcripture hiftory, and gives it the preference to all others, that, as I remarked before, it contains matters the moft weighty and important of any in the world. It treats of things of fuch a nature, that all mankind, before

* Plin. Nat. Hift. l. 34. c. 14.

whom it was laid, would think themselves bound to look into it, and sift it to the bottom. There is no other history like to undergo so critical a scrutiny as the sacred; the reasons of which, I have already hinted at: and, I think, I may justly alledge it as a circumstance in favor of the Bible, and as what gives it a superior credit to any other ancient book.

3. The scripture history has had more enemies than any other, and has stood the test of the most nice enquiry; some of it several thousand years, and all of it several hundred. The Jews and christians have espoused their respective sacred histories, upon full conviction of the truth of each. Their successors have from age to age, and for a great tract of time, acquiesced therein as sufficiently established. Nor have their enemies, for so long a while, been able to discover any fraud, or cheat in the sacred writings, notwithstanding their utmost efforts.

If it be objected, That the adversaries of christianity might confute these things at the time they are said to be done, though we have not now the account of that matter. I answer, 1. We have no proof, no records remaining of any such confutation. Let the objector name by whom this was done, or undertaken; produce any tradition of such a fact, any book wrote on such a subject. If he cannot, there is nothing in the allegation, but it must be looked upon as a mere cavil. 2. It is evident, the enemies of the Bible never pretended to confute or deny the facts therein reported; for instance, the miracles of Christ and his apostles. On the contrary, you find some of them freely confessing them, *What shall we do,* say they, *to these men? for that indeed a notable miracle hath been done by them is manifest to all them that dwell in Jerusalem; and we cannot deny it.* Should the objector turn upon me, and suggest, that I am producing the testimony

DISCOURSE IV.

of a book under dispute, that it is only the Scripture itself that tells us this. I reply, these facts are owned by the heathens and Jews of that time, as has been proved. And besides, the Jews since do not pretend to deny them; but plead, that Christ wrought miracles by the power of magic, or by the mysterious use of the Tetragrammaton, the name Jehovah. I answer further, 3. Had there been any such confutation of the facts in the Bible, the Jews, no doubt, would have preserved the testimony or writings of such opposers; would have made use of them in their disputes against christianity; which yet they never did. So that, I conclude, this character, this superior character of the credit and truth of the Bible, is unquestionable. No other ancient book has been so much examined and criticised upon, and stood the attacks of enemies so long and so much.

4. The Scripture history receives a mighty confirmation from the concord and harmony of its several writers. It was wrote by several persons, in several parts and ages of the world, and every one gives testimony to another; which is a circumstance that cannot be alledged with the like advantage in behalf of any other book or history. Moses speaks and writes of Christ, as he himself tells us, John v. 46. and in his types and prophecies points out and delineates the great events of the gospel dispensation in his song. *He hath raised up an horn of salvation for us in the house of his servant David; as he spake by the mouth of his holy prophets, which have been since the world began.* So Acts iii. 24. *And all the prophets from Samuel and those that follow after, as many as have spoken have foretold of these days.* Moses and the prophets give testimony to Christ and the gospel; foretell and describe the things thereof. The gospel owns Moses and the prophets and gives

testimony to them. So that it is a good argument, that if any part of the Bible be true, all is true; if Moses be true, the prophets be true, the New Testament is true: and on the other hand, if the New Testament be true, so are Moses and the prophets. They have a mutual dependance and give mutual testimony. They stand or fall together. An argument that will serve no other book or history in the world, at least not so fully as the Bible. I might add,

5. God himself hath owned this history, and given it a divine testimony in a manner, that cannot be pleaded in behalf of any other history. He has owned this book to be his; owned the penman of it, and vindicated its truth and authority. But as this belongs to another argument and will be afterwards considered as a proof of the inspiration of the Bible, I shall not here insist upon it. In the mean time it may fitly be observed as one of the particulars that give the Bible a preference to all other books.

And this may suffice for the evidence of the second particular, that the Bible has superior marks of credit and truth in it above any other history. It remains according to what I promised,

III. That I shew, that all circumstances considered, it is morally impossible the Bible should not be true. I say morally, by which I distinguish the impossibility I speak of, from that which is strict and absolute, arising from the nature of things. All human understandings are, and will be, imperfect. If we have the testimony of one man, of an hundred, of a thousand, concerning this or that particular, we may have great reason to believe this or that testimony. But it implies not contradiction when any say, it is false. But notwithstanding this, there may be such a concurrence of circumstances in a testimony or an history concerning

DISCOURSE IV.

past things, as renders it not only highly reasonable to believe it, but even impossible to be false without changing the faculties and nature of man, and the state of things among mankind. And of this kind, I think, is the evidence we have, that the Scripture contains a true history. It is I say, with the distinction mentioned, impossible the Bible should be false. To confirm which position, I shall offer a few considerations.

1. It is not possible that the writers of the Bible should be deceived themselves. They had the help of all their senses and faculties to enable them to discern whether the things they published were true or not. And if so many persons, in so many different cases, were not enabled to make a judgment about what they relate, having all of them their senses and the use of their reason; others in the like circumstances may be deceived, you and I, and ten thousand more, and consequently nothing can be certain in the world.

Moses could not but know, whether he had been with Pharaoh, treating with him time after time in the manner he reports. He could not but know, whether he used his rod for the working such miracles as are contained in his history; he could not but know whether he had been on the mount with God, and received two tables of stone from God there; whether he brought them down in his hands, broke them at the foot of the mount, and had them afterwards renewed. The New Testament writers could not but tell, whether they had seen Christ, heard his discourses, been witnesses of his miracles, seen him hang on the cross, conversed with him after his resurrection, and seen him ascend into heaven; they could not but know, whether they had wrought the miracles they give an account of; and, particularly, could not but know such as were wrought upon themselves, as their speaking with tongues they had never learned; they might know as certainly, whether they received the miraculous gift of languages at Pentecost, as they knew their own existence. To suppose, that a multitude of persons, and that of all sorts, should be deceived in things of this kind, is to destroy the nature of man, deny that he is a reasonable creature, capable of moral government, and reflects the utmost dishonor upon God, the author of his nature. I may therefore conclude, it is impossible these persons should be themselves deceived. If what they wrote was false, they knew it was false, and they could not but know, whether it was true or false.

2. As they could not be deceived themselves, so it is impossible they should mean and intend to deceive others. For, 1. I have shewn they were persons of great integrity and truth. The characters thereof were conspicuous in all they said and did. 2. They were under great obligations to speak the truth. Nothing is more contrary to the religion they propagated, and the doctrine they taught, than lying; not so much as a pious fraud, an officious lie, was allowed by them. When a thing of that kind was imputed to them, they rejected it with abhorrence, *If the truth of God*, says the apostle, *hath more abounded through my lie unto his glory, why yet am I also judged as a sinner? and not rather as we be slanderously reported, and as some affirm that we say, let us do evil that good may come; whose damnation is just.* And you every where find a mark of reprobation set upon lying in scripture, and such as indulge to that vice, appointed to destruction. Thus we are told, *All liars shall have their portion in the lake, which burneth with fire and brimstone.* Now is it possible, that these persons should invent a lie, so prodigious and blasphemous a lie, as that of the gospel, if it be false? Invent, publish, and palm it upon the world in the name of God: that

they should do this in contradiction to their manifest character and avowed doctrine? He that will impute this to them, makes them the most self-contradicting, self-condemned men in the world. 3. They could have no motive to such a vile undertaking. It was against their worldly interest; as is evident to any one that knows their case, and reads their history. What the apostle Paul says of himself, was true of all of them: Christ had forewarned them of it, and they expected it, *viz.* That *bonds and afflictions* did abide them. They were assured, that to follow Christ in hopes of another world, was the certain way to be undone in this; that they should be hated of all men for his name-sake, scourged, every way persecuted even unto blood and death. If it be said, they had not much to lose, I answer, some of them left a very comfortable subsistence. Matthew was a toll-gatherer, an officer of the customs, and, no question, was in the way, not only of living, but growing rich in some measure. Luke was a physician, and the apostle Paul was in so much esteem among the great men of the Jewish church, and so much devoted to their interest, was so learned, exact, and zealous in his profession, that he might have expected considerable preferments: all which he chearfully renounced, accounting all, as he tells us, not only loss, but dung for Christ Jesus our Lord. The rest of the apostles indeed were fishermen; but we are told they had hired servants, which implies, their circumstances were not very mean, at least not necessitous. But the argument is not concerned in this. Whatever their former circumstances were, it is certain, they could not propose to mend them by following Christ. If they had but little, that little must be much with them, because it was their all; and no man can lose more than all. Nor did they only quit their livelihood and means of subsistence, but their ease, their outward peace and their life was facrificed for the fame caufe.

Now I think it not poffible, had they been confcious of a lie, and that the gofpel was a forgery, that they fhould have promoted it upon fuch terms. They could have no motive, no temptation hereto; and confequently to fuppofe them guilty of this, is to fuppofe them to have abandoned the principles of felf-prefervation and felf-love, to do evil for evil-fake: not only without, but againft their own intereft; and to contrive the moft enormous wickednefs, for no other reafon, but to be miferable here and damned hereafter, which I reckon impoffible, as not being confiftent with any principles of human nature that we are acquainted with. If there ever were any that did fuch things as thefe, they muft not be men, but another fpecies of creatures than we have any idea or notion of.

If it be faid, that honor and reputation might fet them at work. I anfwer, that obfcure perfons, fuch as were the firft propagators of the gofpel, and publifhers of its hiftory, are feldom pufhed on to great enterprifes, upon motives of honor and vain glory. They have little fenfe of thefe things. Befides, they could have no expectation of honor from the world. They were told of hatred, of reproach; of the moft infamous, barbarous ufage. And they faw that muft be their lot, if they engaged in the fervice of Chrift. So that, I may conclude, it was not poffible thefe men fhould defign a cheat and impofture. They muft know the truth and goodnefs of the caufe they efpoufed, or they had never efpoufed it. Again, 4. I think it altogether unaccountable, and indeed impoffible, fuppofing fome particular perfons, fhould be capable of fo much wickednefs and vilenefs, that fo many of them fhould agree therein, and that none of them fhould detect the villainy. All forts of perfons, Jews, pagans, multitudes of both, were engaged in the profession and service of the gospel. They had their different sentiments, divided into parties, run into debates, and mutual censures and schisms: some fell into herasies, and were publicly censured by the churches, and excommunicated. The apostle Paul himself had zealous enemies that endeavored to ruin his reputation, among the Corinthians, Galations and others; against whom he was forced to write with some sharpness, for the vindicating himself and establishing the churches. Now, what I remark is, that among all these persons, this multitude of converts, too often drawn up in factions one against another; full of animosities, bickerings, party heats and quarrels, none of them ever undertook to accuse christianity of imposture, or to discover any deceit of confederacy among the professors of it. Think of the case of Judas here particularly. You know he betrayed his master, sold him for thirty pieces of silver. Now, either he knew that Christ was an impostor, and the gospel a forgery or not. If he knew it, would he not upon this account have proclaimed the thing to all the world, and thereby vindicated his own honor? but so far was he from it, that you know conscience flew in his face, and he comes to his abettors with a sorrowful complaint, *I have betrayed innocent blood*, and not being able to bear the load of so much guilt as he found pressing his mind; he throws down the money, goes his way, and hangs himself. Certainly, had the gospel been false, the device of some cunning men, one or other would have spoke out; the provoked and enraged; the apostates, such as Judas, particularly would have done it. It is not, I think, possible they should all persevere in a lie, a known lie; and neither the love of truth, nor love of themselves, nor hatred of such as they accounted enemies, prevail with them to make a difcovery. To which I might fubjoin, that multitudes of thefe perfons carried their teftimony to the truth of chriftianity with them to death, fealing it with their very blood: no fears, no terrors of their enemies, nor remorfe of confcience, could make them draw back or recant.

Now all this confidered, I prefume, I may fay, it is not to be accounted for, it is not agreeable to any thing we know of the human nature; and that indeed it amounts to an impoffibility, that there fhould be any fraudulent defign, in the writers and preachers of the gofpel. They could never, fo many of them thus have agreed, and thus have perfifted in a known lie and falfhood. And then as they could not be deceived or defign to deceive, fo

3. It was not poffible they fhould be able to deceive others. Had the writers of the fcripture intended, and endeavored, to have impofed their hiftory upon the world, they could not have fucceeded in the attempt. This may be fufficiently collected from what has been faid. I fhall however remark two or three things for the proof of it.

1. They had not art enough to manage an impofture. The apoftles of Chrift particularly had not. Their education was low and mean; they were not bred up in the courts of princes, or in the fchools of the philofophers; but were taken from the fifher-boat moft of them to preach the gofpel; and fome have obferved, their employment tended to make them more heavy and dull; for being much upon the water, and in the night, the cold phlegmatic air would have an influence upon them and flatten their fpirits. Hence Plato, when he would exprefs a rude dull man, fays he was brought up among mariners. Add to this, that they lay under difadvantages from their country, being Gallileans, whofe dialect was accounted the moft ungenteel and rude of any; a Gallilean, was a term of

DISCOURSE IV.

diminution, a fort of a nick-name, by which they meant a mean and contemptible rustic.

In short, view them in all their circumstances, and it will appear impossible that such persons, supposing they have the confidence and folly to undertake a cheat of this nature, should ever be able to carry it on. Their enemies took notice they were ignorant and unlearned men. They had neither depth of understanding, nor fluency of speech, were neither scholars, nor orators. And is it to be imagined, that they should be able of their own heads to contrive such a story, as that of the gospel history? and not only so, but persuade others to receive it?

2. They relate facts of such a nature, that it is not possible they should have cheated the world into the belief of them, had they not been true. For instance, they give an account of facts done before a multitude of witnesses, who could not but know whether such things were done, and in that manner done or not. Let us consider, among many other instances, the passage of Christ's crucifixion with the circumstances of it; that at the time of the passover when there was a mighty concourse of people at Jerusalem, he was condemned by Pilate against his conscience, and publicly put to death; that the vail of the temple was thereupon rent, the rocks split, graves opened, and there was a preternatural darkness over the land for several hours; and all this was done, as they pretend, before great numbers of spectators, both Jews and Romans. Now, if these things really were done, as is represented in the gospel, our point is so far gained, the history is true. If false, why did not their enemies contradict them; especially since the honor of some of them was so nearly touched. If this story be false, and Christ was not crucified, and such

and such events did not happen at the time of his crucifixion, it is impossible the apostles should have gained credit to the forgery.

The like I might say of abundance of miracles recorded in the gospel. Let us reflect a little on the raising of Lazarus from the dead, an account of which you have in the eleventh of John: where you will observe he was not only dead, but buried four days; this was publicly known in the neighborhood: and therefore several of the Jews came to the sisters of the deceased to pay them a friendly visit, and to condole with them: upon this you are told of a conference between Christ and Martha; and read of the despair they were in of receiving any help with reference to their brother: yet notwithstanding Christ goes to the grave, calls upon the dead man, and immediately he comes forth. Thereupon, as the history goes on, many of the Jews believed in him. Others lay the matter before the Pharisees, who immediately summon a council, and being alarmed with the report of so surprising a miracle, to prevent the consequence they feared from it, determine to put Jesus to death. *What do we?* say they, *for this man doth many miracles, and if we let him alone all men will believe on him.* And you read in the following chapter, they passed the same resolution with reference to Lazarus; the fame of the miracle encreasing, people flocked to see the dead man now alive, and many believed on Jesus, by reason of Lazarus. Hence they thought it necessary, that he should be dispatched out of the way too, and be put to death. This is the substance of the story, and I think I may warrantably conclude, without much reasoning upon it, that it was impossible to make it pass current had it been false. Here are a great many persons introduced, as having a part in the scene, Lazarus, his sisters, the Jews; some of whom are represented as convinced, and others as taking dishonorable methods to slur the miracle and disgrace the author. Lazarus lives as a standing monument of the divine power of Christ; multitudes are carried by their curiosity to see and converse with so remarkable a person; and of these many are converted, and profess faith in Jesus as the Messiah. Now what I insist on is, that had this story been false, it could never have been admitted as true. Lazarus himself, we may suppose, would have denied that he had been dead, and was raised to life again; his sisters, the Jews, would have been ready to have cried out of the imposture. And upon the whole, I think it is not possible, circumstances considered, that all of them should have suffered a forgery of this nature to remain undetected.*

I might alledge under this head, and for confirmation of the point I am upon, that the writers of the gospel history relate many miracles, which a multitude of persons were the subjects of. For instance, the descending of the Holy Ghost, and their speaking with tongues. Thus Peter tells his hearers, that if they repented, and were baptised, they should receive the gift of the Holy Ghost. And we are informed, that while Peter spake to the people *the*

---

* Upon the occasion of what is here transiently said concerning the resurrection of Lazarus, I cannot forbear remarking, that this is one of the miracles of our saviour that Mr. Woolston has lately endeavored to discredit as much as he can; though was it a proper place to enlarge upon the subject, it would be no difficult matter to shew the weakness and absurdity of his exceptions and cavils. But as the discourse comes in here occasionally, I shall not at present stand to take notice of what he says. Only, I think, I may be allowed to observe, that the hints given in this paragraph are sufficient to vindicate the matter of fact, and manifest the reality of the miracle. But if any desire to see the case considered more particularly, I would recommend to their perusal the Rev. Dr. Harris's two discourses upon it, intitled, the reasonableness of believing in Christ, and the unreasonableness of infidelity, with the appendix.

Holy Ghost fell on all them that heard the word. Now this was a sensible thing; the persons that received the gift could no more doubt of it than of the most obvious, plain and certain truths: they could not be deceived in the matter, could not but know whether they spake with tongues they had never learned, and whether they wrought miracles or no. The thing was evident to others, and therefore Simon Magus desired that he might have power granted him *that on whomsoever he should lay hands he might receive the Holy Ghost.* Others saw it, the persons themselves felt it, and it was impossible that herein they should be deceived.

3. It strengthens the argument and further shews the impossibility of an imposture, that a multitude of persons, and of all sorts of persons, received and believed the gospel history; the Jews, the Gentiles, many thousands and myriads of these; such as had been avowed enemies, owned their conviction and became converts, and that against the most inveterate prejudices. Thus we are told, that *the word of God increased, and the number of the disciples multiplied in Jerusalem, and a great number of the priests were obedient to the faith.* Among the rest, let me only mention the case of the apostle Paul. It is known how deeply he was engaged in another interest, in opposing Christ and the gospel. He was a person of character and eminency in the Jewish church, an Hebrew of the Hebrews, bred up under the famous Gamaliel, entered into the sect of the Pharisees, and exceeding *zealous for the traditions of the elders,* as the rest of that faction were. Hereupon the name of Christ became odious to him, as a person that not only lessened the authority of Moses, but had declared himself an enemy to the traditions and inventions of the Pharisees, condemning them as the grossest hypocrites, and their religion as vain and worthless. This inflamed him

against christianity; and you know how much he set himself to run it down. He was present at the death of Stephen, the first martyr, and was an encourager of it, received a commission from the chief priests to do the honorable work of a persecutor, which he followed with a zeal, that he himself afterwards called madness, haling men and women to prison, and breathing nothing but threatnings and slaughter, and death against them. Now, I would demand of any reasonable man, whether it was likely, nay, whether it was possible, on supposition, that the facts in the gospel had been a forgery to persuade this person and others to have received them. They could not believe the gospel without quitting the most stubborn prejudices which had long possessed their minds; without quitting their honors, their interests, and preferments; without contradicting and condemning themselves, and exposing themselves to all manner of reproach and sufferings. And would persons in such circumstances be gulled and cheated by a company of poor fishermen, and contemptible Gallileans? he that can believe this, is prepared to believe any thing; and indeed believes the most absurd, incredible thing in the world, even whilst he pretends to reject the gospel for want of credibility.

So that I do not think I talk in too high a strain, when I say, that it is impossible the gospel history should be false; and particularly, that if the writers of it had a mind to deceive, it is impossible they should have been able to do it. I may add to what has been said,

4. That it is not possible the gospel history, had it been false, should have maintained its credit in the world to this day. Not to repeat here, what has been observed already, that it was embraced by so many against the strongest prepossessions and prejudices, has been examined by such multitudes

of persons of different opinions and interests. What I would at present remark is, that God himself would not have suffered such an imposture to have been palmed and imposed upon the world. It is not consistent with the divine knowledge, mercy and goodness, to have suffered in his providence a book so full of the strongest evidence to be offered to mankind, a book that looks so like true, that it is impossible by any faculties we have, to distinguish it from true, had it been really false. He would not have suffered his creatures, especially the wisest and best of them, and I cannot forbear accounting them such that have shewn the greatest veneration for christianity and the Bible, to be thus tried, and to have lain under a delusion from age to age.

I grant there are many impostures and cheats in the world; but God is true, wise and good, the best as well as greatest of beings, and he will not neglect, or be wanting, to his upright servants that sincerely desire to be taught by him, and be subject to him in all things. In a word, should we be deceived here, I cannot see but we are deceived by an evidence that is in a great measure irresistable. We cannot reject it without denying our faculties, going contrary to the faculties God has given us, or if I may be allowed to say so, governing ourselves by other faculties than he has given us. And consequently, to suppose the Bible may be false, is to suppose that our very faculties ensnare, and that God has left us to be deceived in the proper use of them, without ever interposing for our relief; which is an horrid arraigning the author of our nature, and issues in no less a blasphemy than this, that if we be deceived, God has deceived us.

And thus I have sufficiently proved that the scripture is true, that it has all the characters of truth that any other ancient history has, and that if we

DISCOURSE IV.

are not to receive it, we can believe no hiftory in the world; I have proved it has greater evidence of truth in it, and that all things confidered, it is impoffible it fhould not be true.

Perhaps fome may be ready to fay, to what purpofe is all this wafte? we do not queftion the truth of the Bible. I anfwer,

1. It is good to be provided againft the day of trial. You do not know what temptations you may meet with on this head; the time may come when you may want your faith affifted and confirmed, and then fuch arguments will be of ufe to you, if you have digefted them and made them your own, whatever you think of them now: and even though you could not recollect many of them, it will be of advantage at fuch a feafon, that this point has been cleared up to you to the fatisfaction of your minds; and that you have feen the evidence of this great point, and have made a judgment concerning it. This may help to repel a temptation to infidelity, when you are not, it may be, able at prefent to anfwer every cavil and fuggeftion. As a perfon may be very eafy, and reft fatisfied in his title to his eftate, after it has been examined, though he fhould have forgot the particulars of his fecurity, and even the very names of the witneffes.

2. You fay, you believe the Bible, but it may be you only take it for granted without believing, or knowing wherefore you believe it. If this be your cafe, as I am afraid it is too commonly the cafe of profeffed chriftians; your faith has nothing rational or divine in it; it ftands upon no better foundation than the faith of the mahometan with refpect to the Alcoran. The Bible has been delivered to you, as a divine book, and accordingly you receive it without examining, which is not truly believing, and only fhews you are chriftians by accident, and that your religion comes to you as many mens

estates do, by succession and inheritance from their fathers. I add,

3. The fuller evidence we have for our faith, the more effectual it is like to be, the more it will influence the heart and command the life. Did we believe the Bible more firmly upon solid grounds and clear conviction of its truth, diligently conversing with those arguments by which the authority of it is established, its doctrines would have greater force upon us, and be embraced with more affection, we should mind it more, study it more, live it better.

Do not therefore think I am mispending your time and my own, whilst I insist on these things. I am so much convinced of the necessity and importance of them, that I account it well worth while to allot a considerable proportion of my time and ministry, as God gives opportunity, to the vindicating and explaining the holy Scriptures. Nor do I know any subject of more use to the serious christian. *The Scripture is profitable for doctrine, for reproof, for correction, and instruction in righteousness:* By the knowledge of which, as it is in the verse following my text, with which I shall conclude, *the man of God is made perfect, thoroughly furnished to every good work.*

DISCOURSE V.

The divine Original and Inspiration of the Scripture.

2 Tim. iii. 16.

All Scripture is given by inspiration of God, and is profitable for doctrine, for reproof, for correction, for instruction in righteousness.

THE subject I am upon, is the divine authority of the Scriptures, my present business being to demonstrate and prove the same. And the scheme I proposed to pursue for this purpose, was,

I. To shew that the Bible is true, or that the facts there related are so.

II. That it is inspired. And,

III. That the books of the Old and New Testament, are the originally inspired books of the Bible.

I have hitherto insisted upon the first of these particulars, and have proved, I hope, to satisfaction, 1. That our Bible is of equal credit with any other ancient history. 2. That it hath greater marks of credibility. And 3. That circumstances considered, it is impossible it should not be true. I do not intend that it is naturally impossible. What is naturally impossible, cannot be otherwise without a contradiction in the very nature of things. Thus it is naturally impossible that the same thing should be, and not be, at the same time; should be true and false at the same time, and in the same sense.

And thus I grant, it is not impossible but the history of the Bible may be false. For instance, it is not impossible but the writers of it might be deceived themselves. They might lose the use of their senses and faculties; their imagination might be disturbed, and the texture of their brain altered. It is not naturally impossible but they might, notwithstanding their fair appearances of integrity, be at the bottom gross cheats. A man may be deceived himself, and he may deceive others; he may be weak and deluded, he may be a knave and intend to delude and cheat. This is true of every man in the world, for all mens faculties are finite and bounded, weak and defective. It is a contradiction and naturally impossible that God, a being of infinite perfection, should either be deceived or deceive, but it is not so with respect to man, the greatest and best of men. It is not naturally impossible that men may mistake their interests, may invent and imbellish an unprofitable lie, that they may run upon their own destruction for no advantage; a frenzy may seize them, or a false appearance of things may carry them on without suspicion of the tragical issue. All this, and a great deal more that might be supposed, is not naturally impossible.

But notwithstanding, it must be asserted, that there are cases, and the case before us is of that nature, in which we have such evidence of the truth and certainty of facts, and of the persons testimony, on which we believe the facts, that it is morally impossible we should be deceived. This is too abstruse and nice a speculation, or I durst undertake the proof and even demonstration of it, that it is morally impossible, that the writers of the Bible have imposed a false history upon us, and that the Bible should be false. I beg leave only to retouch what I have already enlarged upon, which I think makes good this assertion.

DISCOURSE V.

It is morally impossible, that so many persons should be deceived themselves, in so many such instances and in the several facts related by them; that Moses, the evangelists, and apostles should be deceived. The reason is, they have all the evidence that men are capable of having; had the assurance and closest testimony of all their senses. And consequently, if they were deceived all other men may be deceived in all other instances, and there is no certainty of any thing remaining. And if this be granted, there is an end of all converse and of all religion: we can neither have correspondence with our fellow creatures, nor receive any revelation from God. For how do I know what any man saith to me, or that he speaks at all; that God speaks, or what he speaks, if I may not trust my senses and faculties. And if Moses or the apostles might not trust their senses, but might be deceived in the report they make of the miracles and facts that fell under their observation, you and I, and all the world, may be deceived, and that in every thing. The result of which is, that we can depend neither on God, our neighbor, nor ourselves.

It is also morally impossible they should deceive others, or design an attempt to do it. One reason of this may be taken from the consequence of denying the sincerity of these persons. It is certain that man was made for society, with an inclination and love to it: he needs it, desires it, derives his support and comfort from it. And as God designed him for such a state, he has given him principles, or made impressions upon him, suitable thereto. It is also certain that there can be no society without mutual trust and confidence, which is the band and cement of it; nor any mutual trust without truth and integrity supposed, which is the foundation on which it rests. Now what I assert and argue from is this, that the persons I am speaking of, the writers of the Scripture, had the highest characters of integrity. If we do not admit them to be credible, none are, none ever were, or can be credible. The consequence of which, if it be considered will be no less than the dissolution of society. Where there is no truth there can be no trust, and where there is no trust there can be no society. And if we may not trust such men, appearing with such criterions and marks of honesty as Moses and the apostles, we can trust none in the world.

Further, they could have no motive to deceive, which is another reason of my assertion, and shews it impossible they should intend to do it. Men do not use to invent lies for nothing; much less to spend their time, sacrifice their ease, reputation, interest, and even their lives, in propagating an unprofitable forgery, and what they know to be a forgery. And yet this was the case of the writers of the Bible, of the New Testament preachers and writers particularly, if their history be false. The facts they published to the world, and the doctrines they preached, were such as brought all sorts of sufferings upon them. They were told and expected it would be so; and yet stedfastly, resolutely and unanimously, give their testimony, and adhere to it to the last, sealing it with their blood. Now I reckon it morally impossible they should have acted such a part, had they been conscious of imposture, and known they were deceiving the world. It is contrary to the human nature, to the principles of self-preservation, and to that self-love that is natural to every man: for though the will chuse freely and cannot be forced, yet no man can chuse evil as such, chuse misery, sufferings, and destruction. So that we have the utmost security here that these persons were no deceivers, that the Bible is true, and that it is impossible it should not be so.

I shall only mention one thing more, *viz.* that it

DISCOURSE V.

is morally impossible, so many persons of different sentiments in other things, different interests and parties, should agree in contriving an imposture, and so many others still of different interests, and the like, should be imposed upon by it, and none of the former ever confess, nor any of the latter ever detect the imposture. This I affirm impossible. We must suppose mankind to have faculties and natures very different from what they now have, and to be governed by different laws, before we can admit such a case as possible. There is no sufficient cause of such an effect; but on the other hand, there are causes, known, certain, and constant, proceeding from nature, and the governing principles of mankind, that would produce a contrary effect. It is not possible that among the many thousands that owned christianity, some especially when they came to sufferings and death, should not have acknowledged the villainy, had there been any. Surely some of them would have done it, to have delivered their consciences from reproach, or at least to have saved their lives. It is not possible, had their story been false, that their enemies, who were spectators and witnesses of the facts they report, and to whom they appeal, should be silent, and never contradict or undertake to disprove them: but instead of it, multitudes of them be wrought upon to espouse the same cause, and confirm it with their testimony and blood. Lay such a scheme nearer home and among ourselves, and it will be easy to see, that a forgery is impossible in any case that bears a tolerable resemblance to that we are considering.

But I must not dwell any longer upon these things, having considered the matter more fully before; and only designing by this review a little more particularly to limit, explain, and confirm the last proposition I advanced, *viz.* that circumstances considered, it is morally impossible the Bible should not be true. Taking it therefore for granted, as a point I have already, I think, sufficiently proved; that it is true: I now proceed a step further, to the next thing proposed, which was,

II. To prove, that the Bible is the word of God, or, that the books which compose our scriptures were given by divine inspiration. I have enlarged upon the foregoing head, the truth of the sacred history, beyond my first intention, and indeed had I designed to have taken such a compass, I should have cast part of my discourse into a different method. I shall endeavor to be shorter on the present subject, namely, in confirming the inspiration of the sacred scriptures.

What I mean when I say, the penmen thereof were inspired, is that they wrote under the special and infallible conduct of the Holy Spirit; that the prophets and apostles, they that were concerned in delivering to us the truths and doctrines of the Bible, were sent of God and commissioned by him, were stirred up to their respective undertakings and services by God, by whom they were also infallibly assisted, so as, that the things they deliver must be esteemed a revelation from him.

There were indeed different modes of revelation, and different kinds and degrees of inspiration: as I observed in the first discourse from this text. *God at sundry times, and in divers manners, spake unto the fathers by the prophets.* Sometimes he revealed himself to them by dreams, sometimes by visions; sometimes by a voice, an audible voice, thus he spake to Adam, Abraham, Moses, and others: and sometimes by inward impressions upon the mind or understanding, which is more properly inspiration.

Sometimes he suggested the very matter and words to them. Sometimes, I suppose, he left them to the use of their own words, supplying them with

DISCOURSE V.

the matter; and in things they were well acquainted with, and recorded as history, and of which they had been eye-witnesses, all that I think necessary to assert is, that he concurred with them and assisted as there was occasion, and so as might secure them from mistake: just as a guide to a traveller, he needs not direct him in that part of the way he himself knows, it is enough to attend him, and when he is like to wander, to admonish, or reduce when he doth wander. In a word, by the inspiration of the Bible is meant, that it is a divine revelation, a revelation from God. The history of it is infallibly true, and immediately inspired so far as was necessary; the doctrines of it communicated from heaven, in various ways and different manners, I grant; but all from heaven; published by persons that had a divine commission, who were sent of God to make such revelations to the world. The further clearing and stating this point, I am sensible, would require a great deal of time; but as something was said of it before, though very short and defective, I shall not resume it, but directly go on to prove what I am upon, namely, that the Bible is the word of God, or that the books of the Old and New Testament, are divinely inspired. To which purpose, I shall lay before you several arguments.

1. The writers of the Bible professed themselves to be inspired, to be sent of God, and accordingly speak in his name. We have many general assertions with reference to this; as in the text, *All Scripture is given by inspiration of God.* So, 2 Pet. i. 20, 21. *No prophecy of Scripture is of private interpretation. For the prophecy came not of old time by the will of man, but holy men of God spake as they were moved by the Holy Ghost.* It is not of private interpretation, or rather private suggestion or impulse, for so the word *Epilusis* may signify, though some critics think that the text should be read dif-

ferently, and that *Epilufis*, is put for *Epelvfis*, thus Calvin, Grotius, and others, which notes an afflatus or conception within: so that what the apostle intends is, that the prophecy of Scripture, or the written word, was not the product of mens own fancies and conceptions; but was by a divine afflatus, that is, it was given by inspiration of God. And indeed, whether we have recourse to this criticism or not, and change the reading, for which the authority of some copies is pleaded, the apostle's reasoning in the words that immediately follow makes this sense plain, and I think necessary; *For*, he adds, *prophecy came not of old time by the will of man, but holy men of God spake as they were moved by the Holy Ghost.* If by private interpretation we mean the expounding of Scripture by particular persons, and every one for himself, as if that was denied here, to which purpose the papists apply the words, though they have nothing in them favorable to their cause, except the sound, and build upon them a necessity of a public authoritative interpreter; if we understand the text thus, I say, there is no force in what the apostle subjoins. But if we take *Epilufis* for inspiration, as I think we are constrained to do, what follows in *ver.* 21 is a confirmation of that which is said in the 20th. No prophecy is by private impulse, for *it came not by the will of man*, it was not the issue of their own faculties and reasoning, was not from any motion or choice of their own, they did not go upon their several errands, and deliver such and such messages to the world from their own heads; but had a divine impulse, *spake as they were moved by the Holy Ghost.* This I take to be the sense of that text: and so you see it is a full testimony to the truth I am upon, that the writers of the Scripture were inspired.

The same thing we have elsewhere and often asserted, as *Acts* iii. 21. *God spake by the mouth of all his holy prophets since the world began.* Acts i. 16. *The Holy Ghost spake by the mouth of David.* And again, *Acts* iv. 25. *Who by the mouth of thy servant David hath said, why did the heathen rage?* &c. referring to the second Psalm. The prophets were God's messengers, his instruments; he spake by them, by *all of them since the world began.* And we have the same account given of the apostles. Hence they are mentioned jointly with the prophets, as the foundation on which we are built. And Christ says to them, *It is not ye that speak, but the spirit of your Father, that speaketh in you.*

I may add, that they all profess, for themselves, to be sent from God, to speak from him, and to deliver his doctrine and message. Moses gives an account of his commission, of his being sent immediately by God, with the circumstances thereof; he tells how God appeared to him in a burning bush, as he was keeping Jethro's flock, and gave him orders to go to Pharaoh and undertake the deliverance of oppressed Israel. And you know when he afterwards came to deliver laws to that people, he always introduces God as the author of them; thus you read, the *Lord spake unto him out of the tabernacle*, and appointed the laws and services following. And, *God spake unto Moses, saying, speak unto the children of Israel*, which is constantly repeated when any new matter was to be laid before them. Nor did the following prophets of the Old Testament pretend to act without the like authority, the word of the Lord came to them when they prophesied, *thus saith the Lord*, was the common preface to their messages and discourses. The same might be observed concerning them that delivered the doctrine of the New Testament. Christ himself, the great prophet of the church, owns his commission from the Father, and that he received his doc-

S

trine from him, *my doctrine*, says he, *is not mine, but his that sent me*. Again, *he that sent me is true, and I speak unto the world those things which I have heard of him*. And, *I do nothing of myself, but as the father has taught me, I speak these things*. To the same purpose, *I have not spoken of myself, but the Father which sent me, he gave me commandment what I should say, and what I should speak*.

The apostles claimed the like authority; I do not mean, equal to Christ, but a divine mission and authority, as he did; hence when they proceed to the determination of the question debated in the council at Jerusalem, they interest the Holy Ghost therein, *it seems good to the Holy Ghost*, say they, *and to us*, intimating, that what they delivered to the churches the Holy Ghost delivered; or more properly delivered it by and under his immediate conduct and direction. The greatest and most copious writer of the New Testament, was the apostle Paul, and we find him on all occasions asserting his divine authority and inspiration. He tells the *Corinthians* that he had *received of the Lord, what he delivered to them*. That the *things he wrote were the commandments of God*. And to the *Galatians*, that he was *an apostle not of men, neither by man, but by Jesus Christ, and God the Father*. And how direct that to the *Thessalonians, when ye received the word of God, which ye heard of us, ye received it not as the word of men, but as it is in truth the word of God*. And St. Peter, speaking of the gospel, says, *the Holy Ghost sent it down from heaven*.

This is what the writers of the Scripture profess; many of them in the most express terms, and you have heard the same is affirmed of all of them. If it be objected, that impostors have professed the like; many have pretended to inspiration, that were deluded by their own fancies, or by a warm and heated imagination, and how do we know that the writers of the Bible were not imposed upon as well as others. I answer,

1. It is granted, some have been deluded, and have taken their own imaginations for a divine revelation; but this is no argument that all are so; and that none ever had a revelation from God. A man may fancy himself awake when he is in a dream, and have a great many scenes laid before him in his sleep, which he takes for real, though all be imaginary. But it doth not follow from hence, that he cannot know when he is awake, or be certain that ever he is awake, or of any thing that is transacted before him, or that he himself doth when he is awake. No more doth it follow that because some persons of distempered brains have thought themselves inspired, when they were not, that none could ever know that they were inspired.

2. I would ask the objectors here, whether they will allow that God is able to reveal himself to any part of mankind, so that they shall be certain of the revelation? If not, they suppose God has less power and skill than men have, who can express their minds to their fellow-creatures in such a manner, as that they are sure who it is that speaks to them, and what it is they speak. And if God is able to do this, the objection falls to the ground. Some persons may then have a revelation from him, any may, to whom he pleases to vouchsafe it, in which they may rest assured there is no imposture or delusion.

3. The persons inspired might know by inward sensation and feeling, that they were inspired, and that God spake to them; and I doubt not, with as an infallible a certainty as we know when another person, like ourselves, is conversing with us, and speaking to us. God might make such an impression upon their senses and minds as carried its own evidence with it, and though we that are utterly

strangers to such a communication with God, have no idea or notion of it, they that were concerned could feel it, and knew how to distinguish it. To clear this in all the instances of inspiration, by voices, dreams, visions, and more direct and mental inspiration, as I may call it, would require a long discourse of itself, which I know you will excuse me from, though a subject well worthy our serious thoughts, was this a place for it. I will only say, if we allow God is able to make any revelation of himself, we must suppose he can do it in a way that is distinct and certain: and I need not scruple to add, that the person to whom he makes it, may discern it by the faculties to which he applies in his revelation, as clearly as we do our mutual discourse, the communication we have one with another.

4. There was nothing that looks like delusion in the case of these sacred writers and preachers. They had all the marks of a regular head and of a calm sedate mind, that can be; had none of the heats of enthusiasts so far as appears. And particularly they were not credulous, did not seem forward to the work they engaged in; nor to have any preparation and bent towards the service they undertook. You know what objections Moses made against the errand God called him to, *who am I,* says he, *that I should go unto Pharaoh, and that I should bring forth the children of Israel out of Egypt? They will not believe me nor hearken to my voice.* And after God had condescended to give him satisfaction in this matter, still he objects, *O my Lord, I am not eloquent, neither heretofore, nor since thou hast spoken unto thy servant.* And notwithstanding God had promised to be with him and assist him, his reluctancy still remains. *O my Lord, send I pray thee by the hand of him whom thou wilt send.* So little was this person prepared to be played upon

and abused, either by his own imagination or the management of others.

And the like might be observed of the apostles. They were themselves very much prejudiced against the main articles of the doctrines that they were to teach the world, *viz.* the death and resurrection of Christ. Though their master had often spoke thereof to them they could not believe it, nor did they understand him: so far from it, that when it came to pass and he was actually put to death, their hopes seemed to die with him, *we trusted,* say they, *that it had been he which should have redeemed Israel.* Words of despair, intimating they thought their cause lost and ruined. So when they were told of his resurrection, it is said, *the words seemed to them as idle tales, and they believed them not.* This was the case of the apostles at that time. The apostle Paul was not then of their number, but afterwards called to the same office, and had an eminent part in publishing the doctrine of the New Testament, and I need not tell you that he had even stronger prejudices than the rest against the cause he espoused. He persecuted Christ in his members with the utmost fury; and so much had his zeal blinded him, that as he owns in his defence before Agrippa, he *verily thought with himself he ought to do many things contrary to the name of Jesus of Nazareth.* In which temper of mind divine grace, and the call of God found him. Now how little there is in all this of the characters of enthusiasm, how opposite and contrary it is thereto, every one may easily discern. Enthusiasts generally have a preparation in the bent and temper of their mind, to receive the delusion; they readily believe that to be true, which they would have to be true: they are prejudiced in favor of their pretended revelation. Whereas, the prejudices of these persons lay the other way, and were so strong that it is plain they would not act without full conviction of the call of God, and till they were overpowered, as I may say, into the belief of it. I add,

5. That no scruples might remain God gave them such evidence of his speaking to them and of their mission as could not be resisted. Let us suppose, that when God spake to Moses in Horeb out of the burning bush, he might doubt whether it was real or not, whether he was in a dream or trance, whether it was not some unaccountable phœnomenon that had nothing of divinity in it, or the artifice of an evil spirit. Suppose this I say, he could not doubt any longer when God bid him cast his rod upon the ground and it became a serpent. Much less could he carry his scruple with him in all his journey from Horeb to Egypt, and still maintain it after all that passed in Egypt; after he had by the power of God wrought so many miracles there, in the presence of Pharaoh and of the Israelites. He that can suppose this is too great a sceptic to be reasoned with; and indeed it is impossible he should, upon his principles, be certain of the reality of any thing that he sees or hears, or that he himself doth. God reveals himself to Moses, that is the thing I am asserting, and that he might be sure of the revelation, he first summons and awakens his attention by a strange appearance, a bush all in a flame and not consumed. Then he speaks to him out of the bush in a manner that no question, had something great and majestic in it, and brought along with it evidence of divinity. And that Moses might be able to satisfy others, and at the same time be further satisfied himself, for what would do the one, must be sufficient to do the other, he enables him to work a miracle, and afterwards repeat that, and do many more miracles. All which considered, I think it even impossible that Moses should be deceived; and if any are so resolute, as to suppose he might

DISCOURSE V.

be under a delusion, notwithstanding all this security to the contrary, they must be forced to say that God cannot reveal himself to mankind with certainty, or mankind is not capable of receiving the revelation, which comes to the same thing.

I might illustrate the argument in many more instances, particularly in that of the apostles. But I will only observe, that when they were first called to their office they labored under a great many inabilities, wanted light, wisdom, courage; and were no way equal to so difficult a work as lay before them, *viz.* preaching the gospel to and proselyting all nations. This they were but meanly qualified for, and therefore their great master, when he took leave of them just before his ascension, bid them tarry at *Jerusalem until they were indued with power from on high.* What this power was we are told, *Acts* i. 8. *Ye shall receive power after that the Holy Ghost is come upon you: and ye shall be witnesses unto me, both in Jerusalem, and in all Judea, and in Samaria, and unto the uttermost part of the earth.* This he promised, and in the second of Acts you have an history of the great event, an account of the accomplishment of the promise, when the Holy Ghost fell upon them at the day of Pentecost. The consequence of which was their speaking all sorts of tongues which they had never learned, to the amazement of those that heard them, *ver.* 8, 9, 10, 11, 12. Now as this was the power from on high, their master had given them reason to expect, and an eminent instance of their inspiration.; so it was a sensible thing and carried its own evidence along with it; they found that change in themselves, that exaltation of their faculties, that new light in their minds, and that new furniture of strength and ability communicated to them, that they could no more question the thing, nor that it was from God, than that they could question their own beings, and whether they were men or not. If their senses and faculties might deceive them in this particular, they might deceive them in all other things; and I think I may add, all other men in all other instances may be deceived; and consequently it will be true, in the strictest sense, we are, and can be, certain of nothing.

So that thus far, I would hope the way is tolerably clear. The writers of Scripture affirm themselves to be inspired; and they could not be under a delusion, but might know whether they were inspired or not.

But it may here again be asked, how doth this prove the point I bring it for, namely, that they were inspired? they might impose upon us, and take upon them to be inspired, to be sent of God, and to be entrusted with a revelation from heaven, when they were not. We have only their bare word for it. I answer,

1. All the arguments I before produced, to prove their history true, will conclude in their behalf in the present case. I have given you sufficient evidence that there were such persons, that they did the things they relate, that the matters of fact they record were genuine, that they had all the characters of ingenuity, integrity, and veracity, that any historians ever had, or can have, and that if we cannot believe them, and depend on their testimony, it follows, none in the world are to be believed in any of their reports; that there is no such thing as credible history, and as was further argued in a former discourse, no safe converse; all mutual trust and converse is destroyed; and in a word, human society must be dissolved. This it was proved, would be the consequence of denying the credit and refusing the testimony of persons so qualified, as the writers of the Bible were. And, I think, it needs no proof, that if we cannot believe them in this part

DISCOURSE V.

of their testimony concerning their inspiration and divine mission, we may believe them in nothing. So that the result is this, if there be any sufficient witnesses among mankind, these were such; if any true history, the Bible is true, and if the Bible be true it was inspired.

2. To suppose them guilty of forgery, and to pretend to a commission and revelation from God, when they knew they had none, is to make them act contrary to all the principles of human nature that we are acquainted with. It makes them guilty, not only of an unprofitable, but of a destructive lie. They knew, according to the rules of the religion they propagated, they could have no reward in another world; and they knew as certainly they must be undone in this world. And what sort of creatures must we suppose them, if we make them act so extravagant a part, exposing themselves as they did without any motive. For instance, what temptation could Moses have to forego the honors and preferment in Pharaoh's court, and chuse to suffer affliction with the people of God, had he not been assured of a divine call? What could induce the apostles to follow Christ through sufferings, persecution and death, had they been conscious of a lie, questioned the authority of their master, or their own sincerity, in engaging in his service? Would the apostle Paul, think you, have renounced the commission he had from the great men of the Jewish church, with all the advantages he expected from them, and become a preacher of Christ, upon no other prospect but bonds, imprisonment, and martyrdom? Would he have done this, had he not been assured of the justice of the cause he espoused, and of the certainty of the heavenly vision, as he calls it? So that we have not only an argument taken from their veracity, but a strong evidence

arising out of the principles of the human nature. To suppose they were deceivers in this instance, is to suppose them ruining themselves for nothing, guilty of the greatest wickedness without any reason, and doing evil for evil's-sake; which it may be is more than can be charged on the devil himself. Again,

3. They not only said they were inspired, but proved it by a train of facts that alarmed and amazed them. God gave satisfaction to Moses concerning his mission by enabling him to work miracles upon the spot, as you read in the third and fourth of Exodus. And by the same means, *viz.* a course of miracles, he gave the same satisfaction to the Israelites concerning it. Christ sent the apostles, they were assured, as otherwise, so by the *power from on high*, that he had sent them, and by exerting that power in a series of supernatural miraculous works, they gave sufficient evidence to the world of their divine mission, that God had sent them, and spake by them, and that he owned their testimony and doctrine; as I may more fully shew hereafter.

This is the first argument, the authors of the Bible profess themselves to be inspired; wherein I have shown, that they could not but know whether they were or not; and that they cannot reasonably be supposed to deceive us in their testimony. I go on now to another argument, which I shall go through more briefly.

II. As the writers of the Scripture profess to have their doctrine from God, so it could not be the invention of men. This will abundantly appear in the progress of my discourses. What I at present ground my argument upon, is, the inability of men to contrive such a book as the Bible, of men as such, or of any sort of men.

It could not be the contrivance of bad men.

DISCOURSE V.

Had they invented a religion, furely they would have made it more favorable to their own inclinations, lufts and appetites; would not have fettered themfelves, laid themfelves under fuch reftraints as the Bible doth, and denounced fuch tremendous judgments againft the ways they chufe and love; they would not have confulted fo entirely the honor of God, and the reputation of virtue and goodnefs, as we find the Scripture doth; but would have calculated it more according to their own natures and defigns. I may add, could we fuppofe them capable of this, which yet is to make them act contrary to their nature, we cannot imagine they fhould be at fo much expence to promote the caufe of the Bible, facrifice their worldly interefts, and even their lives for the fake of it. Did ever bad men act fuch a part, contrive the greateft good, fuffer and die to advance it.

It could not be the contrivance of good men. This fuppofition involves them in a guilt, perfectly inconfiftent with their character. They fpeak, as you have heard, in the name of God, and profefs to have received their doctrine from him. Now if it was otherwife, and they were confcious of a forgery, they muft be the groffeft impoftors in the world, which is fo directly contrary to all virtue and honefty, that it can never be imputed to any man that deferves the name of good. In fhort, the former fuppofition makes bad men do the beft thing that can be, and this makes good men do the worft; both which are abfurd.

It could not be the invention of any man or men. This might be demonftrated, had I time to ftay upon it; and feveral things will afterwards occur that may confirm the affertion. No man nor body of men could invent fuch an hiftory as that of the Bible. A learned Jew, Manaffeh Ben Ifrael, inftances in the account Mofes gives of the creation, which he maintains could not be his own invention. For no man's reason, says he, will dictate to him that the world was made in six days, and at certain intervals of time, since it is more for the glory of God's power to make the world in an instant. Who can imagine, adds he, that the heavens were made without the stars, and adorned with them on the *fourth day?* What judicious mind can conceive that the plants were created on the *third day*, and the sun on the *fourth*, since naturally they receive their vegetation from the sun? He mentions other particulars, and concludes, the creation of the world was revealed to Adam, and that his posterity had it by tradition from him. But because it was not fit, a thing of such weight should rely on the authority of one man, God in the second place appeared to Moses on mount Sinai, and gave him a clear assurance of these things. Whether this be thought throughout solid or not, the subject he refers to must pass for a pertinent instance of a history that has something more than human in it. Longinus the heathen philosopher, and master of Porphyry, is said to have admired Moses's history of the creation; and he makes the account of the first day's work, an instance of the true sublime. There is indeed more satisfaction in it about the original of the world, the author of it, and manner of creation, than in all the books of Pagan philosophy.

And what shall we say of the many events recorded in the Bible in a prophetic manner? Some of them many hundreds, and some several thousand years before they came to pass. I cannot enter upon the particulars now, though I may do it hereafter, any one that seriously considers the predictions recorded in the Scripture, must see it could be indited by no understanding less than infinite.

I might take notice of the doctrine of the Bible,

and shew how much this exceeds human invention. How majestic and sublime a part of it? How admirably the whole is fitted to the circumstances of man, prescribing to him in every relation and case, answering all his occasions and necessities; and every way adapted at once to promote his happiness and the honor of God. These and a great many other particulars that might be insisted upon, shew that the Bible could not be the invention of any human mind, of any man or men, of whatever quality or capacity; and fully prove what the apostle asserts, that *no prophecy of Scripture is of private inspiration*, or impulse, that it *came not by the will of man, but holy men of God spake as they were moved by the Holy Ghost.*

I have several other arguments to offer, to confirm the assertion, but must leave them to another opportunity. In the mean time I cannot help remarking, how unreasonable the cause of infidelity is. The deists and others, that reject the authority of the Bible, do it upon a pretence that would ruin all the history in the world, destroy all human trust and testimony, and introduce universal scepticism. For if the persons, who published the Bible, might not be certain of what they saw and felt, of the facts they relate, and inspiration they pretend to, no man can be certain of any thing whatsoever. If we may not depend on such testimony as that of those persons, we can depend upon no testimony, nor believe any thing unless we see it, nor indeed then neither. For if they might be deceived and deluded, so may others, all others; it could not be expected that any should have a greater assurance of things than they had, and consequently, there is an end of all evidence, even of that of the senses; an end of all trust, of all certainty: so very absurd is the issue of infidelity.

And I cannot forbear adding, it would be well

for these men, that cannot rest in the evidence of the truth and divinity of the Scriptures, could they carry their scepticism with them into the other world. But their unreasonable cavils by which they now support the worst cause, will then vanish, and all will appear real; the truths they despised real, the distresses they feel real, and neither the one nor the other to be run down with a jest and a banter. O let us believe this before-hand, believe Moses and the prophets, Christ and his apostles, that we come not to the place of torments, and there receive a terrible, as well as unavoidable conviction; believe and reverence the Scriptures, and conduct ourselves according to the glorious rules thereof. It is the Bible that describes heaven and the way to it: it is the light by which a wise and gracious God would guide us through this world, a dark and dangerous place, and the more we love, study and practice the Holy Scripture, the more we shall know of the future heavenly state, and the fitter we shall be for the enjoyments of it. Let the word of God therefore dwell richly in you. *Peace shall be upon all them that walk according to this rule, and upon the Israel of God.*

DISCOURSE VI.

The Divine Original and Inspiration of the Scripture.

2 Tim. iii. 16.

All Scripture is given by inspiration of God, and is profitable for doctrine, for reproof, for correction, for instruction in righteousness.

THE divine authority and inspiration of the Scriptures, is what I am now endeavoring to prove. To this purpose I have observed,

I. That the writers of the Bible profess themselves inspired, and speak in the name of God.

II. That the doctrine they deliver could not be the invention of men. I proceed now to another particular.

III. The Scripture has several internal marks of its divine original; several inherent characters which may be urged in confirmation of the point before us. That it was given by inspiration of God. As 1. The excellency of its doctrine. 2. The spirituality of its design and tendency. 3. The majesty and simplicity of its style. 4. The harmony and agreement of its parts. And 5. Its efficacy and power on the hearts and consciences of men. These are characters of its divinity, such as are inherent, which may be observed in the frame and constitution of the Bible; and all of them proclaim its divine original, though some with more force than others.

1. The excellency of its doctrine, is an internal character of its divinity. The Bible contains the most glorious system of religion. Consider the general scheme of it, and it will appear a revelation admirably suited to the case and circumstances of men, and every way worthy of God.

That we are fallen creatures, and, as such, guilty and defiled, all the world is, or may be convinced by their own experience. The wiser heathens were sensible of this, though how to account for it they knew not. *Whence comes evil?* was a question they could not resolve. What more agreeable to the acknowledged perfections of God, that infinite goodness, kindness, and love we ascribe to the Creator of the world, and Father of all things, than to pity, relieve, and restore his lost creatures? And what method more congruous and suitable to that end, than that which is laid down in the Scripture, namely, by repentance, and remission of sins through the mediation and atonement of the Lord Jesus Christ? What was more necessary for God to do for us, than to forgive our ill, and make us good again? And what way to remove the guilt of sin, but his grace, since it was impossible we should make him satisfaction? As for the method in which he has done it, by the sacrifice of his Son, though we cannot at present comprehend the depth of that design, it appears however a dispensation full of wisdom and goodness, highly tending to advance the honor of God, and secure the gratitude and obedience of the creature. This is the general scope of all the evangelical writings. They represent the plan and council of infinite wisdom for the salvation of sinners through the Lord Jesus, make known the purpose of God for the redemption and recovery of fallen man, the method, means, and terms thereof; a contrivance so wonderfully adapted to the great end it is referred to, and including so profound a myftery both of wifdom and grace as fpeaks its author, and fhews it could not be of man, but from God.

Which would appear with greater advantage, could we here furvey more particularly the doctrines of the Scripture. The Bible is a revelation, a diftinct and full revelation, of all that concerns our duty and happinefs, of all that it behoves us to know and practice. I might illuftrate this, in the three great branches of religion, as it refers to God, our neighbor and ourfelves. With reference to God, we are there inftructed in all the particulars of religion as he is the object of it. For inftance, we have a glorious difcovery of the divine nature and will. I grant that the being and attributes of God are not to be proved from Scripture, a belief and fome knowledge of thefe is fuppofed to the belief of the Bible. The divine perfections, efpecially his goodnefs and veracity or truth, are the greateft fecurity we can have that we are not deceived in embracing the Scriptures as a divine revelation. And thefe perfections are otherwife to be demonftrated and muft be known beforehand. The evidence of them doth not firft and chiefly depend on the account we have of them in the Bible. But notwithftanding, it may juftly be reckoned among the benefits and advantages of Scripture revelation, and among the excellencies thereof, that it gives us fo clear a view of the perfections of the divine nature. *Mofes and the prophets revealed God to the world, and the only begotten Son, that lay in the bofom of the Father, who is the brightnefs of his glory, the exprefs image of his perfon*, hath more fully revealed him. The Bible makes God known in his nature as the one God, the living and true God, infinitely wife, powerful, juft and good; the bleffed and only potentate, who alone hath immortality, whom no man hath seen, or can see. It makes known the glorious mystery of the trinity, represents the three divine persons jointly carrying on the work of our salvation, acting several and distinct parts in this great affair, according to the council of the divine will, and all conspiring in the same design and end. A dispensation of wisdom and grace, that no book in the world can pretend to give an account of but the Bible.

We have here also a full discovery of our duty towards God in the different parts thereof; as, that we must love him with all our heart, soul, mind and strength; that we fear him, and fear him above all others, as being *able to cast both body and soul into hell;* that we trust in him, hope in him, rejoice in him, and the like; that we worship him, outwardly by prayer, praise, thanksgiving and fasting; and as to the manner, that we *worship him in spirit and in truth;* that we *lift up holy hands without wrath and doubting,* and that we *do every thing in the name of the Lord Jesus, giving thanks to God and the Father by him.* A glorious plan of religious worship this! grounded upon the perfections of the divine nature, and mediation of Christ, and admirably corresponding with the case and necessities of sinful man.

As to our duty towards our neighbor, nothing can exceed the rules and prescriptions of the Scripture herein. We are commanded to *love our neighbor as ourselves;* and whatever we would that men should do to us, we are required to do even so to them; which glorious and divine laws the great author of the Bible hath there more particularly explained, and filled up with such instances of justice, charity and love, that nothing can be added to them. He requires, that we put away all bitterness, wrath, anger, clamor, and evil-speaking; that we lie not one to another, nor take up a reproach against our neighbor; that we be gentle and courteous, that we be kind to one another, tender-hearted, forgiving one another, even as God forgives us; that we walk with all lowliness and meekness, with long-suffering, forbearing one another in love; that we owe no man any thing but love; and in a word, that we imitate the great pattern of goodness, our heavenly Father, and with a charity as extensive as the beams and influence of the sun, do good against evil, bless them that curse us; forgive, pray for, and love our enemies, and overcome evil with good.

I might shew at large, what provision is made, in the rules laid down in the Scripture, for the duty and comfort of the several special relations men stand in towards one another. In whatever stations men are placed, by the providence of God, the way of duty is there made plain before them; which did they mind and pursue, the consequence would be the beauty and order of the world, the peace and harmony of society. Every office, was it discharged according to the direction of God's word, would appear glorious and useful among mankind, and every relation amiable and comfortable. The magistrate is here taught how to be a guardian of the society, to defend and serve it in all useful ministries, agreeably to the original design and institution of his office, and therefore he is required to be just, ruling in the fear of God, to be a terror to evil works, and a praise to the good. Parents are here taught, with what tenderness and care, to conduct and provide for their children; to treat them as an holy seed, consecrated to God, bringing them *up in the nurture and admonition of the Lord.* And that most intimate relation between husband and wife is made an emblem and figure of the relation between Christ and the church. The husband is to love his wife, as Christ the church, the wife to observe and reverence her husband, as the church doth

Christ; and both together are to make up a lively image of the love and subjection there is between Christ and the church. And should I pursue the account through all other relations, as subjects and children, ministers and people, masters and servants; and set before you the several precepts and rules of Scripture for the conduct of persons in those relations, the excellency of the doctrine of the Bible might be demonstrated from thence to the conviction of all. It would appear, how well it is calculated to promote the good of society, and that it must proceed, not only from a friend to mankind, but one that perfectly understands the human nature, that knows what there is in man, and what man is; what is the just decorum of every action, and what becomes him in every state; that understands his interests, defects and wants; what belongs to his whole duty, and what would contribute to his happiness.

But to touch a little the next particular, our duty towards ourselves, here the Bible exceeds all other institutes, all the laws and maxims of the moral philosophers, though it is granted, some of them have spoke admirably on this head. The Scripture above all other books teaches us the knowledge of ourselves. It enjoins, that we should not think of ourselves *more highly than we ought to think, but to think soberly, according as God has dealt to every man the measure of faith.* And it hath directed us to make a right estimate of ourselves, preferring the soul to the body, and the interests thereof, to all the little concerns of the present life. Which is the import of Christ's doctrine, *What is a man profited, if he shall gain the whole world, and lose his own soul? or what shall a man give in exchange for his soul?* The Scripture teaches us the proportion of our cares, and the moderation and government of our passions in a most exact and divine manner. Tells us one

DISCOURSE VI. 151

thing is needful, bids us not *labor for the meat which perishes, but for that which endureth unto everlasting life,* to take no thought for the body, saying, *what shall we eat, or what shall we drink, or wherewithal shall we be clothed.* And becaufe the mind of man is too confined and limited to be intent upon two ftudies at once, which tend to divide and diftract it, we cannot ferve two mafters, we are therefore required to give up the one, whenever it comes in competition with the other, and to feek firft the kingdom of God and his righteoufnefs.

And how many and excellent its rules concerning fobriety, moderation, humility, temperance, chaftity, and the like. It enjoins us to *mortify our members which are on the earth, fornication, uncleannefs, inordinate affections and evil concupifcence;* to take heed left our *hearts be over-charged with furfeiting and drunkennefs and cares of this life;* to *poffefs our veffel in fanctification and honor;* to be content with fuch things as we have, and to depend on the providence and promife of God, who hath faid, he will never leave us nor forfake us. In a word, the Bible prefcribes to men in every ftate and circumftance, and lays down moft excellent laws and rules, fuch as tend to reform and perfect their natures, to make them comfortable, ufeful and happy in this and the other world; it regulates their defires, paffions and affections, and as it is in the verfe following the text, *is able to make the man of God perfect, thoroughly furnifhed to every good work.*

Let me add what I obferved before, *viz.* Whatever is excellent in natural religion, and to be found among the philofophers, is all of it taken into the Bible. And further, the Bible reprefents the fame with much advantage; what lies fcattered in the books of the heathen philofophers, and muft have been gathered from thence with much care and difficulty, is here brought to our hands and fet before us in a short summary, truths that were hid under much rubbish and mixed with many mistakes are here pure and clear, and without adulteration. And again, the Bible supplies the defects of natural religion; some of these have been before taken notice of, and I shall now enlarge.

Natural religion, or the light of reason, says nothing of the mystery and redemption of the Son of God incarnate, it discovers nothing certainly of the pardon of sin, the terms and means of it, and nothing at all of the atonement by the sacrifice of Christ; it leaves us very much in the dark about the main article and foundation of all religion, a future eternal state of rewards and punishments; and indeed is lame and imperfect, as to moral duties and virtues. It is observable, that the philosophers have no name for that eminent christian grace of humility. What we call so, passes with them for abjectness and lowness of mind; nay, so unaccountable was their vanity, that they thought a wise man might make himself happy, and was not beholden to God for his virtues. Aristotle places several things in the classes of virtues, which the Scripture brands as vices and sinful disorders; as indignation and displeasure at the prosperity of unworthy men, so expressly censured in many places of the Bible; a disposition to jesting, a lightness of discourse, the philosopher represents as a virtue, and the apostle condemns as not convenient among christians, not being suitable to the gravity with which a christian ought to conduct himself. Greatness of mind, which he defines, a man's judging himself to be worthy of great things, and accordingly pursuing them with an elevation of mind; this also has the character of a virtue and excellency with that philosopher. But how contrary it is to that modesty, abasement, and self-denial, the becoming little children, saying, after we have done all, that we are unprofitable ser-

DISCOURSE VI.

vants, which the Scripture recommends I need not stand to shew.

I might observe, that several of the greatest philosophers allowed lying, theft, fornication, self-murder, &c. Even the famous Cato thought it was a point of honor to make away his own life, rather than fall into the hands of Cæsar: which Seneca, one of their strictest moralists, is so far from blaming in him, that he undertakes his vindication, and applauds him for the greatness of his mind. Thus mixed and corrupted was their divinity, even among those that had most refined it.

But nothing of this can be charged upon the Scripture. It has none of these blemishes and defects. As it supplies what is wanting in their religion, so it corrects what is wrong in their edition of morality. It recommends every grace, prescribes an entire holiness without any blots and stains, according to that of the Psalmist, which he mentions as an encomium upon the word of God, and one reason of his affection to it, *The law of the Lord is perfect, converting the soul; the statutes of the Lord are right, rejoicing the heart; the commandment of the Lord is pure, enlightening the eyes; the fear of the Lord*, that is, the word or law of God teaching religion, or the fear of the Lord, *is clean, enduring forever*. These are properties of the law of God, these are excellencies of the Scripture. It contains a doctrine according to Godliness, admirably suited to promote the great ends of religion and Godliness in the world. And though I will not call this, and the other argument under this class and order, demonstration; yet I think they have a great deal of force in them. It is certain, if we might expect a revelation from God, the Scripture is such a revelation as we might expect from him. It is a revelation every way becoming him; and to suppose it came from an impostor, as must be the case if it be not from God, is very unreasonable and absurd. It is in its contrivance above the reach and capacity of any man, and it is manifest, the structure and frame of it is quite contrary to the gust and heart of a bad man.

2. The spirituality of its nature, its divine tendency, may be pleaded to the same purpose, and reckoned among the internal characters and marks of its divinity. And here I might take notice that no book condemns sin like the Bible, and appears against it with so strong an opposition. It strikes at the very root of it in the thoughts, heart and desires, and pursues it through every part of the conversation and life; represents it as the abominable thing which God hates, and threatens it with eternal death.

I might also remark, that no book so much and so effectually teaches us to deny self and exalt God, as the Bible doth; to refer all to him, and give him the glory of every attainment.

Thus the apostle, *by the grace of God I am what I am*. And having taken notice of his labors, his more abundant labors, in the service of the gospel, he adds, nevertheless, *not I, but the grace of God which was with me*. And elsewhere, *I am less than the least of all saints*. And again, *though I be nothing*. Where will you find any strains like this in all the volumes of the philosophers. So far from it, that pride and self-exaltation was their great idol; honor, applause, and glory, the main spring of all their actions; even of their more generous atchievements, when they sacrificed their lives for the good of their country. But the Bible breaths all self-denial, it teaches, that whether we eat or drink, or whatever we do, we should do all to the glory of God; that we should not receive honor from men, but be content with the honor that cometh from God only.

DISCOURSE VI.

I will only subjoin under this head as a glorious character of Scripture, that it every where recommends and promotes a right frame and posture of soul towards God, and what I may call a devotional temper. The main scope of heathen philosophy, was to regulate the passions, which it is granted was a noble subject; or to direct them in homiletical and social virtues. The first tended to fit them for converse with themselves, and the other with their fellow creatures. But for converse and intercourse with God in the exercise of divine graces, those moralists knew little of it. There is a deep silence in their writings about it. And I am sorry to find there is so much of the like defect in the discourses and writings of others, whose business and profession it is to explain the Bible, and recommend the religion there taught to the world. In the mean time, the Scripture has this mark of divinity in it throughout; every part of divine revelation leads to God, to a devout communion and converse with him; and in order to this it directs us to beg for the holy spirit, to sanctify the nature, impress, renew, and transform the mind, and thereby prepare us for this divine and heavenly employment. It prescribes rules of inward and outward purity, that we may not lose the devout frame. It appoints solemn ordinances as so many means and opportunities of intercourse with God. And I might shew you that this has been the temper of good men in every age of revelation. How much it was of David particularly, under the Old Testament, every one knows that has read and considered his Psalms. You often hear him speaking in these, and the like strains, *As the Hart panteth after the water-brooks, so panteth my soul after thee, O God. In thy favor is life, thy loving-kindness is better than life. A day in thy courts is better than a thousand. My soul thirsteth for thee,*

X

my flesh longeth for thee, to see thy power and thy glory, so as I have seen thee in the sanctuary. Nor are these expressions of the peculiar experience of David, but pious breathings that in some measure suit all good men, and describe the heart and frame of the church of God. And you have a great deal to the like purpose in the book of Canticles, which must also be understood in the same latitude.

In short the Bible is a book of devotion: so it may not unfitly be termed. It not only prescribes it, but seems very much calculated to promote it. Its principles and articles of faith, its rules and laws, its ordinances of worship, are all directed to this end; to elevate and raise the mind to God, to bring him and his soul near together. The spirit and grace it bestows are for the same purpose given to refine the nature, purify the heart, and fit the soul for the divine presence and embraces. And accordingly all the great heroes of the Bible, those divine souls that have lived under the impression of its doctrines, have been men of devotion, a temper that the greatest among the philosophers, as I have hinted, were very much strangers to.

Now from hence without further enlargement, I think I may justly place this among the characters of divinity, that we may discern upon the Scripture. It is pure and spiritual, wholly savors of God. It so directly leads to him in the design of it, that one cannot but infer it comes from him. It teaches to live godly, as well as soberly and righteously. It prescribes an high point, the dignity and glory of human minds, which the light of nature and the philosophy of the heathens fell short of, *viz.* a friendly commerce with God.

3. There is something in the style of the Scripture, that savors of divinity. As for instance, the majesty and grandeur of it. I do not mean with respect to pompous figures, or any rhetorical flou-

DISCOURSE VI.

rishes and flights of oratory: but with respect to the authority with which it speaks. It speaks in the name of the great God, the maker of heaven and earth, and demands the attention of the whole world. Some have observed there is a great deal of majesty in that often repeated expression of our Saviour, *he that hath ears to hear, let him hear.* Which is a solemn admonition to mankind of the mighty importance of the thing spoken. What I would chiefly remark, is the awful sanctions with which this book enforces its laws and precepts, no less than eternal rewards and eternal punishments. *Hear, and your soul shall live. He that believeth shall be saved; and he that believeth not shall be damned.* Such as this, is the language of the Scripture, and hereby it is too sublime and great for any human lawgiver. How far any might have gone in this way, personating the supreme majesty of God, and abusing the world with a counterfeit of his divine authority, is not easy to say. But it has been observed, that no book has ever yet come forth, that has spoke with such a sublimity and height of sovereignty, as the Bible doth.

Further, there is an admirable simplicity mixed with the authority. This appears in the laws contained in the Scriptures, particularly, the ten commandments. Every thing is delivered with an air of greatness, and yet with a plainness that cannot be enough admired. *Thou shalt have no other gods before me. Thou shalt not make unto thyself any graven image, &c.. Thou shalt not take the name of the Lord thy God in vain, &c. Thou shalt not kill. Thou shalt not steal,* and the like. I know some make this, which they call a lowness and flatness of style, an objection against the divinity of the Bible. But it is a cavil without all reason. There is really a grandeur in such simplicity. Even human lawgivers would think it a diminution to them to deliver their laws in the strain of an orator, Speeches from the throne, the edicts of princes, and acts of parliament, come forth in naked plain terms, and the greater their simplicity and plainness, the greater marks of authority they have in them. Persons whose business it is to persuade, addrefs to the passions of men, and make use of their art; but where the highest authority speaks, and the will of the speaker is a law, the more plainness there is in the style, the more authoritative it appears.

There is the like simplicity in the narrations and history of Scripture. The writers delivered things without disguise, relate facts, even the most wonderful and surprising, and their several circumstances, with freedom and boldness; like men that are conscious of their integrity, and depend upon the dignity and importance of the things they report, and the authority of him that sent them. They make use of no artful apologies, nor studied addresses, to posses their readers in their favor. When they command it is with a majestic plainness, as those that speak in the name of God, and when they relate past things it is with the like simplicity, as those that speak in the name of truth, as I may say.

Now this is so far from being the manner of impostors and cheats, that it is not really the manner of common men. I do not think any men, left to the conduct of their own wisdom and understanding, would have represented such things, as the Bible contains, in the way the writers of it do; making their reports, and delivering their messages with a freedom and indifference of style, that may seem rather to favour of carelessness, than any thing of affectation. And though I do not say, that these, and the like properties and characters of the Scripture style, are a full argument of its divinity; yet I cannot help thinking the style thereof has a great deal in it recommending; it is something worthy of God, and what one might expect in a divine revelation.

4. The harmony and agreement of the several parts of the Bible is another mark and character of the inspiration of the writers thereof. Particularly, there is an harmony in the greatest point of all, I mean exact truth. Survey the Scriptures from the beginning to the end, examine the part every penman has born in this composure, and there is nothing to be found, but what can stand the test of the most severe and critical judgment. It may be affirmed of all the sacred writings without exception, what is affirmed of some part, *these sayings are faithful and true.* Let us reflect a little on this matter. The Scripture consists of three sorts of subjects, doctrines, histories, and prophecies. And in none of these can it be convicted of falsehood. As to its doctrines, you have heard that it comprises a very glorious and large system, articles of faith, rules of practice, all were concerned to know, believe, and do; our whole duty towards God, our neighbor, and ourselves. And in all this there is no flaw, no false doctrine. No caviller in the world is able to pronounce upon evidence concerning any principal, maxim, or rule laid down in the Bible, that it is corrupt and erroneous; what cannot bear the trial of sound and impartial reason. As to the historical and prophetical part, it is of great extent, takes in a compass of some thousand years; and yet here one may challenge all the adversaries of the Scripture to produce a single instance of mistake, any facts misrepresented, or any predictions given forth, disgraced by the event; which is a circumstance that distinguishes it from all human composures, and gives it a sort of triumph over all competitors. In the best writings of uninspired men there are marks of frailty and infirmity, weakness of judgments, slips of memory,

inconclusive arguments, mistaken facts, and the like. But there is nothing of this in the Bible. All is without a blot, true and irreproveable.

Further, this harmony is among all the writers of the Scriptures. They not only speak truths, but many of them the very same particular truths. When they touch the same doctrine they give the same account of it, the same in the main, no one contradicting or interfering with another. They teach the same things concerning God, his nature, attributes, providence and government; give the same account of the creation, apostacy, general flood, and other facts of ancient date. The New Testament writers deliver the same things concerning Christ, his incarnation, death, burial, resurrection, ascension; his doctrine, miracles; the coming of the Holy Ghost, and the like. Not that they copy from one another, or express the same particular thoughts upon every subject. But there is no repugnancy among them. They harmonise in every thing. One may enlarge upon and explain what another has said, add to his account and carry it further; but he never contradicts him.

Again, this harmony is among a great number of persons, living in very distant places and ages of the world; so that they could not act by confederacy and combination. The prophets that follow Moses, and who confirm his history, laws and predictions, had, many of them, never seen him. Christ and his apostles, that lived above a thousand years after Moses, all agree with him. In short, they are all of a piece; their revelations, their doctrines and narrations, accord as much as if they had lived at the same time; had done every thing by concert and contrivance before one word was written. This will appear afterwards with more advantage when I speak of the prophecies of the Bible, and their accomplishment. I shall only at present mention one instance for the illustration of what I am upon. Moses writes that the *seed of the woman should bruise the serpent's head.* This was a promise made to our first parents in paradise immediately upon the apostacy, about four thousand years before it came to pass. This Moses records, places in his history, lays his credit upon it, and leaves it to the examination of after ages. The succeeding prophets likewise, all with one voice bear testimony to the same thing, point out the same glorious event till it was actually accomplished. They resume the subject and comment upon it, one after another, and in one age after another, still enlightening it more and more, one adding this, another a different circumstance; as of what family he should come, of what person, namely, a virgin, where he should be born, at what time, and the like; which I take to be an irresistable evidence of their inspiration, and that their *prophecy came not of their own will,* but that they *spake as they were moved by the Holy Ghost;* otherwise they could never have agreed in an event so strange and surprising as this. Had Moses spoke of it on his own head, what could induce the other prophets to venture upon the same prediction, with more particular and determining circumstances. This would never have been the doctrine of one prophet, retouched and enlarged by others, and confirmed by all, had they not been guided by the same spirit, and proceeded under the conduct of God. In a word, all the parts of the Bible are in close connection, and like the several parts of a regular building, give strength and support to one another. The Old Testament contains the New in types, shadows and predictions; and the New Testament is an accomplishment of the Old. Hence the apostle takes notice in his defence before Agrippa, that he had said no other things than what Moses and the prophets had foretold should come to pass. *Even all the prophets, that have been since the world began, spake of these things.*

I might subjoin, that this harmony appears the more beautiful and divine, as it is with some circumstantial variety and difference. They preach the same doctrine, but not in the same manner, relate the same facts, but not with the like circumstances; and often foretell the same events, but place them in a different light and cloath them with different circumstances, which is so far from disparaging their writings, that it really gives reputation to them, and is an argument of their sincerity and inspiration. Had they acted with a fraudulent design they would have been more cautious in this respect, and avoided all appearance of discord: had they contrived a deceit, they would have laid it closer together, and not have exposed themselves to any suspicion of contradiction. Common writers think themselves obliged for their credit-sake to guard every expression, are timorous and anxious, especially if there be any design of falshood and imposture. But the sacred writers conduct themselves with a noble freedom of expression, as being secure of the truth and justice of their cause, and that under all this variety, the same divine truth would appear and triumph upon examination.

Well, as this is the case of the Bible; as there is such a wonderful agreement and harmony among the writers of it; it must, I think, imply and infer their inspiration. It is not to be conceived, that a weak and fallible understanding, as that of man is, should go through such a variety of matter, doctrines, histories, prophecies, of exceeding great latitude and compass, and always be consistent with itself. We do not find that two persons can write on the same subject, especially if it be copious and diffusive, without clashing; nor can one man write on a multitude of subjects, but he will forget himself, and show his weakness and infirmity. Whereas the Scripture is clear of all imputation of this kind, I mean all just and well grounded imputation. As to the objection of contradictions therein, I may afterwards consider it; at present I take it for granted there are none and thence argue, that they who wrote it were under the special and infallible influence of the Holy Ghost, who led them into all truth.

5. I may offer to the same purpose, or as a further proof of the inspiration of Scripture, that efficacy, power and authority, it has on the hearts and consciences of men. Indeed this may be thought an effect of the Scripture, and accounted extrinsic; and consequently, not here in its proper place. But it must be considered, that the efficacy I am arguing from, is owing to the internal constitution of the Bible, and to the divine spirit that breathes in it. Now take this in conjunction with the other arguments, and I look upon it a great confirmation of our faith, that it is the word of God. I shall beg leave to enlarge a little here. And,

1. I observe, that the Scripture is attended with a penetrating light; has a great deal of efficacy and power in this respect. It shines into the mind, and lays open the most secret, concealed treasures of it; the good or evil treasure of the heart. Thus the apostle speaks of it, as many understand that text, *the word of God is quick and powerful, and sharper than any two-edged sword, piercing even to the dividing asunder of soul and spirit, and of the joints and marrow, and is a discerner of the thoughts and intents of the heart.* God that made the heart, is perfectly well acquainted with all its workings, desires and motions, *he knows our thoughts afar off;* he knows all that is in man, and has in his word, as

in a map or glass, delineated and represented the various movements of his soul, what is formed in his heart, and lodges at any time there. Thus St. Paul, speaking of prophecy, or the opening of the Scripture by virtue of that afflatus or gift of the spirit which some had at that time, tells us, that by the means thereof, *the unlearned and unbeliever is convinced of all, and judged of all.* It follows, *and thus are the secrets of his heart made manifest, and so falling down on his face, he will worship God, and report that God is in you of a truth.* The word of God often finds the sinner out, and when it is displayed before him, God co-operating therewith by his spirit, there is a discovery made of the heart and conscience, and of the thoughts and purposes lurking there, that often astonishes and amazes. What the king of Syria's servant told his master, *viz.* that the prophet Elisha made known to the king of Israel even the *words that he spake in his bed-chamber*, may be said of the Scripture, it makes known to men the language spoken in the secret chambers of their hearts; their most retired thoughts and affections. It discloses the hidden things of dishonesty, anatomises and dissects the conscience, brings into open and full light, what the sinner before was not aware of. This thousands can witness that have been seriously conversant with the holy Scriptures, and especially such that have sat under a lively searching ministry. They find their sins, their secret sins, set in a clear light, find themselves struck at, and described in the word of God with great exactness, as if the writer or preacher had known their hearts, and been some way privy to what passes there. The reason of which is, that the Scripture, proceeding from God, the author of the human mind, that is acquainted with its most secret springs, and inmost recesses, is able to penetrate into it, and lay all open.

DISCOURSE VI.

I might observe that the light there of equally reaches the hearts and cases of good men. It shews them what they are, what they want, what they suffer; describes their graces, their conflicts, and fears. In short, it is a glass in which both good and bad may view themselves, and see what manner of persons they are. Now had it been a mere human writing, a contrivance of men, though of never such great and wise men, it could not I think have had this property in it. It would not have been a searcher of hearts, as it every where pretends to be, and we find it to be, had it not proceeded from him that framed the heart and knows it perfectly.

2. The Scripture has a wonderful power and efficacy to convince and awaken conscience. A great deal might be said here, agreeable to the experience of thousands and myriads among mankind. The world hath had a real and sensible experiment of this property thereof for many generations. It has been gloriously instrumental to discover the fig leaves, and detect the delusion of blinded sinners, and to demolish those refuges of lies wherein they trusted. How many mountains hath it thrown down? how many sons of pride hath it abased? how many obdurate and hard hearts hath it broken? many a soul hath the Scripture covered with the shadow of death, even of those who thought themselves full of light, and while they have exalted themselves to heaven, it hath brought them down even to hell. Thus the Scripture hath often been to the secure sinner, as the hand writing on the wall to Belshazzar, *it hath made his countenance change, and his thoughts trouble him, the joints of his loins to be loosed, and his knees to smite one against another.* Something of this it is supposed the apostle intimates, when he says, *I was alive without the law, but when the commandment came, sin revived, and I died. Then the commandment which was ordained to*

life, I found to be unto death; that is, when the law was sent home to my conscience in its spirituality, purity and authority. When God carried it to my heart, and removed the ignorance, prejudice, and blindness which kept the law from reaching me; when it was thus I died, I was filled with amazement and horror at the view of myself upon this discovery the law made of my heart, state and condition; and I became as a dead man. Now this the Scripture has done in innumerable instances, with a strange sovereignty and authority, ransacking the hearts of men, casting them down from their high towers, and laying their pride in the dust. And is there nothing of God in this? is it not manifestly his finger? can any human writings pretend to such a force? must not a word armed with so much power be the word of God? It is observable the Hebrews call thunder the voice of God, *the voice of the Lord is powerful, the voice of the Lord is full of majesty, the voice of the Lord breaketh the cedars of Lebanon.* And the reason why it is termed his voice seems to be, because of the majesty and terror that sometimes attends it. *Hast thou an arm like God,* saith he himself to Job, *or canst thou thunder with a voice like him.* Now certainly to thunder in the minds and consciences of men, and to make such terrible commotions and concussions there, as the Scripture doth, cannot but argue something of divinity, and import that it is the voice of God.

If it be said, men may have terror from other causes, and without the ministry of the Scripture, I grant it; God can strike the conscience of a secure sinner immediately, or by what means he pleases. But I believe I may justly observe, that trouble of mind, of a spiritual nature, and about another world and the concerns of it, is seldom the exercise of any but such as are conversant with the Bible: and it is mostly the exercise of those that have the word of God brought closest to them under a lively ministry. Whilst Peter preached, his hearers were *pricked in their hearts, and cried out, men and brethren what shall we do.* It is the Scripture read or preached, laid open and applied, that gives the compunction and makes sinners inquisitive what they must do to be saved. Such as live in ignorance of the Bible, and enjoy no faithful preaching, seldom know any thing of this: No, their *goods are in peace, they are alive without the law;* but when he *that commands light to shine out of darkness, shines into* their *hearts;* when the word of God which is *quick and powerful* pierces the conscience, former delusions vanish, former strong holds are broken down; and there is an inward awakening, an inward light, and often a terror that may be called divine. And as this is a known property of Scripture, what it claims, and what the church of God has all along more or less found in it, it is an argument of its inspiration. Again,

3. It shews a mighty efficacy in quickening and comforting good men. Read the hundred and nineteenth Psalm, and you will see how much of this David experienced in the Scriptures that were extant in his time. Hereby God quickened him, and hereby God supported him, as he abundantly declares, particularly, *ver.* 92. *Unless thy law had been my delight, I should then have perished in mine affliction.* And thousands can say the same thing. They have felt these powers of the world to come, have found a divine power breaking out of the Scripture in the serious perusal, or in the faithful ministry of it, like lightning out of a cloud, by which their hearts have been revived and raised, as it were, from the dead. Sometimes they have been strangely eased in their minds; freed from their darkness, burthens and fears: at another time gloriously strengthened in the inward man:

sometimes, when they have been in sackcloth, under darkness and terror, the Scripture has cheared their drooping spirits, girded them with gladness, and filled them with joy in believing. If this be fact, and I am persuaded some of you can rise up and give testimony to it, if the Scripture has been of this efficacy to you; if you have found it to be a word of power, of life, peace and consolation; you will not easily doubt whether it be the word of God or not. When John the Baptist sent some to Christ with this question; *Art thou he that should come, or do we look for another?* Christ answers, *Go, and shew John the things you hear and see, the blind receive their sight, the lame walk, the deaf hear, the dead are raised up, and the poor have the gospel preached to them.* Intimating that such things as these were a sufficient attestation to him, that he was the Messiah. The things were too glorious, and of too great a reputation, to attend an impostor. So if the question be, whether the Scripture be the word of God, it might be a sufficient answer methinks, if we are able to say, that by them the souls of men are enlightened, comforted, the dead spirits of men are raised up, and made to live again, that many who were in chains and fetters are set free by them, and by them the world filled with joy and gladness. A tree that bears such fruit must have been planted by God's right hand. I will only add,

4. That this efficacy is still the same. The Scripture has the same quickening, reviving, comforting power that ever it had. The church has lived upon it some thousand years; and it has the same light, life, and consolation in it that it had at first. What the statutes of the Lord were to David, so long ago, they are still to all the faithful; *a lamp to their feet, and a light to their paths*, their rejoicing and their heritage forever. Nay, the more we know of the Bible, the more we meditate in the

law of God, the more we shall delight in it, discovering still new and rich mines; being like its author an inexhausted store-house of all supplies.

Well, these are the internal marks and characters of the Scripture's divinity. How far they may be depended upon, and what argument they afford for the establishing this doctrine, I designed at this time to have enquired; but that would lead me farther than your patience and attention may be prepared to follow; and therefore I shall defer it to another opportunity.

In the mean time it is easy to observe, that good men have a mighty advantage above others for understanding and believing divine revelation. They can discern its innate excellencies and beauties. They have *the witness in themselves*, an inward experience of the glories of the Scripture; they have felt its power, tasted its sweetness, and therefore can say a thousand things on its behalf that others cannot, and consequently will not be staggered with every little sophistical cavil; but when attacked by gainsayers, will be ready to reply, as the man born blind did to those that were wrangling with him concerning Christ, *It is a marvellous thing that ye know not from whence he is; and yet he hath opened mine eyes.* Endeavor that you may find the power and efficacy of the Scripture on your hearts, and it will very much assist your faith, and confirm you in it, you will never question whence it is, nor whether it be of God, since it hath opened your eyes. *I will never forget thy precepts*, says David, *for with them thou hast quickened me.* The more we experience of the power and usefulness of the word of God, the more we shall value and love it, and the more steadily we shall adhere to it: we shall not forget it, nor be drawn off from our regard to it, because thereby God hath quickened us, thereby he hath comforted us, restored and established us, and many ways faved us. And if this be the cafe, if the word of God has got this hold of us, of our hearts and affections; and recommends itfelf to our experience, we fhall not be moved with every flirt of wit and little jeft that the author may think brifk and lively. God's teftimony to the Scripture without, in his works and providence, has a glorious evidence in it, as you will afterwards hear. But his teftimony within comes nearer and clofer to the confcience, and is of mighty ufe to thofe that have it. Endeavor for this, and for more of it; and if you do the will of Chrift, and feel the authority of the Scripture in your hearts, you fhall know of his doctrine, whether it be of God.

DISCOURSE VII.

The Divine Original and Inspiration of the Scripture.

2 Tim. iii. 16.

All Scripture is given by inspiration of God, and is profitable for doctrine, for reproof, for correction, for instruction in righteousness.

IN my last discourse on these words, I laid before you the internal marks and characters of the divine inspiration of the holy Scriptures. Some call them, the self-evidencing light thereof, and lay so great a stress upon them, that they not only think all other arguments insufficient without this, but that this is sufficient without them, and exclusive of them all. There are, they think, those characters and impressions of divinity upon the Scriptures that it manifests itself by its own light, to be from God. " The authority of God, the supreme Lord of all, " saith a learned divine*, speaking in and by the " penmen of Scripture, evidenced singly in, and " by Scripture itself, is the sole bottom and foun- " dation or formal reason of our assenting to these " Scriptures as his word, and submitting our hearts " and consciences to them. He adds, God's voice " to the penmen of Scripture was accompanied " with its own evidence, which gave assurance to

* Dr. Owen's self-evidencing light of the Scripture.

"them; and God speaking by them, or their
"writing to us; his word is accompanied
"with its own evidence, and gives assurance to
"us, his authority and veracity did, and do, in the
"one and the other sufficiently manifest themselves.
"And again, as God in the creation of the world,
"and all things, hath so made and framed them,
"hath left such characters of his eternal power and
"wisdom on them, filled with such evidence of
"their author, that without any other testimony
"from himself or any else, under the naked con-
"sideration of what they are, they declare their
"Creator. So in the giving out his word, he hath
"by his spirit implanted in it, and impressed on it
"such characters of his goodness, power, wisdom
"and holiness, of his love to mankind, truth and
"faithfulness, with all the rest of his glorious ex-
"cellencies and perfections, that at all times, and
"in all places, where the expansion of Scripture is
"stretched out over men by his providence; with-
"out any other witness or testimony given there-
"unto, it declareth itself to be his, and makes good
"its authority from him. So that the refusal of
"it upon its own evidence, brings unavoidable
"condemnation on the souls of men. This is di-
"vine testimony, accompanying the true voice of
"God, evidencing itself, and ascertaining the soul
"beyond all possibility of mistake. Wherever
"the Scripture is truly received, as the word of
"God, it is received upon the evidence of that
"light it hath in itself; it is all one by what means,
"by what hands, whether of a child, or of a church,
"by tradition, accident, or special providence, the
"Scripture comes to us; come how it will it hath
"its authority in itself by being the word of God,
"and hath its power of manifesting itself so to be
"from its own innate light." A great deal more
in the like strain occurs in the same learned wri-

ter. He particularly hints wherein the power and authority of the Scripture confists, by which it proves itself to be divine. As its driving into the hearts, consciences, and secret recesses of the minds of men; its judging and sentencing them in themselves; its convictions, terrors, conquests, and killing of men; its converting, building, making wife, holy and obedient; its adminiftring confolations in every condition, and the like. These he accounts such an impress of God on the Scripture, that they may be looked upon as so many infallible signs, diftinguiſhing it from the product of any creature. To the fame purpose another ingenious writer, " the Scripture, fays he*, appears in divine " and heavenly characters, and by thefe it bears " witnefs to itfelf that it is the word of God." So Calvin putting the queftion how we fhall be perfuaded it comes from God? anfwers, it is the fame thing as to afk, how we can diftinguifh light from darknefs. And adds, another author of confiderable name, I mean biſhop Leighton, † " They are " little verfed in the holy Scripture that know not " that it is frequently called light, and they are " fenfelefs that know not that light is feen and " known by itſelf. *If our gofpel be hid*, fays " the apoftle, *it is hid to them that perifh;* the God " of the world having blinded their minds againſt " the *light of the glorious gofpel*. No wonder if fuch " ſtand in need of a teftimony. A blind man " knows not that it is light at noon day, but by " report; but to thofe that have eyes, light is feen " by itſelf." I mention thefe paſſages more particularly, that I may give you the argument they lay fo great weight upon in its full ftrength, as reprefented in their own words. Thefe learned men

---

* Polhill's Precious Faith, p. 35.

† Sermons, p. 85.

you see suppose the Scripture to bring with it its own proof; and its internal characters, that impress it has upon it of the majesty and authority, purity, wisdom and holiness of God, they suppose a sort of a divine light, and requires only open eyes to discern it. Now before I dismiss this argument I shall make a few remarks upon it; in which I mean not to set aside or weaken it, but guard it. No doubt there is a great deal in the doctrine of Scripture to recommend it to us, as a revelation from God. It has internal characters, that shew its excellency, and imply divinity. But whether the notion of self-evidencing light, as you have heard it stated, be not carried too far may be questioned; I shall briefly propose my thoughts concerning it in the following particulars.

1. It must not be asserted, that the Scripture appears to all men with this self-evidencing light. They, that insist most upon it, grant that the special illumination of the spirit is necessary to our discerning the evidence. The eyes of our minds must be opened or we shall not see this light, how clear and strong soever. So that the argument from hence is rather for the confirmation of good men, than the conviction of all. Though the sun shines with the utmost brightness, it cannot enlighten those that want eyes. And the case is allowed to be the same, with reference to the Scripture's internal light and evidence. Consequently, this argument cannot be of general use. And yet I question not the Scripture may be proved, not only to be true, but to be inspired even to the conviction of carnal men, that have only use of their rational faculties, without special grace and illumination. Not that they can receive it, or indeed any other point or particular doctrine of religion with a divine faith; but it may be demonstrated by strong arguments, the force of which they may dis-

cern, even before they receive the spirit of illumination. How far they may discern the internal marks of its divinity, I cannot digress to enquire. No doubt they may discover much of the beauty and excellency of the Scripture, and own it. It would be presumptuous, I am afraid, to affirm, that all who have wrote with great learning in defence of the Bible, and particularly have with great skill displayed the internal excellency of its doctrine were sanctified and good men. However, whether this be granted, or not, as the self-evidencing light, in the judgment of those authors I have mentioned, shines only to them that have the illumination of the spirit, and no question it shines most eminently to them, it must not be looked upon as an argument proper to convince every one. Whatever light there is in the Scripture, or how much soever it partakes of the nature of light, it cannot enlighten them that have not eyes, or want the faculty of discerning. And yet even these are bound to receive the Scripture, and are capable of apprehending sufficient reason and evidence upon which they ought to believe it.

2. When it is said the Scripture is self-evident, it must not be understood, that the evidence is as easy and obvious as in the case of those propositions we call self evident; as that two and three make five, or that the whole is greater than a part. Even good men, notwithstanding their illumination from above, need a great deal of reasoning, and consideration, and the help of much and long experience before they can satisfactorily discern the internal light of the Scripture; so discern it as to make it an argument of the divinity thereof. We must not therefore apply the metaphor of light, to which the Scripture is compared, too strictly; as if every spiritual and good man, that opens the Bible, might see characters of divine inspiration there, as

plainly as he can see when the sun shines. Those expressions, that import any thing of this kind, I cannot think sufficiently guarded.

3. I apprehend this self-evidencing light doth not run through the whole Bible, and appear in every part alike. And I know not but I might say it doth not sufficiently appear at all in some parts of it. If the light and evidence be placed in the assertions of Scripture, that it is from God, this cannot be admitted as evidence enough that it is so; because other books not inspired, as the Alcoran for instance, assert the same. And besides there are some parts of Scripture that do not assert this. If the impress of God thereon be made the self-evidencing light, I am afraid it will be difficult to discern this in every book and chapter of the Bible, as in the Kings and Chronicles; and it will be no less difficult for any one, by this impress appearing in the book itself, to pronounce that the Proverbs is the word of God, and not the book of wisdom, that Ecclesiastes is divinely inspired, and not Ecclesiasticus. I subjoin,

4. That this internal evidence of the inspiration of Scripture results from the constitution and frame of the Bible in general; from the doctrines and history of it, the excellency of its matter and style. Take the Bible together, consider it in its whole plan and design; and it has glorious characters of divinity upon it. Its doctrines, laws and histories, have something so great, so pure and spiritual in them; it has such marks of wisdom and goodness; it is so wonderfully suited to the necessities and occasions of sinful men, and so well fitted every way to subserve the professed end of such a revelation, that one may conclude it to be a revelation from God, and above human contrivance. And this will appear with greater force and conviction to those that have lived under the impression of it, and

have long experienced its power, and tasted its comforts.

5. Though this be a good confirming argument of the divinity of the Bible, we ought not, I think to lay the main stress here, much less to make it the only argument. We find our Lord appeals to other evidence, namely, that of his miraculous works; *I have greater witness*, says he, *than that of John; for the works, which my father hath given me to finish, the same works that I do, bear witness of me, that the Father hath sent me.* And again, *the works I do in my Father's name, they bear witness of me.* And, *If I do not the works of my Father, believe me not: but if I do, though you believe not me, believe the works.* You see he doth not demand their assent and faith upon his own testimony, or the testimony of John, but produces his works as his credentials. The Scripture is a doctrine worthy of God, and appears in its own innate light and excellency worthy of our acceptation. But, as God has been pleased to recommend it by many other arguments besides his own image and impress thereupon, these ought not to be neglected. Christ brings in his works among the evidences of his divine mission: and certainly whatever tends to prove, that God sent the writers of the *Bible*, should be admitted on their behalf, and as a plea for their inspiration. Nor can I think it any service to the cause, to lay all the weight upon a single argument, rejecting others that may have equal, if not superior force. Once more,

6. It must however be allowed, that the internal excellency, or what some call it, self evidencing light, is at least a strong motive of its credibility. I do not say, it is no more, for I think the Scripture Revelation, considered in the whole of it, is too sublime and divine, has too many characters of wisdom, holiness, &c. to own any author, but God. So that it is more than a motive of credibility.

In the mean time, it is that in a very high degree. Indeed no external arguments of the divinity of the Bible could conclude and determine any reasonable creature's belief of it, as from God, was it not a revelation every way worthy of him. It is a pertinent paſſage to our purpoſe of the great Chillingworth " I profeſs, ſays he, if the doctrine " of Scripture did not appear as good, and as fit " to come from God, the fountain of goodneſs, " as the miracles by which it was confirmed were " great, I ſhould want one main pillar of my faith, " and for want of it; I fear, I ſhould be much " ſtaggered." In ſhort, there is nothing a chriſtian can reſt in with more ſatisfaction, touching the divine inſpiration of the Bible, than this, that he finds it ſpeaks to him in a way becoming God, commands with an authority becoming God, ſearches the heart and conſcience with light and force becoming God, directs with a wiſdom and knowledge God-like, ſupports, quickens, and comforts in a manner that plainly ſhews a divine influence attends it.

But thus much for the third general argument, the internal characters of the Scripture's divinity; which I have ſtayed the longer upon, becauſe I apprehended ſome difficulty in it; whether I have cleared it or not, I ſhall not ſay. I have however offered what occurred, at preſent, moſt proper for that purpoſe. I proceed now to another argument.

IV. The divine inſpiration of the Scripture may be argued from ſome external marks and characters, ſome outward circumſtances, and from the providence of God eminently intereſting itſelf in behalf thereof: as the antiquity of it, the preſervation of it through ſo many ages, its ſurpriſing accompliſhment in all the parts of it, and the like.

1. The antiquity of it. I am far from thinking this, one of the beſt of our arguments. But as it

is generally produced in favor of this cause, I do not think fit wholly to neglect it; though I shall but touch it briefly. It is agreed, I think however I am satisfied nothing tolerable can be offered against it, that the Scriptures, I mean part of them, are the most ancient writings of any in the world. Justin Martyr, a learned father, who lived in the second century, within about one hundred and thirty years after Christ, as some compute, in his exhortation to the Greeks, proves by comparing the times of all human writers, poets, philosophers, historians, and lawgivers, the most celebrated for their antiquity, that the laws of Moses and his writings were long before any of them. And at the same time shews, that whatever is excellent in any of them, as Orpheus, Homer, Solon, Pythagoras, or Plato, they derived from Moses, lighting their candles at his lamp. Eusebius, another primitive writer, evidences at large the superior antiquity of Moses, and concludes, that Moses is found to be more ancient, even than all the gods and heroes of the Greeks. To the same purpose Tertullian and others. And indeed, there are none of the heathen authors that can vie with Moses in this respect. He begins his history and account of things, from the creation, and continues it through the first two thousand years of the world, and more. And though we have no written records of the affairs of the patriarchs before the time that Moses wrote, yet it is certain his book is of earlier date than any other. His Pentateuch was extant before Thales, Hermes, Sanchoniatho, Homer, or any of the famous pagan antiquaries were heard of, indeed before they had a being; which Tertullian * enlarges upon, and thereby

* The whole passage of Tertullian being so very remarkable

triumphs over the gentiles; shewing them their religion was but a novel upstart thing compared with that of the christians. Moses, he tells them, lived some hundred of years before the ruins of Troy; that all the rest of the prophets succeeded Moses, and yet some of the last of them were of the same age with their first wise men, lawgivers, and historians.

If it be asked, what evidence doth this afford of the divinity, or inspiration of the Bible? I answer, as mankind needed a revelation from God, immediately upon his apostacy, and had reason to hope

and full to the purpose it cannot be amiss to insert it here; "Be-
"fore any of your public monuments and Inscriptions, says he,
"before any of your forms of government, before the oldest of
"your books, the original of many nations, the foundation of ma-
"ny famous cities, and most ancient historians; yea, before the
"invention of letters; and, as if I had hitherto said but little, be-
"fore the very being of your gods, your temples, oracles, and
"sacrifices, were the writings of one of our prophets extant;
"which are the treasury of the Jewish religion, and by
"consequence of the Christian. If you have heard of Moses the
"prophet, I will tell you his age, he was co-temporary with Ina-
"chus the first king of the Argives, older by three hundred nine-
"ty-three years than Danaus the oldest in your histories. About
"a thousand years before the destruction of Troy, or, as others
"reckon, about five hundred years before Homer; the rest of
"the prophets, though later than Moses, yet the latest of them
"fall in with some of your Sages, lawgivers and historians."—
Nor did he say so without reason, since Isaiah, Hosea, and other of the prophets lived at the time when the Greeks first began their Olympiads, before Rome was built; and the very latest of the Old Testament writers flourished before Socrates. To which I may add, that as the other two fathers here mentioned, Justin Martyr and Eusebius, to say nothing of Clemens Alexandrinus, Cyril, St. Austin, &c. who urge the same argument, insist more at large upon the subject, so they fully prove Moses of much greater antiquity than the most ancient pagan authors. And indeed, this is universally owned not only by Jews and Christians, but also by heathens themselves. Even Porphyry, one of the most learned and shrewd adversaries christianity ever had, was forced to allow him older than his favorite Sanchoniatho, whom yet he places before the Trojan war.

for such a favor, from the divine mercy and goodness; and as the Bible is the most ancient revelation, beginning with man's necessities, and providing a suitable remedy for them, it is most likely to be from God. Not to say, that antiquity has always claimed a sort of veneration, men agree by common consent, to rise up before the hoary head thereof. Hence Tertullian pleads with the gentiles, that as it was matter of religion and conscience to give credit to things according to their age and antiquity; therefore the Christian religion, having marks of the highest antiquity, deserved their greatest honor, and they ought accordingly to reverence it. But what I think of the greatest weight here, is, that the Bible being the most ancient book in the world, has gone through a course of the longest examinations. It has, some of it, bore the test of many thousand years, and has stood its ground, after the severest and most critical trial.

Now had it been false, it is not to be imagined it would have escaped without discovery. After it has undergone the scrutiny of so many ages, of so many thousands and millions of persons, both of friends and enemies, from one generation to another, one cannot reasonably suspect it; nor can we think it consistent with the wisdom and goodness of God, his love of truth and hatred of falshood, and his regard to mankind, to suffer a cheat to reign and triumph so long in full glory and reputation. No, had it been a cunningly devised fable, he would surely have interposed in his providence and have defeated it. As time is a consumer of things, so it is a touchstone to discover what they are. A cheat may pass for a while, but it was never known that a cheat, such a one as the Bible must be, if it be a cheat, ever passed long without disgrace. So that it is really a probable argument, and I carry it no farther, whatever others have done, that as the Bible is the most ancient book, it is a divine book.

If any object, this only speaks for the writings of Moses. I answer, it is granted. But then it must be considered that Moses' books contain the substance of the rest. The apostle tells us, the gospel was preached to Abraham. It had an edition then. We find in the Pentateuch the lineaments, and a more imperfect draught of the whole Bible. And besides, it has been shewn before, that the several parts of the Scriptures give testimony to one another. So that what confirms and proves one divine, derives a sort of an Authority to all the rest.

2. The preservation of the Bible through so many ages is another circumstance, that may be urged to prove the same thing. If it had not been of God, we cannot think he would have concerned himself so much about it, and employed his providence for its security all along, as we are assured he has done. That we have the several inspired books brought down to us safe and entire, in the main, I shall hereafter shew. At present, I suppose this to be fact, and may, I think, ground an argument upon it in favor of the Bible.

Several things might be offered to illustrate this; as, that it is the most ancient book, and so has had the more time to decay and perish in. It has gone through a longer state of trial, as I may say, and has stood exposed to all casualties and hazards for more ages than any book besides.

Farther, the subject of it would create it more enemies. Some books so little concern mankind, they treat about such mere amusements, matters of no importance, or at best little speculations; that they are not like to raise the enmity of the world against them. Indeed mens carelesness about things that deserve no care, may suffer them to perish; but their supposed interests, or real enmity will never rife up againſt them to deſtroy them. Whereas the *Bible* is of a different conſideration. It treats of higher important things, to which the paſſions and corruptions of men ſtand in a direct oppoſition. It is a ſtanding record for God, and againſt Satan and his kingdom; a conſtant curb and check to vicious men in their purſuits, and ſometimes a terror to them. And conſequently, ſuch a book would have many enemies that would be glad to get rid of it; to ruin its reputation, and deſtroy its very being, if they could.

I add, this has actually been the caſe of the Scripture. Not only bad men have always hated it, but ſome of its enemies have appeared againſt it with a power equal to their malice. The attempts of *Antiochus Epiphanes* under the Old Teſtament, and of Diocleſian under the New, to this purpoſe, are known. The former, when he had ſacked Jeruſalem, profaned their temple, and made the daily ſacrifice to ceaſe, as Daniel propheſied of him; made diligent ſearch for the law; burnt all the copies of it he could find, and threatened the ſevereſt torments to thoſe who ſhould conceal it. And the very ſame thing did Diocleſian, ſo famous, or rather infamous, for his rage againſt chriſtians, and who triumphed in his ſuppoſed ſuccefs. After the moſt barbarous havoc of them, he put forth an edict commanding them to bring in their *Bibles* to be burnt and deſtroyed: which multitudes out of fear complied with, and thence had the reproachful name of Traditores, thoſe that delivered up their *Bibles*, and in caſe of failure, he threatened all ſorts of tortures and death. Well, notwithſtanding theſe and all other aſſaults, notwithſtanding the enmity and malice of wicked men and devils againſt the Scripture, it has been preſerved pure and uncorrupt, in the main, to this day. We have the same law God delivered to Moses on mount Sinai, the same statutes and judgments he gave to Israel, we have the true history left by the immediate followers of the Lord Jesus, and those sacred books that contain the genuine records of their doctrine. These God has preserved to us, and lodged in our hands, by a care and sovereignty of providence, that one need not scruple to call divine. They have been often in danger, * and sometimes almost bundled up and brought to the funeral pile. The implacable and avowed enemies of religion, who at once had all human power and terror in their hands, have decreed their extirpation, and accordingly set themselves to accomplish it. But God has defeated all their designs; still the Bible exists and is triumphant, and, I doubt not, will as long as there is a church in the world, that is, till the end of time, and consummation of all things.

Now hence, I think, one might form an argument that amounts to a demonstration of a moral kind. God's providence in preserving the Bible is a public signification that he owns it. Such have been its hazards, that it could never have been preserved, had not God undertaken its defence. And such is the justice, truth, holiness, and goodness of God, that he would never have espoused

---

* The greatest danger they were ever in of being lost, was in the days of king Josiah, if those learned men are in the right who think there was only one copy of the law of Moses then left, which Hilkiah the priest casually found in the temple, 2 Kings xxii. 8. But there are others to whom it seems much more probable, that the book there spoken of, was either the Autograph of Moses, that authentic copy that was expresly ordered to be laid up and kept by the side of the ark in the most holy place, Deut. xxxi. 26. or else some other sacred copy used in the service of the temple and preserved there, like as was afterwards done in the second temple, where we are told that copy was kept, which Titus carried in triumph to Rome. Joseph. de Bell. Judaic. L. vii. cap 24.

it in the manner he has done, had it been a forgery, and not from himself.

3. Another particular, under the general head of external marks and characters of the divinity of Scripture, is the wonderful accomplishment of it in all the circumstances thereof. I say, in all the circumstances of it; which I question not is true, though we may not be able fully to make this out. We may want capacities sometimes to understand the text, and often to expound the providence that is an exact accomplishment of it; and so cannot discern the harmony between the one and the other; which yet is real and certain, and reaches even to very minute and little things, had we penetration enough to discover it. However, notwithstanding our defects here, so much is evident to a diligent observer, as is sufficient to give this argument its due force. The Bible has been fulfilled in all ages, from the beginning of the world to this day. It has been so in many instances, as must appear to the satisfaction of all, that will allow themselves seriously to consider these matters, and we have reason to conclude, it is so universally.

I shall a little expatiate on this head; and let you see wherein the Scripture is fulfilled, and then make a few remarks, shewing you how the accomplishment thereof proves its divinity. Now the Scripture has been fulfilled, 1. In the natural and material world. And, 2. In the moral world or world of mankind.

1. It has been fulfilled in the natural or material world. The account the Bible gives us of the heavens and the earth, so far as they fall under our observation, has been answered in providence through all generations hitherto. I shall mention a few particulars out of many.

1. We find, according to Scripture, the ground

laid under a curse upon man's apostacy, *And unto Adam he said, becauſe thou haſt harkened unto the voice of thy wife, and haſt eaten of the tree of which I commanded thee, ſaying, thou ſhalt not eat of it: curſed is the ground for thy ſake; in ſorrow ſhalt thou eat of it all the days of thy life. Thorns alſo and thiſtles ſhall it bring forth unto thee: in the ſweat of thy face ſhalt thou eat bread, till thou return unto the ground.* This the Scripture tells us ſhould be the future ſtate of the earth, and we have the experience of ſeveral thouſand years atteſting the truth of it. Had not mankind ſinned, we may juſtly ſuppoſe the earth would have been more fertile, and would have yielded the conveniencies of life with leſs labor and pains. But as a puniſhment of his tranſgreſſion it was doomed to a ſort of ſterility, or barrenneſs. Thorns and thiſtles are its ſpontaneous production. It brings forth theſe of its own accord. But if man will enjoy its more uſeful fruits, it muſt be with greater expence than was neceſſary heretofore. He muſt labor in cultivating it, and eat thereof in the ſweat of his face. Thus the Bible intimates it ſhould be, that the earth would undergo a change for the worſe in this reſpect; being curſed for man's ſake. And thus all have found it through every age ſince.

2. When mankind had lived upon the earth for fifteen or ſixteen hundred years, and their ſins had provoked the wrath and vengeance of heaven againſt them, the Scripture foretells the amazing judgment of an univerſal deluge, or flood, which God would bring upon them for their wickedneſs. The denunciation of this judgment you have, Gen, vi. 5, 6, 7, 13, 17. That it was fulfilled, and how, you read in the next chapter. I will only obſerve, that the fact that there was a general deluge, at the time aſſigned by Moſes, is not only affirmed in the Bible, and referred to over and over again there,

both in the Old and New Testament, but we have the concurrence of the most ancient heathen writers to the same truth. One of them, of great reputation, tells us, that Osiris, or Noah, went into the ark on the seventeenth day of the Egyptian month Athyr, when the sun passes the sign Scorpio, which is the very same day mentioned by Moses, the seventeenth day of the second month, as some have shewn from astronomical calculations. Nor have we only full testimony for the fact; but a kind of demonstration of it from the numerous shells of fishes, from plants, trees, and other remains of the antideluvian world; which are to this day found buried in the bowels of the earth; and, I do not think, can be so rationally accounted for, as upon the supposition of a general deluge.

Now if it be considered, that this was threatened above a hundred years before it came to pass, when there were no tokens and intimations of it in nature; that Noah, that preacher of righteousness, was employed to give warning of it all that while, and that the judgment was executed in the very manner, and at the very time foretold; we may, I think, place this among those remarkable providences that confirm the truth and divinity of the Scripture. None but the great Author of nature could bring about such an event, and none but he could predict and insure it. He alone could do the thing, and he only could foretell it.

3. After this dreadful and amazing judgment had taken place, God was pleased to give a solemn assurance to mankind, that he would not again destroy them in such a manner, and inflict the like calamity of an universal deluge; and as a token and pledge of his promise he tells them he would set his bow in the heavens. *I will remember*, says he, *my covenant which is between me, and you, and every*

living creature of all flesh; and the waters shall no more become a flood to destroy all flesh. And the bow shall be in the cloud; and I will look upon it, that I may remember the everlasting covenant between God, and every living creature that is upon the earth. This was God's promise to the world after the flood, and one may observe it carries an air of sovereignty and authority in it, that seems to intimate it could come from none but God; could not be the fiction of Moses, or any impostor, inserted as an embellishment in his history. For who but the great Sovereign and Lord of nature, that had spared a very sinful world for above sixteen hundred years, and just now destroyed it, could pass an act of indemnity, and grant a security against the like judgment for all future time; and not only so, but place the rain-bow in the clouds, as a pledge of his faithfulness in this instance: a token, a federal token between God and man, that the world should never more perish by water.

This is the record of Scripture, and every generation since, for more than four thousand years, has seen the accomplishment of it in both the parts, *viz.* a freedom from an universal flood, and the frequent appearance of the rain-bow: if it be said, the rain-bow is no new thing, it appeared as much before the flood, as since, and could not but appear, if they had rain, it proceeding from natural causes, and being the necessary result of them. I answer, that at least it was appointed for a new service and purpose after the flood. If it appeared in the clouds before, it was not as a sign of God's covenant and promise till afterwards. But, I answer further, that it does not appear probable to me, there ever was a rain-bow before the flood. The manner of introducing it, *behold I do set my bow in the clouds,* and the end it was to serve for, *it shall be for a token of the covenant between me and the* *earth.* This I think implies, it had not been seen in the clouds before, and that it was then first, and ever after upon occasion, to appear as a pledge to mankind, that God would make good his promise. Nor are the late discoveries in philosophy concerning the rainbow, any sufficient objection against this. We need only suppose, that the state of the air before the flood was different from what it is at present, and then the objection is removed. And that it might be so, is not at all improbable; and that it actually was so, I have the authority of some modern philosophers of no little reputation for skill in these matters. One * of them speaking of the subject, has these words. " Who, but the great " governor and disposer of all the works of nature, " could so alter the constitution of the air after the " deluge, that whereas all the former generations " had never seen nor heard of such a thing as the " rain-bow, the future should never be without that " glorious signal of divine goodness, and instance of " the divine power." He supposes, that the rainbow is a new appearance, that it is a special work of the divine power and providence, and that to produce it God changed the state of the air. And if this be the case, as I reckon probable enough, that the bow is a new phænomenon, never seen before the flood, it was the fitter when it appeared, to be a sign of God's covenant, and a confirmation of his promise. And the constant appearance of it now, is a glorious instance of the truth of the Scripture. We should accordingly improve it, and when we behold the bow in the clouds; such a reflection as this cannot be impertinent. How faithful is God in all his promises! How certain, how divine the record he has given of himself in his word! This God promised before any such thing was

* Whiston's Scripture Prophecies, p. 103.

known in the world; and every age has seen the performance. Thus true is the word of God, and thus sure are his promises. I may subjoin, as what is nearly connected with this head.

4. The assurance the Scripture gives us of a regular succession of day and night, and of the various seasons of the year. This was promised immediately after Noah came out of the ark, and had offered sacrifice to his great preserver, *while the earth remaineth, feed-time and harvest, cold and heat, summer and winter, and day and night shall not cease,* that is, there shall be no such confusion of things as during the late catastrophe and desolation occasioned by the deluge, but he will preserve nature in its regular course to the end of time. This I take to be the import of that promise or prophecy, and every age since has had the comfortable experience of the accomplishment of it to the present day, and we may depend upon it, it shall always be accomplished, even till that period the apostle speaks of, *when the heavens shall pass away with a great noise, and the elements melt with fervent heat, the earth also and the works therein shall be burnt up.*

This account and representation that the Scripture gives of the natural world, some great and important phænomena and events therein: To which much more might be added to the like purpose did I apprehend the discourse would be acceptable and useful to the auditory; this account, I say, gloriously confirms the truth of Scripture, and evidences it must have a divine original. Had the writers thereof invented their own materials, they would not have drawn such a scheme of things, and so boldly have pronounced concerning future events of providence, wholly out of their power and prospect, about which they could have no certainty themselves, nor give security to others. In the next place,

2. The Scripture has been fulfilled in the moral world, or the world of mankind. The account it has given of men and their affairs, has been verified and answered with great exactness through every age, so as to make a beautiful harmony between the word of God and providence. It would be no small pleasure to contemplate and view this, as far as our knowledge and observation can carry us. But I shall restrain myself, and only offer a few hints. The Scripture has been and is fulfilled in several instances, that concern mankind in general. It has been fulfilled in some special instances towards particular families, nations, and people, towards particular persons, and towards the two different sorts, in the grand division of mankind, bad men and good men.

1. It has been, and continues to be fulfilled in several instances that concern mankind in general; as the universal taint and defilement of nature. This the Bible mentions as fact. *God made man upright, but he found out many inventions.* And it gives an account of the occasion and rise of it, *viz.* the apostacy of our first parents; by which the human nature was corrupted in the fountain of it. That this has been fulfilled, every man in the world has had experience, more or less, according to his time in the world, and his sense and understanding of these matters. *This only have I found*, says Solomon in the place I now refer to, that *God made man upright; but they have sought out many inventions.* He was a person of eminent wisdom, of great observation, and very inquisitive; and he could find nothing more certain, than the degeneracy and depravation of mankind. And this every one finds in himself, and may observe in others. The heathens found it and complained of it, though they could not find out the cause of it; which the

Scripture acquaints us with, and herein is fulfilled in the experience of the whole world.

I might instance in the labor, toil and sorrow, mankind was doomed to upon his sin and apostacy, which every one tastes of in one degree or other. As also, in the vanity and disappointment that attends every undertaking and state. Nothing can be attained without labor and sorrow, nothing enjoyed without vanity: a sort of curse flows down upon it, and mixes with the enjoyment. This is implied in the sentence pronounced, Gen. iii. 16, 17, 18, 19. Witnessed to abundantly in other Scriptures, particularly in the book of Ecclesiastes, and confirmed by the experience of the whole world. Nor is it impertinent to mention here with respect to one sex, her pains in child-bearing, which are greater than those of any other females in the world, and were appointed as a peculiar punishment for the part the woman had in the transgression; together with her more uneasy subjection to her husband. This the Scripture speaks of with authority and certainty, at the very beginning of the world: and it has had a constant confirmation during a succession of many thousand years.

I may add, the sentence of death passed on all mankind. And let it be observed, that according to the Scripture account, this was pronounced before there was one example of death in the world; and before it could be known by any, but the great Lord of life, or those to whom he would reveal it, whether any of the human race should die or not. And yet, this has been fulfilled universally, excepting two instances, where the great lawgiver interposed, and where the persons underwent some kind of an equivalent, a translation instead of death. It has been fulfilled, I say, in every age and place, and continues to be so, at this day. And it is very remarkable, that as the life of man, was prolonged for

DISCOURSE VII.

several hundred years, in the first ages, the better to serve the purposes of the wise providence, that governs the world, and was at last reduced to three score years and ten, as being the common standard, that is, the time of a full age, when nature should appear decayed and spent; so that if men do not die then, they will however, be languishing and dying: as, I say, the standard was thus fixed, it has been found the common measure of life ever since, and men have died, as I may express, according to the word of the world. The Scripture has pawned its truth and veracity upon this point, and that when there was no example of dying, as you have heard, that all men should die, should return to the dust, and that in the revolution of seventy years, they should at least be ready to fall into it.

Now, could men, any men, by their own understanding and foresight, not let into the secrets and purposes of the great governor of the world, could they draw such a scheme of things? could they have recorded such matters? have given such an history of providence, for many ages and generations to come, which is so fully and punctually answered in the event? was it possible they should have done this, if they had not had intercourse with the divinity, and had not spoke from God, who saw the end, from the beginning?

2. The Scripture has been fulfilled in some special instances, towards particular families, nations, and people. The subject here is too large for me to trace through the particulars, that are known and certain: or, it would afford an ample confirmation of the divinity of the Bible; and not having room for it in this discourse, I must leave it to another head, where it may be urged not less pertinently. In the mean time, I shall observe in general, that the state of Abraham's family, the surprising increase of it, when as yet he had no child, and according to

the course of nature, was likely to have none. The sojourning of his posterity in Egypt, for four hundred years, their deliverance thence and settlement in the promised land, with a great many amazing circumstances, concerning their settlement, their apostacies, and punishments, their several captivities and restorations, with a multitude of things relating thereto; even till the coming of the Messiah, and their final destruction: all these are set forth and described in the Scripture, with so much positiveness, so distinctly, and with such an air of sovereignty, as leaves no room to question, by whose authority the Bible was written. And, as it describes the state of the Jews, in all their revolutions, so it paints the various scenes of the christian church, that have been, and that shall be; I presume to the end of the world. These we have in the books of Daniel, Ezekiel, and the revelations of John; to say nothing of the fate of the several kingdoms of the Gentiles, against whom the prophets denounced judgments, the burthens of the Lord, as they express it, against Idumea, Tyre, Sydon, &c. all which prophecies, have been fulfilled, even in the most minute circumstances, as we are assured, in regard of the main branches of them; and in a manner, that gives the Scripture a triumph over all the cavils of infidel objectors, and will warrant, I think, this conclusion, that either the Bible is true, or God doth not govern the world. For, I cannot see but providence and the Bible, are in such connexion, that they stand or fall together: and that whoever denies the one, must give up the other also. Further,

3. The Bible has been fulfilled towards particular persons, in some very memorable instances, as towards Abraham, instanced in before, whose concerns reach through many generations; where-

DISCOURSE VII.

in there are such marks of divine providence, as plainly imply, the persons who wrote the accounts, were under a divine conduct. To this, I may add, that denunciation of wrath against Eli's house, which was to this effect, that God would certainly reject his family from the honor and dignity of the high priesthood, for their profanation of sacred things, and substitute another family in their room; that he himself should live to see the ark of God, that glory of Israel, depart from them, and fall into the hands of the Philistines; that all the branches of his house should die in the flower of their age, and that there should not be an old man among them, and that instead of the plenty they now lived in, and which they so much abused, they should be reduced to a piece of bread, and be forced to beg some mean employment of the high priests, his successors about the sanctuary, to keep them from starving; and that as a confirmation of all this, his two wicked sons, Hophni and Phineas, should both die in one day. This is the threatning, the description laid down in Scripture of a future event; as you have it, 1 Sam. ii. 31, 32, &c. and chap. iii. 11, 12, 13, 14. How it was fulfilled in all the parts of it, the Scripture history of Eli's house lets us see, though neither my time nor your patience, will allow me to consider it. I shall only take notice of one passage, very remarkable, related by a grave author, that a certain family among the Jews being observed to be short lived in an unusual manner, all of them dying about eighteen, they consulted a learned rabbi about the occasion of such a judgment. He advised them to enquire into their genealogy, and see if they were not of the posterity of Eli, to whom such a punishment was threatened of old; which they found to be their case, and thence learned the cause of that severe dispensation.

Of the same nature is what Joshua denounces against the builder of Jericho, that his eldest son should die when he attempted the work and laid the foundation of the city; that the rest of his sons should perish during the progress of the building, and his youngest at the fitting up the gates. The threatning is recorded, Josh. vi. 26. and the accomplishment, 1 Kings xvi. 34. So exactly all along has divine providence commented upon the Bible, and verified its predictions.

I shall only mention farther under this head, the threatning of the prophet against his servant Gahazi and his posterity, viz. That the leprosy of Naaman should cleave to him and to his seed forever, 2 Kings, v. 27. The inflicting of which judgment, as we have reason to expect it would be certain from the authority of him that denounced it, so we have an intimation of it in a story, not unlike that I mentioned before, concerning the short lives of Eli's house, viz. That a family of considerable note being leprous one after another in a long succession, enquiry was made into their descent, and it was found that they were of the posterity of Gahazi. Thus true and infallible is the holy Scripture. What it predicts, it insures. An argument it could not be of human contrivance, but must proceed from an all-comprehending mind, that had knowledge to foresee and discern what would be, and right and authority to determine what should be. In a word, the Scripture is the disclosure of the divine purposes, and contains the model and plan of the divine government. It points out future events, and is a sort of a prophetic register, as I may say, of all the vicissitudes and changes there are in human affairs, and of the proceedings of divine providence, whether in a way of rebuke and judgment, or mercy and deliverance, towards the world, towards the church, and towards particular

DISCOURSE VII.

perſons. And, as it has been hitherto verified, we may conclude, it ſhall be ſo ſtill, not one word ſhall fail, nor one iota paſs, till the whole be accompliſhed.

The laſt particular under this head remains, which I muſt be forced hereafter to reſume. As it contains matter of ſo much inſtruction and confirmation to chriſtians, I cannot ſatisfy myſelf to paſs it over lightly. I ſhall therefore in another diſcourſe ſhew that the Scripture has been fulfilled, and continues to be fulfilled in numerous inſtances in the two different ſorts of men, good and bad. It gives the character, lays open the heart, principles, ſtates and frames of both. Wicked men are exactly ſuch as they are there repreſented to be. Their inward thoughts, deſires, affections are ſuch as the word of God deſcribes them, And as for good men they find the Scripture a bright mirror wherein they view themſelves in all the varieties of their caſe; at leaſt, they might do ſo, and would do it more fully, did they ſtudy the Scripture more, and underſtand themſelves better. So that the ſenſible, ſerious chriſtian has a witneſs in himſelf that the Bible is the word of God. He finds it fulfilled in his own heart every day in ſome meaſure; fulfilled in the conſtant experience of his life; whence he is aſſured it is true, and thence infers that it is divine.

DISCOURSE VIII.

The Divine Original and Inspiration of the Scripture.

---

2 Tim. iii. 16.

All Scripture is given by inspiration of God, and is profitable for doctrine, for reproof, for correction, for instruction in righteousness.

AS an argument of the inspiration or divine original of the Scripture, I mentioned the accomplishment of it in all the circumstances thereof. I observed, that it has been fulfilled in the natural, material world, and in the moral world, or world of mankind. Under this last particular, I shewed you,

I. That it has been, and is fulfilled, in several instances that concern mankind in general.

II. That it has been fulfilled in some special instances towards particular families, nations, and people. And,

III. Towards particular persons. I proceed now to shew,

IV. The Scripture has been, and continues to be fulfilled in numerous instances in regard of the two different sorts in the great Division of mankind, Bad men and good men. It has been fulfilled in the Representation it makes of the hearts, principles, condition, and frame of both.

I. It has been fulfilled in bad men, and is constantly fulfilled in them. I shall touch upon a few things to make this appear.

DISCOURSE VIII.

1. The Scripture is fulfilled in the account it gives of their inward principles and frame, with refpect to God and Religion. As, that they know not God; that their carnal minds are enmity to him; that they are of this world, have the fpirit of the world, their portion in this life, and mind earthly things. That they are fenfual, not having the fpirit; that they live without God in the world; that he is not in all their thoughts; they call not upon him. It reprefents them as void of the fear and love of God, deftitute of all divine graces; having dark minds, hard hearts, feared confciences, and being reprobate to every good work; and in confequence of this, wanting the great diftinguifhing ornaments of the new and divine nature, their hearts are faid to be little worth, and they are compared to the chaff which the wind driveth away, and that fhall be burnt up with unquenchable fire. Now how evidently is all this verified in a large body of mankind. It is granted, the character being taken from the heart, it is not fo legible to us; but it is true of all the ungodly; they exactly anfwer this defcription, and their conformity hereto is in part obvious to the obfervation of others; their carnal minds and earthly frame are in fome meafure manifeft in their practice. And every one that has had the experience of both ftates, has the confirmation hereof in his own breaft. He knows what that darknefs, ignorance, enmity, and carnality is, the Scripture makes the character of the wicked and unfanctified. What he fees fuch woeful fymptoms and indications of in others, once he experienced in himfelf. He was once alienated from the life of God; dead in trefpaffes and fins; once darknefs, though now he be light in the Lord; and though he has not warrant to fay precifely of fuch and fuch perfons, that they have the characters of the ungodly; yet he can be affured he was

once one himself; and comparing what he observes in others about him with what formerly he found within him, he remains convinced that the Scripture account of this matter is true, and that were the hearts of wicked men laid open, as they will be at the great day, it would be evident they are there painted to the life.

2. The Scripture is fulfilled in the description it gives of their antipathy to good men; their hatred of them, and opposition to them, that Enmity God put between the seed of the serpent and that of the woman, has been working ever since. It shewed itself early in Cain, and has appeared in all following ages. There has all along been a generation of men, that may properly be called a serpentine seed; full of enmity against the sincere worshippers of God, and followers of the Lamb: and though their enmity has been, and is disguised under various pretences, it is really levelled at the religion of the principles of piety and virtue in good men. This the apostle remarks concerning Cain, *he was of that wicked one, and slew his brother; and wherefore slew he him, because his own works were evil, and his brother's righteous.* This was then the ground of the quarrel, and it remains so to the present day. *As he that was born after the flesh, persecuted him that was born after the spirit, even so it is now,* says St. Paul. So it was in the apostle's days, indeed, always was, and always will be. Thus the Scripture has told us of one sort, at least of wicked men; and I appeal to the observation and experience of every age, whether it is not fulfilled. *The wicked in his pride doth persecute the poor.* Sometimes they persecute with the tongue only, calling names, inventing invidious distinctions and terms of reproach; and sometimes they proceed to more open methods of violence. But the enmity still reigns in the heart, which way soever it breaks forth.

3. The Scripture is fulfilled in the character it gives of this body of men, as to their outward circumstances; placing them on higher ground, and representing them as the great men of this world. This character they have often in the Old Testament, but more commonly in the New. *Ye see your calling, brethren, how that not many wise men, after the flesh, not many mighty, not many noble, are called.* Where you will observe, the persons of this condition, the rich, the mighty, are left out of the church. So elsewhere, *do not rich men oppress you? do not they blaspheme that worthy name by which you are called?* And again, *go to, ye rich men, weep and howl for your miseries that shall come upon you. Ye have lived in pleasure on the earth, and been wanton. Ye have nourished your hearts, as in a day of slaughter.* Thus the Bible speaks of that body of mankind, which it distinguishes from the church. And no man, I think, can read the history of former times, or observe the occurrences of his own, but must see an exact accomplishment thereof herein. Not that all rich men are bad men, or all bad men rich. But in that division I am speaking of into two classes or kinds, bad and good, the church and the world; it is evident according to Scripture, that bad men will have the greatest portion of this world. In short, the Scripture sets forth the danger of riches, in the most lively terms; tells us, a rich man shall hardly enter into the kingdom of heaven; represents such as often abandoned to sensuality, pride, oppression, to forgetfulness of God and religion. All which we have seen so punctually fulfilled hitherto, as may convince us there are no random guesses in Scripture; that it is a divine revelation, makes known what shall be; containing the dictates of an infinitely wise, foreseeing, I may add, of a sovereign mind.

4. The same may be said of their inward disqui-

etude, want of proper tranquility and rest of mind. The Scripture tells us, *There is no peace to the wicked*, that they *are like the troubled sea, when it cannot rest, whose waters cast up mire and dirt*. For the accomplishment of this, I appeal to those that once were in such a state, and are happily got out of it. I appeal to the persons themselves, whether they do not find a thirst and craving that cannot be satisfied among the creatures : whether they have not many a time been weary of pursuing vanities and grasping shadows ? whether their inward lusts do not vex and disturb them ; their outward enjoyments disappoint them ? and in a word, whether they be not utter strangers to the solid rest and satisfaction of pious, devout souls ? They may indeed endeavor to quiet conscience, divert and amuse themselves by little arts, and cheat themselves into a false peace ; but after all, they find it will not do : their peace is a dream, their joy a flash. Nor can they rest till they return to God, and rest in him.

Thus the Scripture is fulfilled in regard of bad men : it is fulfilled in their moral character, in their outward state and circumstances, in their enmity towards the church, in their disorder and uneasiness of mind.

II. It is fulfilled likewise towards good men. I have here a large field, but must satisfy myself with the bare mention of such heads of discourses, as would admit of great enlargement. It is fulfilled towards good men in general, and towards particular believers.

1. The Scripture is fulfilled towards good men in general, the whole church of christians. I shall illustrate this in a few instances.

It represents the church of Christ, as consisting of persons mean and low, as to their circumstances in the world. *Not many wise men after the flesh,* says the apostle in the text I have quoted before, *not many mighty, not many noble are called.* And *hath not God chosen the poor of this world, rich in faith, and heirs of the kingdom which he has promised to them that love him.* This is the constant language of Scripture. It every where intimates, that the followers of Christ would be of the meaner sort. Indeed, every thing was at first so contrived, and the scene so laid, as plainly imported and signified this. Thus, when the Lord and head of the church came into the world, it was in circumstances of great outward meanness. He did not appear with any of the pomp and grandeur of a temporal prince, but assumed the character of an ordinary mechanic; was called the carpenter's son, and the carpenter. The prime ministers of his kingdom were chosen from among fishermen. And it is remarked, at the beginning of his religion, that the *poor had the Gospel preached to them*, that is, were gospellized, or brought to receive the gospel. All which was a sort of a type, as I may call it, or intimation of what he himself expressly declares, that his *kingdom was not of this world.* He did not intend to set up a worldly kingdom, nor would the men of this world, that were fond of its distinctions and enjoyments be among the subjects of his kingdom. And a little observation, I think, may convince any competent judges, that in this instance the Scripture has not wanted its accomplishment. Not that the members of the christian church are the abject and miserably poor; but generally they are of the meaner sort. Nor is it to be understood, as I hinted before, that none of the great men of this world belong thereto; but that not many of them do so. This is what the Scripture affirms, and the event agrees to the account it gives. It may be otherwise, indeed, before the end of the world, when the kings of the earth shall bring their glory into the new Jerusalem, which is but according to the Scripture prediction, and will be the accomplishment of it. But, at present, the church of Christ is the congregation of the poor, as they are called, I mean the invisible church, the true genuine members thereof. For, as for mere professors and pretenders, that usurp the christian name without the christian nature, by whatever title they are distinguished, whether catholic, christian, or most christian, it is no objection against this; *he is not a Jew, that is one outwardly*, nor are all christians, that bear that character.

The Scripture represents the church also as the less, as well as the lower part of mankind. *Fear not little flock,* says Christ, *it is your Father's good pleasure to give you the kingdon.* And elsewhere, *many are called, and few are chosen.* If it be understood of the church compared with the world, the true church of Christ, the invisible church, compared with the rest of mankind, the great body of hypocrites and false professors; there can be no question of its accomplishment.

Again, the Scripture represents the church, the real genuine members of it, as generally in a state of conflict, exercise and sorrow; whilst the men of the world are in circumstances of great freedom and ease, that appear more plausible and agreeable to common judges. Thus, *ye shall lament and weep, but the world shall rejoice.* And this is the constant strain of Scripture; *Blessed are they that mourn,* says our Lord, *for they shall be comforted.* They that will live godly in Christ Jesus must suffer persecution, and *through much tribulation we must enter into the kingdom of heaven.* And even when we are told, that they who *forsake father or mother, &c. shall receive a hundred fold in the present life, and in the world to come eternal life:* it is added, with persecutions, Mark x. 30. intimating, that the church in this world would be in a state of suffering, and will be so, more or less, whilst it is militant. The accomplishment of which has been matter of experience and observation through every age: good men have generally been the butt of the world's malice. They *called the master of the house Beelzebub, how much more them of the houshold?* They have had *wrestling, not only with flesh and blood; but with principalities and powers, with the rulers of the darkness of this world, with spiritual wickedness in high places.* Add to this, the constant conflicts in their own minds, with their infirmities, lusts, and corruptions. Great inward peace and consolation, I grant, sublime and pure joys good men are partakers of, according to the measure of their attainments. But notwithstanding these, they have their exercises, burthens, fears, their hours of weeping and humiliation, their deep abasements and self-annihilations, as I may call them, such as the world knows nothing of. In all which the Scripture is gloriously fulfilled. We see two sorts of men in the world; some bearing the cross and following Christ, denying themselves, crucifying the flesh, sowing in tears: others secure, thoughtless, living in pleasure, putting far from them the evil day, without care, thought, burthen or fear; which is just the scene described in Scripture, agreeable to the plan and state there laid down.

Further, the Scripture represents the church of God, as immoveably secure and safe, notwithstanding all the dangers that threaten it, whether without, or from within. The *gates of hell*, we are told, *shall not prevail against it.* It shall never be extinguished and die, whatever extremities it may be reduced to. No, Christ's *sheep hear his voice, and they shall never perish, neither shall any pluck them out of his hand.* And thus it hath been hitherto. The *bush has been in flames, but not consumed.* The church has been preserved in the midst of all its adversaries. Two things add a lustre and glory to this providence. It has met with the most powerful opposition. Never had any body such formidable enemies, and yet it has survived all. And further, other kingdoms have sunk under a far less weight. The four famous monarchies, the Assyrian, Medo-Persian, Greek, and Roman, that thought themselves invincible, and had all external advantages to render them so, are perished and come to nothing. And yet the church destitute of all human help, headed by a carpenter, as he was called and appeared in the world, and by a few poor fishermen, has stood its ground and weathered the point to this day. The billows have raged and the mountains been cast into the midst of the sea; but God has always been in the midst of his church, *a river has made glad the city of God.*

The Scripture represents the Church of God as mixed with hypocrites, a company of pretenders, joining in profession with the upright followers of the Lord Jesus; that have the Lamb's mark on their foreheads. This we have in various parables as well as in other texts; as in the parable of the *net cast into the sea, the tares sown among the wheat, the wise and foolish virgins.* And I need not stand to shew you, that it has had its accomplishment hitherto, that the church has herein exactly answered the description of the word, and appeared in the form, or according to the model drawn by the great Lord and founder of it.

I add, The Scripture represents the church in a great variety of states; as undergoing sundry changes, and appearing in different shapes. At first it was like a grain of mustard-seed, little and obscure, and then was to grow up to a great tree, and in different periods to put on different faces: sometimes to be oppressed, its witnesses lying in sackcloth, and prophefying in fable ; and then to be enlarged : fometimes to apoftatife and grow lukewarm, fecure, and carelefs ; and then again to revive, and appear in its luftre and glory. This we have defcribed in feveral prophecies and particularly in the Revelations, under the type of the feven Afian churches. And the providence of God has been fulfilling the fame in every age fince the going forth of the word of prophecy ; part of which we have feen, and the reft we wait for. You read when the church was only a grain of muftardfeed, you have feen it a great tree. You have heard of its general defection, and have feen its reformation in fome meafure. And we have reafon to expect it will appear in greater glory than it has ever yet done. But what I offer, is, that the Scripture points at all thefe revolutions, viciffitudes, and changes ; and that the Sovereign Ruler of the world has ordered events anfwerable to the predictions and characters given of things therein. Thus it has been with reference to the church in general. And I am now to remark,

2. That the Scripture has been fulfilled towards particular believers ; and that with reference to their call into the church, their character and principles, their infirmities, the promifes made to them, and the threatenings denounced againft them for their chaftifement and correction.

1. The Scripture has been fulfilled in their call into the church. And here I may take notice that the Bible reprefents the different characters of the perfons called, fome as notoriously wicked, finners before the Lord exceedingly ; as the prodigal fon, Mary Magdalene ; fome among the Corinthians, as the apoftle tells us, 1 Cor, vi. 9, 10, 11. Some as lefs infamous and fcandalous, as the apoftles of Chrift, Nicodemus, Jofeph of Arimathea, Philip, and Lydia, who are not mentioned with any nota-

ble blot upon them, or mark of infamy: some as persons of purer morality, walking with greater caution, according to the light of their own minds, which was the case of the apostle Paul, and it is likely of other of the converts from among the Jews.

The Scripture also represents the different manner of their call; some with more terror and consternation, as Peter's converts that were pricked at their hearts, the gaoler who cried out, *Sirs, what must I do to be saved?* These were recovered and brought home to God in a more awful manner. He prefaced the work with the voice of thunder. Others were called with a small still voice, feeling little of the terrors of the Lord, as Philip, Zacheus, Lydia, and it may be, most of the apostles. Now as these things happened for examples, they must be considered as a kind of Scripture type of future conversions in the different manner and circumstances of them. And I doubt not but herein the Scripture has from time to time been fulfilled; as the experience of christians can witness; whilst some are able to say, this was my case, another that was mine. And no question, if we take in the whole body of the faithful, every case will be found touched and described in Scripture. Nor is there a true convert in the world, but the word of God points to him; shews him in the various postures of his mind, and in all his tendencies towards God. A glorious argument of the divinity of the Bible, though all do not understand it, and it may be some will laugh at, and despise it; glorious will it appear when the church is complete, and the saints come to compare notes in heaven.

2. The Scripture has been fulfilled in the character, and principles of believers. A christian has the *law of God written in his heart,* and is a sort of living Bible. Time will not allow me to enlarge

much. But let me remark, that the Scripture every where speaks of a generation of persons distinguished from the rest of the world, by an inward sanctification. It calls them saints, believers, the righteous children of light, the sons of God, the excellent of the earth, and the like. And as bad as the world is, there still are, and always have been some that appear to belong to this body, and shall be to the end of time. Farther, the Scripture describes them by such characters as are a sufficient distinction between them and the rest of mankind, by which they may be known certainly to themselves, and probably to others: as that they *are not of the world*, that they *do not commit sin*, that they *have crucified the flesh with the affections and lusts*, that they *set their affections on things above, and not on things on the earth*, that they *hunger and thirst after righteousness*, that they are sensible of present infirmities, and *forgetting things behind, and reaching forth unto things before, they press towards the mark for the prize of the high calling of God in Christ Jesus*. It represents them as aspiring after God, making him their centre, breathing after him, and resting in him, and as cloathed with all divine graces, all glorious within. Nor are these accidental strokes that belong to some rare saints, but the proper character of all believers; though indeed with much variety; some having the several graces in greater eminency and lustre, others more faintly and with greater alloys, according to the distinction the Scripture itself mentions of babes, little children and fathers.

Well, thus the Scripture speaks of the church, and thus the church has been from the very foundation of it to this day. There is not one member thereof, but appears with the characters the word of God has provided for him; he has the heart, the frame, the principles, there appointed and set forth as the ornament of believers.

3. The Scripture is fulfilled in their infirmities also. Though they be saints, that speaks of them, as imperfect saints; represents them as having a *body of sin, a law in their members, waring against the law of their minds; the flesh lusting against the spirit; as not having yet attained nor being already perfect.* It represents the heart deceitful above all things and desperately wicked, which is true of good men in some measure, as well as others. *The spirit that is in them lusteth to envy,* and other vices. Whence they have their inward conflicts, and frequent struggles with their corruptions.

It represents them in a great variety of frames: sometimes their hearts following hard after God, triumphing in his favor, and exulting in his presence; at other times, overspread with clouds and darkness, filled with fear, and wholly indisposed for spiritual converse and acts of devotion. It represents the best of them as weak and defectible, as sometimes off their guard, secure and presumptuous, and thereupon falling into sin. To which purpose the miscarriages of the saints are left upon record in Scripture; not merely to tell us what they have done, but what others would be like to do in the same circumstances, when for their pride and self-confidence, God leaves them to themselves; and they are written for the admonition and caution of the church in future ages. In the mean time, they shew the frailty of believers, in their present imperfect state. In short, the Scripture represents them as falling out by the way, running into parties and schisms; uncharitably censuring one another, and indulging mutual passions to the disgrace and scandal of their profession. A great deal of this is hinted concerning them in the New

Testament. And that these particulars are accomplished, is matter of constant and universal experience; I appeal to every heart and conscience among the generation of God's children, and am satisfied there are too many witnesses of the truth to need any further confirmation.

4. The Scripture is fulfilled in the promises thereof towards believers. And here I have a subject that I could with pleasure employ an hour upon. But I must be forced to pass it over in a good measure, and leave every christian to supply the defect out of his own experience. All the promises of God, *the exceeding great and precious promises are in Christ Jesus, yea and amen*. All are true, faithful and sure; as every one has found that has tried them, every believer from the beginning of the world to this day. Let me observe very briefly, that there are some general promises constantly fulfilled towards all believers; as that God *will never leave them nor forsake them;* that he *will not suffer* them *to be tempted above what* they can *bear, but will, with the temptation, make a way for their escape;* that *all things shall work together for good to them that love God,* that he will give them his Holy Spirit; that he will *manifest* himself to them, *be their God,* and they shall be his *people*.

Further, there are occasional promises, as I may call them, adapted to the circumstances of particular persons, and which they, in those circumstances, happily experience the accomplishment of; as support under burthens, direction and conduct in difficulties, when sensible of our own weakness, we trust in the Lord with all our hearts, and lean not to our own understanding, help in prayer, answers of prayer, comfort in tribulation, and the like. A multitude of promises there are in the Scripture, wonderfully suited to all the cases of christians that I must not stand now to collect: all which have been accomplished in every age of the church. Every christian can set to his seal in this matter, though with more or less clearness, according as he is more or less exercised and experienced in the divine life.

5. I might shew, that the Scripture is accomplished in the threatnings of it towards good men, in the corrections and chastisements frequently intimated in case of backsliding, the omission of duty, carelessness in the performance, restraining prayer, want of watchfulness, attention and seriousness in their walk and conduct. In these cases, God threatens he *will visit their transgressions with the rod and their iniquities with stripes*. Nor have we only general, but even particular threatnings, designed as a rebuke to particular failings and transgressions. All which, in their time, season and manner, are fulfilled in God's discipline, towards his children and servants. In short, this is a general experience, and it is a perfect accomplishment of the divine word; that if the christian grows secure and careless, less prayerful and watchful, God withdraws and hides his face; the spirit is grieved and stands at a distance: in consequence whereof the christian finds his chariot wheels taken off, he has neither light nor comfort, little strength for duty, and little enjoyment in it.

Thus the Scripture is fulfilled in all the parts of it: fulfilled towards the world, towards the church, towards particular believers, in the characters, promises and threatnings of it.

I promised to make some remarks upon these particulars, in order to shew the force of this argument for proving the divinity of the Scripture. Had it been a human writing, proceeded from men, without any intelligence from above, it could never have described the state of the natural and moral world so accurately as it has done, and so agreeably to the events and issues of things. The Scripture exhibits and gives us a plan and scheme of the divine government of the world ; of the different states of the world and church ; of the church in general ; and of the several members of it ; of good men and bad men. It represents them in their various frames, principles, and dispositions ; in their various outward circumstances and conditions ; in their various spiritual states, their conflicts, trials, temptations, sufferings and comforts. This it doth in such a manner, and with such a perfect agreement and correspondence to the providence of God in the constant course thereof, making such beautiful harmony between the divine providence and the holy Scripture, as is a full evidence that the Bible is from God, and that he who governs the world indited it. Now that this argument may appear in its proper light and force, I shall subjoin a few observations without dwelling long upon them. As,

1. That the great author of nature and governor of the world had in his own mind a full view and comprehension of his works. A perfect scheme, idea, or model thereof, as I may call it. This, I think, we may conclude from the exact wisdom, regularity, and order with which he proceeds in all of them ; and the Scripture gives intimations of it. Thus in the history of the creation, after the forming the several classes and parcels of his creatures, it is said of each, *God saw that it was good ;* and at the close of all, when the great Creator came to review his work, it is said, *he saw every thing that he had made, and behold, it was very good,* that is, was just what God designed it, proportioned and fitted to its place and station among the creatures, and to the end of its maker. And we are told by the apostle, that God *worketh all things according to the counsel of his own will.* When he purposed and willed that there should be a world, there was a

DISCOURSE VIII.

counsel of his will, a wise plan and scheme, according to which he determined all things should be made, and all things should be governed. Now he governeth all things in nature, providence and grace, according to this *counsel of his will*.

2. The counsel of God, this plan of the divine works and government, is in part laid down in Scripture. I say in part, for I know not that I have warrant to affirm, that the Bible contains all God's purposes, and the whole scheme of his counsels and decrees. But it contains what concerns our world, the great maxims of his government, the different states of his subjects here, and the chief events of his providence towards them from time to time. In the Scripture the Book of the divine decrees is opened, as it were. We are there told of his creating a world according to his purpose; in what manner he proceeded in that work; and how he would proceed in the government of it. And I reckon the course of his providence in the main revolutions and changes there would be in the world, and in the several grand dispensations of it, at least, are there described as they have been, and will be, from the beginning of the world to the end thereof.

3. As the Scripture was written chiefly for the use of the church: and it may be, I might add, the world continued and governed with regard to the interest and concerns of the church; so the scheme of divine providence exhibited and laid down there chiefly respects it. Not that the rest of mankind are passed over wholly. The Scripture frequently takes notice of the affairs of the world in general, and of particular kingdoms and nations without the pale. Nor do I suppose all the affairs of the church, nor of the several members of it, are represented in Scripture and included in its map. But the general state thereof, its

vicissitudes and changes, the main instances of providence and grace towards it, and the particular members of it; these things the Scripture represents. It tells us, what the state of it has been, and what it shall be in the successive ages; what the several members of it always have been, and will be; what they fear and suffer, and what they enjoy; what their warfare would be; what their conflicts, toils, and victories: and in short, in what way they should be disciplined and prepared for heaven.

4. Every thing contained in the Scripture, as part of the divine counsel for the government of the world; supposing the Scripture is God's word, and really contains such a scheme, will be infallibly accomplished. The purposes of God shall stand. His words will not, cannot, fall to the ground. Hence we read, that such or such a thing was done, or came to pass, that the Scripture might be fulfilled. It is as necessary, according to the hypothesis, or supposition, I am now upon, that the Scripture should be fulfilled, as that the world should be made. For as the creation of the world was an accomplishment of God's purpose and counsel in that particular; the same may be said of every event in the government of it; especially as it is ensured to us in the Scripture. Not one iota, or tittle, shall pass till the whole be fulfilled. The reason is, it proceeds from God, the God of truth and wisdom; and nothing can fall out to disappoint an infinite understanding. I add,

5. The fulfilling of the Scripture is a gradual thing, not done all at once, but successively. For it contains God's scheme of providence and government for many generations. Some of it is fulfilled in one age; such parts of it, as refer to particular events, that were to take place at this or that time: as, the destruction of the old world by

water; the slavery of Abraham's posterity in Egypt; their settlement in Canaan; their captivity and deliverence; the coming of he Messiah; and the like. Some of it is constantly fulfilled; as, what concerns the state of the natural world in general; and the world of mankind, of good men, and bad men; who always were, and will be, such as the Scripture describes them, answering the characters there laid down of their respective states, principles, and manner of acting. Some of it, indeed a great deal of it, as it points out particular events, has been fulfilled; and some remains to be fulfilled, and will have its accomplishment in its proper time, in the several successive ages of the church and periods yet to come: as, the fall of Antichrist; the last great struggle of the followers of the Lamb with the followers of the beast: the Millennium; the resurrection of the body; and the final judgment. The Scripture is an entire Synopsis, or general view of the whole course of providence, towards the church especially; and consequently will not all be fulfilled till the last scene is acted.

6. When the whole work of God in the method of providence is finished, and the entire scheme or wise council of God, as laid down in Scripture, is perfected; and all has taken place in regular and orderly events, the argument from hence, that the Scripture is from God, or given by divine inspiration, will appear with greater advantage; partly as it will be more full and strong, being grounded upon the accomplishment of all the Scripture; partly as it will stand in a fuller light, without being obscured by that darkness, prejudice, and want of experience, which now attend persons and hinder them from discerning the evidence of this matter. I doubt not, but in that more amiable state of things which we expect in this world, as

the church will see more of the accomplishment of the Scripture, so it will see it more clearly. But, when the end cometh, when the whole mystery of providence is compleated, and the *Son shall give up the Kingdom to God, even the Father*, this argument will appear triumphant, the whole Bible stand in a glorious light, and a perfect harmony between Scripture and providence be seen to the conviction of all. The contemplation of which will probably be some of the business of heaven, and among the entertainments of the saints there. In the mean time,

7. So much of the Scripture is already accomplished, and evidently appears to be so; as is sufficient at present to give this argument great weight. There is a surprising concurrence between the Scripture and providence. They have hitherto run parallel. The world has been such as the Bible represents it should be. It has been governed in the manner that describes, and a multitude of wonderful events have taken place in the very time and way the Scripture sets forth. Now it ought to be considered, that these things were foretold, spoken of there as what should be, certainly be, and be in such a manner, long before the things themselves came to pass. What David says with referrence to divine providence in his formation, may be accommodated to this purpose, *thine eyes did see my substance yet being imperfect, and in thy book all my members were written, which in continuance were fashioned, when as yet there was none of them*: the same may, in a sense, be said of the writers of the Scripture, they saw, as it were, the substance of all future things, all the great transactions of providence upon the theatre of the world in the various states and changes of human affairs, and they wrote down all the members and particulars thereof, which in time come to be finished, and receive their

being while yet there was none of them. Now who could do this but God ? or, which is the same thing, those that saw with his light. In short, the Scripture holds before our view the various faces of the world: the various states and postures of affairs therein, and the various tempers of mens hearts. And the experience of several thousand years, the constant daily experience of all good men perfectly accords therewith. And this, I think, to be in its kind, next to a demonstration, that the writers of the Bible did not speak of themselves, from private impulse, like weak and short sighted creatures, as all men are, not knowing certainly what shall be on the morrow; but they spake from God, and as they were moved and taught by the Holy Ghost.

And thus I have set before you the fourth argument I proposed, to prove the Scripture is given by inspiration of God, viz. the external marks and characters that attend it: and have insisted somewhat copiously on one branch of it, the accomplishment of Scripture. The usefulness and importance of which argument, I reckon to be such, that it well deserves a volume by itself. Nor do I think any one could better employ his time, and with more service to the church of God, than by setting it forth in its strength. Which must be my excuse that I have said so much upon it; as a regard to your patience is the best excuse, that I can make, that I have said no more.

DISCOURSE IX.

The Divine Original and Inspiration of the Scripture.

───────

2 Tim. iii. 16.

All Scripture is given by inspiration of God, and is profitable for doctrine, for reproof, for correction, for instruction in righteousness.

I HAVE already offered several arguments to prove the divine original or inspiration of the Scriptures, and having gone through those I proceed now to another.

V. This truth may be argued from the testimony that God gave to the penmen of the Scriptures, as by miracles, prophecy, the spreading of their doctrine, and the glorious effects of it upon the hearts of men in their sanctification. Hereby he has set to his seal that the Scripture is true, is divine, and is his word. I shall go over the particulars in their order, beginning with the first of them.

I. God has borne testimony to the writers of the Scripture, and to the things there written, by miracles. I have stood too long on former arguments to insist largely on this. I shall briefly represent the matter of fact; shew that the penmen of Scripture wrought miracles, and what miracles they wrought. And then consider the argument from hence, how this proves they were inspired.

1. I shall briefly represent the matter of fact.

shew that the penmen of the Scripture wrought miracles, and what miracles they wrought.

What a miracle is, what are the proper distinguishing characters of those works that we admit as miraculous, it must be owned, is a matter of some difficulty to determine. The common difinition of a miracle, is an extraordinary operation, contrary to the settled laws of nature, wrought by the infinite power of God. "It is," saith a learned man,* "a work above the power of nature, and "above the reach of any creature whatsoever" And another says,† "it is that which properly can "have no second cause for its author." Such as no second cause, in the judgment of reason, can effect. Another calls it,‖ "a production of some-"thing out of nothing, either in the thing itself or "manner of producing it;" which he affirms can be effected by no less than an omnipotent arm. And on this account some critics remark, miracles are termed in Scripture, powers, being works of a divine and infinite power. And this is the more generally received account of the matter. A miracle is thought to be something above the ordinary power of nature, as it is contrary to the laws of it. And whenever it is wrought, or by whatever instrument, it is the work of God and proclaims omnipotence.

It must be granted, that some others are willing to come lower. The ingenious Mr. Lock defines a miracle thus: "It is, says he, a sensible opera-"tion which being above the comprehension of "the spectator, and in his opinion contrary to the "established laws of nature, is by him taken to be "divine." But acknowledging there is a real difficulty in stating this point, arising from our not

* Bishop Kidder.   † Sir Charles Wolseley.
‖ Stillingfleet.

DISCOURSE IX. 223

understanding fully the laws of nature, and the power of second causes; and, consequently, what things are contrary to those laws, and above the capacity of created beings; I do not think this much affects the present argument, for certainly many of the facts we have to alledge, as performed by the authors of the Scripture Revelation, and those that were employed in it, must be admitted to be such as could proceed from none but God. Either they are divine works, extraordinary miraculous operations, or never any such were laid before mankind, and offered to the test of human judgment. So that, without philosophising over nicely here, and fixing the exact bounds between created and uncreated power, determining the utmost that a creature, a man or an angel can do, and what God only can do, I think it must be allowed, the facts recorded in Scripture, and that we place to the head of miracles, must pass for miracles, or I cannot see that there ever were, or can be, any miracle in the world, or that any use can be made of those extraordinary phænomena and displays of divine providence that have always in the accounts of mankind been esteemed miraculous.*

---

* Since these discourses were composed, the notion and nature of miracles has been much better stated, than ever before by the Reverend Mr. Samuel Chandler, in his ingenious vindication of the christian religion. Who defines a miracle in general, " an action " done, or an operation visibly performed, by any being, that is " really and truly above the reach, power and capacity of that " being who doth it, to perform of himself, and without the as- " sistance of some superior agent." And a miracle when done by a man in confirmation of a divine mission, is, according to him, " somewhat visibly performed by him in order to prove himself " to be sent of God, which is strictly and truly above all his natural " powers and capacities, and which he could not of himself per- " form without the influence and assistance of some superior a- " gent." So that what is or is not a miracle is to be determined by the agreement and proportion between the action performed, and the capacities and powers of the agent. If the action done

Having premised thus much for stating the point and obviating cavils, I shall briefly touch the facts themselves, those things which the Scripture records as miraculous operations. And here I would observe, that all whom God employed to make known any new laws, or reveal any new doctrines to the world, came with the power of miracles, which were their credentials, or the certain tokens that he sent them. Thus did Moses, thus did Christ, and thus did the apostles. Moses delivered a body of laws to the Jews, which he professed to receive from God; to prove which, he wrought miracles among them.

Let me observe again, that the miracles, which these persons wrought, were numerous, open, and manifest in the face of the world; and had the highest characters of divinity in them that any facts ever had, that have been proposed to the world, under the character of miracles. I shall not give you the list of them. They are known to such as are conversant with the Bible. Moses offers a specimen of his power immediately upon his call to his office; his rod is turned into a serpent, and then turned into a rod again. The ten miraculous judgments inflicted on Pharaoh and his people,

---

be certainly above all the powers of the agent, of himself, and unassisted to perform it, is a true and proper miracle, and proves the co-operation and assistance of some invisible and superior being. That may therefore be a miracle in regard of one agent, that is not so with regard to another of greater ability and power; that may be a miracle when done by a man, that would be none if done by an angel. For since no beings can possibly of themselves perform any thing beyond their natural powers and capacities, whenever they are instrumental in doing any thing of this kind, it must argue the concurrence and assistance of some other and higher being. If a man doth what is above the reach of human abilities, he performs a real miracle, and must necessarily be assisted by some superior agent. Now this is manifestly the case of those wonderful works here urged in behalf of christianity and the Bible.

every body has heard of. You have them recorded in Exod. vii. 8, 9, 10, 11. He afterwards divides by his rod the waters of the Red Sea. In the wilderness he appears glorious, as the minister of heaven, by a power of miracles that constantly attended him, and which he exerted on all occasions. Thus he cured the bitter waters at Marah, by casting a tree into them, Exod. xv. 24, 25. brought waters out of the rock by smiting it with his rod, Exod. xvii. 6. subsisted forty days on the mount without food, when by his heavenly converse, his face acquired an angelical lustre. And you find when his authority was disputed, and his pre-eminence unreasonably cavilled at, God was pleased to interpose, and by a miracle, make a decision in his favor, punishing Miriam with the leprosy, Numb. xii. and afterwards upon occasion of another instance of the contempt of his authority, and of an affront to his mission, the earth opens and swallows up the contenders; and Aaron's rod is made to blossom as a public signal of God's election and appointment of him and Moses, Numb. xvi. 17. Thus you see Moses the first lawgiver to the church, and first writer of Scripture, was a worker of miracles. God hereby bore testimony to him, owned his ministry, and sealed his mission.

And what miracles Christ wrought, who came to establish a new law, and deliver a new system of religion to the world, I need not tell you. *Go and shew John*, saith he, to one of his disciples, *those things which ye do hear and see, the blind receive their sight, and the lame walk, the leapers are cleansed, and the deaf hear, the dead are raised up, and the poor have the gospel preached to them*, Matt xi. 4, 5. In short, he shewed a power over universal nature, wrought all sorts of miracles, and that in the most surprising manner. He did the works that never man did; and yet tells his disciples, the same, and greater works they should do in his name, which their history confirms.

It is further observable, that this power of working miracles was continued with the church, and was exerted by those that professed the christian religion for some ages. Many instances I might give of this, but must forbear.

I shall only take notice of a bold challenge which the christians sometimes made to the greatest emperors, that if they were brought before the seats of their gods, if they did not force them to depart and make them confess themselves to be devils and wicked spirits, they would suffer all sorts of punishments. They pretended to cast out devils in the name of Christ, to triumph over the heathen oracles; and so confident were they of their power herein, that in their disputes with their heathen adversaries, they offered to put the credit of their cause upon their success in this matter.

I add, the most considerable miracle of all was the resurrection of Christ from the dead. This he himself foretold before it came to pass, even when his disciples themselves neither understood it, nor believed it. He bid them *destroy* that *temple,* viz. his body, and he would *build it up again in three days.* And he did so accordingly: which single fact is a sufficient confirmation of the christian religion. It doth not indeed directly prove, that the Scripture is inspired, that the prophets and apostles, and the several books that go under their names were inspired; but it proves Christ was what he professed himself to be, the son of God: that the doctrine he preached was true; and that he had authority from heaven for all he did.

I cannot stand to prove the certainty of this fact that Christ rose from the dead. It has all the evidence that a thing of this nature is capable of. And I am confident, no reasonable person can lay any weight upon the sorry pretence of his enemies, the affidavit they hired the watch to make, viz. that *while they slept his disciples came and stole him away.* It was utterly unlikely, that the disciples should attempt such a thing. Next to impossible that they should succeed in it: and besides the very pretence is senseless. Men asleep, are as men absent and at a distance, or even men so far and so long dead; and what credit is to be given to their testimony? how could they tell what was done when they were asleep?

These, and the like, were the miracles by which the doctrines of the Bible were ratified and confirmed. Moses, Christ, the apostles, and primitive christians for some ages wrought miracles. I am now,

II. To consider the force of the argument from hence, and to shew how miracles prove the inspiration or divine mission of those that wrote the Scriptures. And,

1. We find that miracles were wrought for this purpose, as an evidence of a divine commission, and accordingly appealed to. Thus when God enabled Moses to work miracles, he tells him it was that the Israelites might believe the God of their fathers had appeared to him. And accordingly we see the miracles he wrought in Egypt, at the Red Sea, and in the wilderness, were the great means, not only of establishing his authority, but of vindicating it when called in question. When Corah, Dathan, and Abiram mutinied against him, he has recourse to miracles, as his credentials, and puts the decision of the dispute between himself and his competitors thereupon. *Hereby,* says he, *ye shall know that the Lord hath sent me: if these men die the common death of all men, or if they be visited after the visitation of all men, then the Lord hath not sent me.*

But if the Lord make a new thing, and the earth open her mouth, and swallow them up, with all that appertain unto them, and they go down quick in the pit; then shall ye understand that those men have provoked the Lord. In the following verses you have this new thing, a wonder of providence, as God's attestation to his servant Moses. *And it came to pass as he had made an end of speaking, that the ground clave asunder that was under them: and the earth opened her mouth, and swallowed them up, &c.* And the same may be observed in a multitude of instances concerning Christ and his apostles. They appeal to miracles as God's witness to them. *Believe me,* says Christ, *for the work's sake.* And again, *if I had not done among them the works which none other man did, they had not had sin.* The apostle Paul pleads for himself and in behalf of his mission, that the *signs of an apostle were wrought* by him. And the evangelist remarks with reference to all the apostles, that *they went forth and preached every where, the Lord working with them, and confirming the word with signs following.* They preached in the name of the Lord, and he owned them by the power of miracles that attended them.

I might here observe that the famous impostor Mahomet, as he was defective in all other proofs of a divine mission, so particularly in this. When some of his country-men that were aware of the vile designs he was carrying on, under the specious pretence of a call and revelation from heaven, set themselves to oppose him, the more effectually to try and gravel him, they demanded he would shew them some miracle. " Moses, say they, and Jesus,
" and the rest of the prophets, according to your
" own doctrine, wrought miracles to prove their
" mission from God. And therefore, if you be a
" prophet, and greater than any that were sent be-
" fore you, as you boast yourself, make the dead

"to rife, the dumb to fpeak, and the deaf to hear.
"Let us fee come down from heaven, fome of thofe
"punifhments you threaten us with. Let us fee
"the book come down from heaven that you would
"have us believe you receive from thence ; or
"fee the angel defcend thence which you tell us,
"doth bring it unto you; and then we will be-
"lieve your words." But nothing of this could
he pretend to. Nor indeed did he ever venture
upon a public miracle, but knowing himfelf to be
utterly difqualified for any fuch work, he endeavors to evade the objections they brought againft
him on that account, as well as he could : fometimes infinuating, that he was only fent to preach
to them, the rewards of paradife, and the punifhments of hell. Sometimes he infinuated, that their
predeceffors contemned the miracles of Salek, and
the other prophets, and that for this reafon God
would work no more among them. At other times
he told them, that thofe God had ordained to believe, fhould believe without miracles, and that
thofe whom he had not ordained to believe, fhould
not be convinced, though all the miracles they required were wrought in their fight. And when he
found this would not fatisfy, he goes to work another way ; takes up the fword and refolves to make
ufe of that as his only argument for the future.

But the writers of the Scripture, and thofe that
were employed in delivering to us the doctrines
thereof, do not put us off with fuch flames and forry
pretences as thefe are. They do not defire we
fhould believe them upon their bare word, but appeal to their works, the power of miracles they were
intrufted with, and exercifed as there was occafion.

2. Let me obferve, that the miracles thefe perfons wrought, are certain evidences of a divine
power concurring with them. It was the juft rea-
foning of Nichodemus, *Rabbi, we know thou art a*

teacher come from God ; for no man can do these miracles that thou doest, except God be with him. A miracle suppoſes the courſe of nature ſuſpended and altered, which can be done only by the author of nature : it is the finger of God, an operation of infinite power, whoever may be the inſtrument in it. The apoſtles *went forth and preached the goſpel,* ſays the evangeliſt, *the Lord working with them, and confirming the word with ſigns following.* He worked with them, or they had never wrought the things they did. Now,

3. I think the argument hence fully concluſive, that theſe perſons were undoubtedly ſent of God. They wrought miracles, and that by a divine power; and we may be ſure God would not lend his power, as I may expreſs it, to confirm an impoſture. Had the perſons we are ſpeaking of been cheats, forged the doctrine which they delivered to the world in the name of God, can we imagine that he would have concurred with them in the manner he did? have enabled them to ſpeak all ſorts of languages they had never learned, and that on purpoſe that they might propagate and ſpread the religion they had contrived and forged ; enabled them to heal all ſorts of diſeaſes, and raiſe the dead, as we know they frequently did ? would God have been thus preſent with cheats and impoſtors, that came to abuſe mankind in the groſſeſt manner ? would he have ſupplied them with power for ſuch a horrid purpoſe ? we cannot ſuppoſe this, without changing our ideas and notions of God, and deſtroying his eſſential characters of wiſdom, holineſs, and goodneſs.

In ſhort, the miracles wrought by Moſes, the prophets, Chriſt and his apoſtles, are the ſtrongeſt proof and evidence that can be given, ſo far as we know, of a divine miſſion. None ever did ſuch works as they. And I reckon, when any come in the name of God, with such a power accompanying them, mankind not only may receive them, but are under a necessity of doing it; otherwise, they reject the testimony of God, and oppose his authority.

What shall we say, for instance, of that great confirmation of the christian religion, the resurrection of Christ? had he not rose from the dead, his religion had died with him. Whereas the miracle of his resurrection is such a proof of his commission, as one would think the most stubborn infidel could not withstand. Had he been an impostor, it is certain, he could not have raised himself. And can we suppose, that God would have raised him, that is, have employed his power, the exceeding greatness of his power, to establish a lie, and give credit to a cheat: no, all the notions we have of God oblige us to believe, that if Christ had not been the faithful witness, sent and approved by him, he would never have given so high a testimony to him: but rather have withdrawn from him, and left the temple of his body, when it was destroyed, to have lain in its ruins forever. I remember a passage, which may serve for the illustration of this argument, of an impostor, called El-David, that gave out he was the Christ, and drew many followers after him. It is related by Maimon in a letter to the Jews at Marseilles. His pretences making a noise in that part of the world, he was brought before an Arabian prince, who asked him, " what miracle he " shewed, that they might believe in him?" He answered, " cut off my head, and I will live again." To which the prince replied, " thou canst not give " us a greater sign, and if it so fall out, that thou " dost rise again to life after I have cut off thy " head, I and all my people, nay, all the world sure, " will believe what thou sayest is true." And presently the experiment was made. He commanded him to be beheaded, and there was an end of the cheat. But it was not thus with our blessed Lord. He put the credit of all upon this one single event, and came off with glorious success. He told them often he would rise again on the third day. Accordingly, he did so at the time appointed; triumphed over the grave, and was declared to be the Son of God with power thereby.

Now this miracle, and the others so wonderfully shewn in the ministry of Moses and the prophets, of Christ and the apostles, are such public authoritative vouchers for the persons concerned, that God acknowledged them, owned them, and sent them; that their doctrine was true and divine; that nothing can be greater. It may be affirmed of all the rest, what was said of Jesus of Nazareth, namely, that *he was a man approved of God by miracles, wonders, and signs, which God did by him.*

I am sensible many objections may be and have been raised against this doctrine; and it is granted, it is not without its difficulties. But as I am determined to hasten through this subject as fast as possible, I must not enter upon the consideration of these things, which would not only require more time than I have for them; but it may be, more attention and judgment, than I can promise myself from the generality of the auditory. In the mean time, I hope none will think this is an evasion, and that I am willing to pass over objections, because I know not what to say to them. I can truly declare, I know no difficulty, that may not easily be removed; no objection against miracles, that doth in the least invalidate, and disable the argument from them. As an instance of this, though I cannot now stay to examine all the objections, or cavils that are brought in upon this account, I shall however mention the chief and strongest of them.

1. It is objected, that we do not understand the extent of created powers; do not so well compre-

hend the philosophy of nature, as to determine what is a miracle, according to the common definition of it, that is, what is contrary to the established course and laws of nature, what can or cannot be done by any finite being, men or angels. Consequently, should it be granted, that God only can work a miracle, yet if a cheat can do such things, as no skill of ours is sufficient to distinguish from a real miracle, we are left under the same difficulty; a miracle can be no satisfactory proof of a divine mission: since an impostor can perform things so like miracles, that we know them not from miracles.

This is the strongest objection, that I know, against the doctrine, and I have given it in the strongest terms. In answer to it,

1. I grant, that created beings, evil spirits for instance, may do a great many strange and surprising things. We find juglers among men, can by mere legerdemain, perform feats that puzzle the nicest observers. And no question, the devil can do far greater things. He understands more secrets in nature, than the most skilful philosophers or physicians do, the virtues of natural means, and knows when and how to apply them with more advantage; and consequently may be allowed to perform, what may be to us utterly unaccountable; what we may think above the powers of nature, though it may not be so. But then we must consider for what purpose these things are done, in what manner they are done, and what other evidences of divinity go along with them. We are to attend to the circumstances of such signs and wonders, that we are now supposing may possibly be done by wicked spirits; and thence make a judgment of them, which we may not be qualified to make, upon the mere contemplation of the facts themselves. But I add,

2. That no powers but those that were divine, ever performed such things as we have recorded in

Scripture. Neither men nor devils ever wrought wonders any thing parallel to the miracles there related, or that deserve to be compared with them. Suppose any could give the color of wine to water, make it look like wine: did ever any turn a great quantity of water into real wine, into the more generous sort thereof, as our Lord did at the marriage of Cana in Galilee. *Thou haſt kept the good wine till now,* saith the governor of the feaſt, speaking of the wine to which Chriſt had miraculouſly converted the water. Supposing any could by magic, or the devil by his own power, could calm the sea; yet, who ever knew this done by a word speaking? Supposing a person of ſkill could open the eyes of the blind; yet to do this as Chriſt did, by clay and spittle, is a thing unknown in the world. Who ever attempted to speak a dead man into life, or call him out of his grave? What virtue has a *Lazarus come forth!* to command back a departed spirit, and re-unite it to its body? Life, cannot be restored, but by the author of life; at leaſt we have no instances of any power effectual for this purpose, but the divine power: nor do we find it was ever delegated to impoſtors, or put forth by evil ſpirits, on any occaſion. Diſeaſes may be cured by natural means, and the proper uſe of medicines. But our Lord cured all ſorts of diſeaſes, and ſome have obſerved, ſuch as were naturally incurable. A learned Phyſician has wrote a book to prove this. And he cured them without medicines, or waiting the leiſure of nature; only by speaking a word: and ſometimes when the patient was at a great diſtance. How ſurprizing that, *he ſtood over her, and rebuked the fever, and it left her, and immediately ſhe aroſe and miniſtred to them?*

If it be ſaid, how do we know but ſpirits, and angels may do as much? I anſwer by aſking another queſtion, whether God deſigned to preſcribe a diſtinction between created and uncreated power? between his own power and that of his creatures? if not, how should he govern the world? at least, how should he make himself known in the government of it, since we cannot discern his works from those of his creatures? In a word, though I will not take upon me to say, how far the power of this or that creature, of angels, good or bad, may go; and to fix the precise bounds between the divine power, and that of second causes: yet I think it no presumption to affirm, there are many things creatures cannot do; and that the miracles we have an account of in Scripture, both in the Old and New Testament, are of this sort. They cannot by a rod, or stick, stop streams of water, and make them stand up like a wall. They cannot command water out of a rock; make the ground open and swallow up a company of men; rebuke fevers and other distempers, and make them depart immediately. They cannot make a man that has been dead four days rise out of his grave by only calling upon him, and bidding him come forth. They cannot say to a cripple, that has been lame from his mother's womb, rise and walk, and thereby restore him, as Peter did. These and the like works are such instances of power, such inroads upon the established laws and course of nature, and so much above any capacity that second causes are possessed of, so far as we know; that we can ascribe them to none, but the author of nature, and great Lord of the world. I answer once more,

3. Whatever may be possible to created beings, it is certain, they can do nothing without God: and I think it demonstrable from the divine perfections; his wisdom, truth, goodness; that he will never suffer them to delude mankind by such works of power, as those recorded in Scripture, employed

to confirm falsehood and lies. Suppose Satan and his accomplices could heal the sick, and raise the dead; which yet, I am persuaded, none will undertake to prove they can, in the manner that these things were performed by Christ and his apostles. I ask, for what purpose they did this? If the Scripture be true, and they hereby meant to establish it, it makes them take part against themselves, represents Satan as divided against Satan, and ruining his own kingdom. If the Scripture be false, and they concurred with the writers of it to give credit to their fictions; this must be done, at least, by divine permission. It supposes the great and wise governor of the world standing by, and not only so, but I think, assisting, every one must own permitting; while the devil and wicked men, his instruments, abused the name of God, and imposed on mankind in the grossest manner; performing such things as none in the world can distinguish from the works of God; and yet all is let pass without any interposition of providence to discover the cheat. This I think not consistent with an acknowledgment, that God governs the world, and with those attributes and perfections of his that are inseparable from his nature and government.

2. It is farther objected that impostors have wrought miracles, Appollonius Tyanœus particularly, and the magicians in Egypt that withstood Moses.

I answer, as to the first, we have no good evidence of the truth by the facts alledged. What is related by Philostratus is manifestly of very doubtful credit. Besides, those pretended miracles were few, obscure, and in no respect to be compared with those we have in the Scripture. As to the magicians in Egypt, supposing they were real miracles, which yet it is not necessary to grant, nor, so far as I know, is it necessary to deny that they were.

DISCOURSE IX. 237

But suppofing they were, they are no difparagement to the miracles of Mofes, and others in the Scripture. The cafe I take to be this: there was a trial of fkill, as I may fay, between Mofes and thefe men, Mofes works feveral miracles before them. God is pleafed for the proving of Pharaoh, or for other purpofes and ends known to himfelf, to enable them to do the like: but then, exerts a fuperior power, by his fervant Mofes, and fo triumphs over them. He firft fent them his power and then withdrew from them, leaving them to manifeft their weaknefs and fraud. For after the fpecimens they gave, they were nonpluffed, and could proceed no farther. So that the iffue of this conteft was the defeat of thefe pretenders; their conviction of a divine power with Mofes, and I may add, the eftablifhment of Mofes's authority. God left the magicians, fuppofing they acted before by his power, continued to affift and own Mofes; and thereby declared whom he had chofen. And as Mofes was hereby confirmed in his office, and had his commiffion fealed from heaven, fo it was with the reft of the writers of Scripture: God bore teftimony to them by miracles. But I haften to another point.

3. God bore teftimony to the penmen of Scripture, and to thofe that were the inftruments and means of the revelation it contains, by prophecy. Something has been offered on this head, when I fpoke of the accomplifhment of Scripture; and I have at prefent only room for fhort hints. The fubject is copious and important; but I fhall confine myfelf. Any one that converfes with his Bible will fee how much it runs in a prophetic ftrain, it abounds with prophecies; and divine providence has fhewn us the accomplifhment of them: thereby proving, I think, the infpiration I am pleading for. Give me leave to mention a few inftances out of many.

It was prophesied and foretold, that Abraham should become a great nation; that God would multiply his seed, even as the *stars of heaven*, and as the *dust of the earth;* as it is expressed. And it is to be observed, at the time of this assurance given him, Abraham had no child, nor had reason in an ordinary way to expect any. He being old, and Sarah naturally past child-bearing. And yet the word of God took effect, and the prophecy proved a *sure word of prophecy*. God built him up into a nation, and increased his posterity above any people in the world, as we are often informed in their history. The apostle gives us this summary account of it, Heb. xi. 12. *Therefore sprang there even of one, and him as good as dead, so many as the stars of the sky in multitude, and as the sand which is by the sea shore, innumerable.*

It was prophesied, that the descendants of Abraham should be sojourners in a strange land for four hundred years; should live in a state of great affliction and slavery; and that, at the end of that term, God would punish their oppressors, and work deliverance for them. This was foretold, Gen. xv. and in other places. How it was accomplished, you read in the book of Exodus. I will only observe, that God not only visited his people, and visited their enemies with his judgments, according to his word; but kept day with them: *it came to pass,* says Moses, *at the end of the four hundred and thirty years, even the self-same day it came to pass, that all the hosts of Israel went out from the land of Egypt.*

It was foretold, that great body of men, the people of Israel, whom God had delivered out of Egypt in so wonderful a manner, should all of them that were above twenty years old, die in the wilderness; and none of them, save Joshua and Caleb, enter the promised land; that they should wander in the desart forty years, and there perish for their frequent murmurings and rebellions. This was foretold, Num. xiv. the accomplishment of which you have, chap. xxvi. of the same book.

Jacob foretold the settlement of the tribes in the promised land, and in a prophetic map, as I may call it, represented their several conditions there; where they should be fixed; what their state should be; and what changes they should undergo. This you have, Gen. xlix. and the accomplishment of it in their after history.

The state of the children of Israel in Canaan, their success, and all manner of prosperity, whilst they continued obedient; their punishment, frequent captivities and final destruction, upon their apostacy. This was foretold in the most exact manner, and was accomplished with the like exactness; as might be shewn had I time to enquire into these things. You have the prediction, Lev. xxvi. Deut. xxviii. and other places: and the accomplishment of it in the constant course of Providence towards that people afterwards.

As their captivity, so their return from captivity, with the time and circumstances thereof, was foretold: that God would deliver them up into the hands of their enemies for their sins, and afterwards bring them back and restore them. All this was prophesied of, over and over again, and every word of it fulfilled.

The rise, continuance and fall of the four famous monarchies, the Assyrian, Medo-Persian, Grecian and Roman, was exactly foretold by Daniel; the heads of these monarchies described, and the great events and revolutions under them represented, as if the prophet had been an historian, and had written after the things were come to pass.

A great many things were foretold concerning particular persons, which were verified in the event. Thus Josiah was prophesied of by name above three hundred years before he was born, that he should execute the judgment of God upon the altar at Bethel, which Jeroboam had set up, and upon the priests that officiated there, 1 Kings xiii. 2. This was fulfilled, as you see, 2 Kings xxiii. 15. Cyrus was prophesied of by name above a hundred years before he was born, as the person that should restore the Jews and rebuild the temple, Isa. xliv. 28. There are a great many wonderful and unlikely things in this prophecy; as indeed in all the rest, could I here enquire into them: as, that his birth should be foretold so long before; his name given him; that he should conquer so potent a monarchy as that of Babylon; and that though an heathen, he should favor and restore a religion his predecessors had set themselves to crush and ruin. This could proceed only from him that knows all things, and to whom future things are present.

We have a glorious collection of prophecies concerning the Messiah; the illustrating of which would more than require a discourse by itself, and fully prove what is said, that the *testimony of Jesus is the spirit of prophecy*. It was foretold of him, that he should be the seed of a woman, born of a virgin, which was accordingly fulfilled: that he should be the seed of Abraham and of David, born at Bethlehem, and brought out of Egypt. In short, most of the circumstances of his life, his sufferings, his death and resurrection, the opposition he would meet with, the success of his doctrine, and the like, were foretold: every iota and tittle of which predictions was accomplished.

I add, Christ and his apostles were distinguished with the same spirit of prophecy, and foretold a great many wonderful events, which the christian church has seen take place in the way and manner described. Thus Christ foretold his own death with the circumstances thereof; that all his disciples should forsake him; that one of them should betray him: and this he signified when none of them had any suspicion concerning the traitor; nor the traitor, it is likely, any suspicion concerning himself. He foretold the manner of his death, and his resurrection, with the time of it. He foretold that those who believed in his name, should work miracles, speak with tongues, heal diseases, and cast out devils. How punctually this was accomplished, the history of the New Testament, and the most primitive writings of the church inform us. Nor were these extraordinary gifts confined to the apostolical ages; but were common in the ages next succeeding. " To restore " to health, says Irenæus,* by imposition of hands, " to cure the weak, the lame and paralitic, and those " that labor under any other malady, is a thing " frequent in the church." To the same purpose Origen.† " We have seen, saith he, people freed " from a thousand dreadful symptoms and ca- " lamities, from which neither men nor devils " could recover them, by the invocation of Christ's " name." And for the casting out of devils, the fathers over and over again mention it in their apologies, as a thing confessed by their adversaries. They appeal to their consciences and knowledge, and tell them that many hundreds were still living of their own superstition as well as christian proselytes, who by their personal experience could attest it.

Christ foretold the preaching of his doctrine through the world, that there should arise false prophets, and false Christs, that should come in his name and deceive many, which accordingly was fulfilled. He foretold the destruction of Jerusa-

* L. i. c. 56.   † In Celf. l. 1. p. 34.

lem, and the temple; the signs and prodigies that should go before it, the calamities that should attend it; and that the destruction should be total and final; that there should not be left one stone upon another that should not be thrown down; that Jerusalem should be trodden down, and the Jews led captives into all nations. How this has been fulfilled the world has seen. And was I not now in haste to get through the subject, it would be no small pleasure to shew you the exact parallel between the prophecy and providence, the prediction and the event. I shall only observe, that the Jews have often attempted to rebuild their temple, though in vain. The last attempt was by Julian the apostate, who out of spite to Christ, and to defeat the prediction, gave orders for rebuilding it; but was baffled by the immediate hand of heaven. The story is related by several, particularly by Ammianus Marcellinus, an heathen who lived at that time. He tells us, that Julian endeavored to rebuild the temple at Jerusalem, and gave it in charge to one Aliprius of Antioch, assisted by the governor of the province, and a vast treasure by the Emperor to hasten and promote the work. But, he adds, they were soon forced to desist from the enterprise, by balls of fire issuing from the foundation, which terrified and destroyed the persons employed therein. So much authority was there in these prophecies, that God would not suffer men or devils to interpose and slur them, or by any acts and powers of theirs, hinder their accomplishment. And how strong an argument is this of the divine mission and inspiration of the persons by whose ministry we have the Scripture doctrine and revelation. They had the seal of miracles as you have heard, and the seal of prophecy, a demonstration that God was with them, and had sent them. In the one instance he lent them his power, in the other his

DISCOURSE IX.

knowledge: neither of which he would have honored impostors and cheats with.

Let me farther remark, that the spirit of prophecy that runs through the Scripture concerns generally such things, such events, as depended wholly upon the will of God, and the will of free agents, which could not be known at that distance by any but God himself, and those to whom he was pleased to reveal them. Who could foretel, for instance, that there should be a man born called Cyrus, so long beforehand? that he should conquer Babylon, that he should have it in his heart to restore the Jews and rebuild their city? There were no natural causes then existing of such an event: nor could any foresee it but the infinite all-comprehending mind, who has the whole tract of time and series of events under his eye at once, and to whom all his works are known from the beginning to the end. In short, to foretel future events is the prerogative of God. Hence we find him triumphing over idols upon this account; *Let them shew us what shall happen*, says he, *shew the former things what they be, and shew the things that are to come hereafter, that we may know that ye are Gods*. Intimating, that to be able to foresee and positively declare events and occurrences of things merely contingent, that depend on the will of man, or the pleasure of God; to declare these at a great distance of time before they come to pass, argues divinity, or at least, special communion with and instruction from the divine mind, who from his throne views and takes a prospect of all time, and has all events placed in order before him.

I shall not now consider the objections that may be offered from diviners, the heathen oracles, and the like. It is known there was so much uncertainty in their answers, as very much disgraced them even with their votaries, and occasioned the giving the nickname of "crooked speaker," unto the devils that presided in their oracles. It is true the devil and his prophets endeavoured to imitate God and his prophets. But the whole history of their management shews, they knew no secrets, but what he was pleased to instruct them with, for the trial and punishment of mankind. And after all their pretences, the events frequently blasted their credit. I think I may therefore with great safety and assurance conclude, that *the testimony of Jesus*, and indeed the proof of the Scripture's divinity and inspiration, is the *spirit of prophecy*.

DISCOURSE X.

The Inspiration of the Scripture proved, and the Canon of Scripture vindicated.

2 Tim. iii. 16.

All Scripture is given by inspiration of God, and is profitable for doctrine, for reproof, for correction, for instruction in righteousness.

I AM arguing the divinity or inspiration of the Scripture from the testimony that God gave to the penmen thereof. I have already considered the two remarkable instances of miracles and prophecy, and now go on to another particular.

III. God bore testimony to the writers of the Bible by the spreading of their doctrine, and the mighty success it had in the world. I must here premise, that it is the christian religion, or doctrine of the New Testament, that this argument chiefly respects. The revelation God made to the Jews was very much confined to themselves. Not that others were wholly excluded. They admitted proselytes, and taught their religion to them. But there was not that general communication made to the world, as after the coming of Christ. When the partition-wall was broken down, and the inclosure God set about his ancient people was laid open. The apostles had a commission in the largest terms to go and preach the gospel to every creature, and proselyte all nations. God designed the revelation, he made to the world by the ministry of Christ and the apostles, should be universal for the use of all mankind that would receive it. And it is this part of the divine revelation that my present argument peculiarly relates to, the success and spreading of the gospel, the doctrine and religion of the New-Testament.

Though I may further premise, that if the argument from hence be good with respect to one part, it doth by consequence prove the whole Scripture to be divine. For the New Testament confirms the Old, as I observed before. If Christ and his apostles were sent of God, it is certain Moses and the prophets were so too; for the former bear testimony to the latter. Let me add, I do not lay the stress of the argument upon the mere spreading of their doctrine, but on the manner and circumstances of it. Having premised these things, I shall set the argument before you in a few particulars without enlargement.

1. It is a certain and known thing that the christian religion had the most surprising success when first preached, and was spread through a great part of the world in a little time. This appears from the ancient monuments of the church; from the testimony of friends, and acknowledgment of enemies. Tertullian tells the Roman senate, that though the christians were but of yesterday, yet they had filled all places and offices, that they were strong enough to master the Roman empire; nay, that so great were their numbers, that if they should but agree to retire out of it, the world would wonder at its own solitude. And in his book against the Jews, he says, " the christian religion had enlarged its " conquests beyond those of the Roman empire, " and had subdued those places that were inacces-" ble to their armies." Pliny takes notice in his letter to the emperor concerning the christians, that " there were such multitudes of them, that the

DISCOURSE X.

"temples and facrifices of the gods were almoſt "forſaken." Tacitus fpeaks of an immenſe number, even iu Nero's time, the very firſt age of chriſtianity. In ſhort, the prevalency of the chriſtian religion was ſuch, that it gave occaſion to the heathens to call it, "the powerful and prevailing ſect." Nor,

2. Did it prevail among the vulgar only, but among the moſt inquiſitive and learned. All ſorts of perſons, Jews, Gentiles, the ignorant and untaught, and even the greateſt philoſophers, embraced chriſtianity. Indeed, its ſucceſs then, and ever after, has been moſtly with perſons of a lower ſtation in the world. But there have always been fome of the greateſt name that have owned and eſpouſed it. It was ſo, particularly, at the firſt planting of it. I might give a large catalogue of philoſophers and men of fame for learning that came into the church, and employed all their abilities in the ſervice of the chriſtian cauſe. Juſtin Martyr before he became a diſciple of Chriſt, was converſant with all the ſects of the philoſophers, and was at laſt a zealous Platoniſt; but left all to follow Jeſus, and upon his acquaintance with the doctrine of Chriſt, profeſſes, that he found that to be the only ſure and profitable philoſophy. Origen, another father in the chriſtian church, was in ſo great fame for his learning, that even after he profeſſed himſelf a chriſtian, many of the philoſophers attended his lectures at Alexandria, and fome of them dedicated their books to him. It is ſaid of Plotinus, a famous Platoniſt, that while he was reading lectures, diſcovering Origen among his auditors, he bluſhed and was daſhed with ſo great a preſence, ſo as to break off abruptly. I might inſtance in a great many more of confiderable reputation for their learning; but I forbear. All that I mention theſe things for, is to obſerve to you, that as the chriſtian

religion was propagated through the world in a little time, so some of the greatest men, persons of the highest name for wisdom and knowledge, became proselytes to it.

3. The success that attended the gospel in its first publication was the more remarkable and glorious, I might say, divine, on the account of the mighty difficulties it had to encounter, and which it surmounted. Had I time to pursue this argument, and to illustrate it with such particulars, as might be insisted upon, it would amount to a sort of a demonstration, that the christian religion is of God. For instance, to give a few hints, it had the strongest prejudices of mankind, of Jews and Gentiles, to overcome.

Among other prejudices among the Jews, there were three that stood directly in the way of the gospel, and that were so deeply rooted that I cannot see any power, less than divine, could ever have conquered them.

One of them was, that the Messiah should appear with the character of a sovereign earthly prince, whose business it was to deliver them from their enemies, restore the kingdom of David at Jerusalem, and there reign in great splendor and power over the house of Israel; the rest of the world being in a great measure subject to their nation. This was the notion they had formed to themselves of their Messiah and it still possesses their minds, as Maimonides, one of their own rabbies, informs us.

It was another of their prejudices, that their law should abide for ever; that the Messiah should be so far from abrogating, that he should establish it; and that the glory of his kingdom should chiefly consist in the exact performance of the legal worship. The forementioned Maimonides, tells us this shall belong to his office, whenever he comes; to rebuild the temple, and gather the disperfed of

Israel; to re-establish the legal rites and Constitutions; to restore sacrifices, the sabbatical years and jubilees, according to every precept delivered in the law.

It was also an opinion among them, that had got hold of every mind, that the Jews only should partake of the blessings of the Messiah's kingdom. The Gentiles they accounted as dogs, unholy and unclean; and we find in a multitude of places in the New Testament, they could not bear the thoughts of their calling and admission to an equal state and equal privileges with themselves.

As for the heathens, they had prejudices too many to be here enumerated; and which were like mountains in the way of the christian religion. The gods they worshipped in this or that country, the rites with which they worshipped them, and all the forms of their religion were become venerable with them by a pretended antiquity. And so much were they inslaved to antiquity and tradition, that even the famous Tully* introduces Cotta as thinking the plea thereof sufficient to supply the want of all other arguments, and to give a sanction to every thing that had obtained among them; *this alone will be sufficient for me*, says he, *that our fore-fathers have thus handed it down to us*.

I will only observe, besides the influence of education and custom, and the slavish subjection, that hereby they were brought into, to their religion; there were two things in it, that gave it a full possession of their hearts. It was pompous, and had a glorious exterior, and was calculated to gratify their fleshly inclinations.

Now let it be considered that before christianity could get any footing in the world, all these prejudices must be removed. The Jews must quit

* De Natura Deorum; l. 3.

their darling notions of a temporal Meſſiah, and believe in a crucified Saviour: the pagans renounce the gods of their countries, the eſtabliſhed rites of their religion; the maxims they had received by tradition from their fathers; and which was a further difficulty, renounce their beloved luſts. Upon theſe terms chriſtianity was preached to the world, and with all theſe diſadvantages did it prevail and triumph.

I might ſhew, that it had, not only the prejudices of mankind againſt it, but human laws, and all the power and learning of the world. The *kings of the earth and rulers* of the people *ſet themſelves againſt the Lord and againſt his Anointed.* The heathen philoſophers, the Jewiſh doctors, with all the authority of the greateſt emperors, were united againſt Chriſt and chriſtianity, and yet it prevails, thouſands and myriads bow the knee to the holy Jeſus, and profeſs themſelves the diſciples of a crucified maſter. I am perſuaded you will not put me upon proving there muſt be the finger of God in this ſucceſs. Let me obſerve again,

4. The doctrine of the goſpel in itſelf had a great deal in it to incumber it, and obſtruct its ſucceſs. It was built upon the utter ruin of the heathen religion; declared the Jewiſh religion void and antiquated, and decently laid it in its grave. It overturns all the forms of idolatry and ſuperſtition the world was ſo fond of; calls from pageantry to ſimplicity; and from looſeneſs and fleſhly indulgence to the greateſt ſtrictneſs and purity. Some of its doctrines were not a little ſhocking to the reaſon of mankind, as it was at that time trained up, and blinded by inveterate prejudices. As for inſtance, ſalvation by a crucified chriſt; this was the great fundamental point of the goſpel, and we know what entertainment it met with in the world: it was *to the Jews a ſtumbling-block, and to the Greeks*

foolishness. Pardon of sin, justification and life, by the death and righteousness of another person, the resurrection of the body, &c. To say nothing of the duties prescribed in the christian religion, as humility, meekness, self-denial, forgiving and loving enemies, and the like: these were things that lay cross in the minds of men, most opposite to the great maxims of wisdom established among the philosophers, and promised no kind reception to the gospel.

It may also be remarked here, that instead of honors, preferment, and temporal advantages; it ever speaks of contempt, sufferings and persecution, as the lot and portion of them that embrace it. Now, that such a doctrine as this should obtain in the world, bear down all opposition, gain proselytes without number among both Jews and Gentiles, is an event that, I think, it is impossible to account for without having recourse to a divine hand. Especially, if I add,

5. That the instruments of this great work were low, mean, and contemptible persons You know the character of the apostles, and I need not insist upon it. The founder of our religion sent forth not twelve princes or philosophers, but twelve fishermen; men destitute of all human advantages, void of learning, arts, language, reputation, power, and authority: these receive a commission from him. And what was it to do? why, to teach all nations and convert the world. Now you will please to remember what your Bible tells you, and what is confirmed by the most authentic records of the church, that these persons went forth, twelve poor fishermen, preaching the gospel in the name of Christ. And in a few years they overturn Satan's empire, silence his oracles, baffle all the philosophy of the heathens, and cavils of the Jews;

and subdue a great part of the world to their Lord and master. I leave every one to make the inference from hence which I design, viz. that God approved them, that it was his doctrine they published, that he sent them, and was with them. The whole history of their proceedings, I think, demonstrates this.

Two things are evident concerning them, to mention no more, viz. that they had a supernatural courage, otherwise they would not have undertaken the work. Suppose twelve mechanics, among us, should now be sent by any to go into Turky or Persia, and convert the Mahometans, can we imagine that men in their senses would engage in such an enterprise? they might object they wanted subsistence, they wanted a guard to secure them from danger; they could not speak the language of the country; nor was it likely they should have any other reception, but to be insulted and sacrificed for their impertinency. The like objections might rise in the minds of the first preachers of the gospel, had they not known they were called of God; had they not received power and courage from on high. Nor would they have persisted in their enterprise, as they did, through all sorts of terrors and deaths, had not God been with them, and stood by them, strengthening them *by his spirit, with might in the inner man.*

Further, it is evident, had not God sent them, and owned them, they could never have succeeded in the manner they did, and under the difficulties they met with. So that I reckon I may conclude with good authority, that the success of the christian religion is a strong argument, that it is divine. And if so, the Scriptures must have a divine original.

I am sensible it may be objected, that the imposture of Mahomet has spread over a great part of

DISCOURSE X.

the world. But I shall easily shew this does not at all weaken the force of my argument. The case of the one is no way parallel with the other. Though, as I determine now to conclude the proofs I design to mention of the inspiration of the Bible, I shall defer the consideration of this objection taken from the spreading of Mahometanism, till I speak to the objections in general; and hasten to another particular.

IV. God bore testimony to the writers of the Scripture, by the glorious effects thereof upon the hearts of men, in their constant sanctification. This is a standing proof of the truth of christianity, and indeed of the truth and divinity of the Bible. And as it is an argument that every christian, how unskilful and unlearned soever he may be, may understand, and which he carries in his own breast, it well deserves to be distinctly considered. I shall only at present take notice, that the christian religion, wherever it came and was heartily embraced, wrought a very glorious change. As it teaches to deny ungodliness, and worldly lusts, and to live soberly, righteously and godly in the world; prescribing the most exact rules of holy living. So it was attended with an inward power and efficacy; subduing the minds of men to a conformity to those rules. This was eminently seen in the first ages of the gospel " shew me a drunkard, says one of the " fathers, shew me a passionate man, one that is " lustful; and with a few words of God, I will make " him sober, calm, temperate, chaste, &c. Such was the divine energy and virtue that generally went along with the gospel at that time. And though we have reason to lament it, that the word of God has not so sensible, and visible an effect upon those that profess christianity now, as it seems then it had; yet still the gospel of Christ is the *power of God to salvation to every one that believeth.*

God still owns it as his instrument in renewing the minds of men; and thereby gives testimony to his word. But as this is a testimony of the highest importance, and what tends not a little to confirm christians of every sort in the behalf of their Bible, I shall resume it upon another occasion; and therefore now dismiss it without any farther enlargement.

There is one thing more I shall subjoin, as the last argument I intend to offer of the inspiration of the Scripture.

V. That all this evidence is strengthened and confirmed by the gross absurdities that attend the scheme of unbelievers, who deny the truth and divinity of the Bible. They alledge and object difficulties in believing the Scripture; and yet they themselves believe against Scripture with far more difficulties in their way. This might be shewn in a great many instances. I shall mention and touch upon a few. As,

That God notwithstanding the confessed bounty and goodness of his nature, and his gracious and merciful inclinations towards mankind; should yet suffer them to remain under their present darkness, ignorance, and prejudices, without affording them any supernatural revelation. That mankind need a revelation from heaven, I have at large proved. I have proved, that if the Bible be not that revelation, there is no such thing in the world. So that this is one absurdity that attends their scheme, who reject the authority of the Scriptures, that God has given no revelation of himself to the world.

Another is, that a book should be offered to mankind, attested in such a manner as the Bible is, so full of strong evidence, and yet be false.

Again, That so great a part of the world, the wisest and best part of the world, should lie under a delusion for so many ages; embracing the Scripture as a revelation from God, when it is a mere imposture, and yet the cheat never be discovered.

That the persons concerned in delivering to us the doctrines of the Bible, should impose upon us by known designed juggle and imposture; and that without any prospect of advantage to themselves. This is to make them guilty of the greatest wickedness, the vilest iniquity upon no motive, but to be undone in this world, as they found would be their case, and undone in the next, supposing they believed any thing of another world.

Farther, that so many impostors and cheats should unite in the same black and horrid designs; invent lies and impose them upon the world in the name of God; and that none of them should ever recant, and discover the fraud, that neither the love of life, nor the terrors of a violent death, which was the lot of many of them, even on the account of their religion, should have any influence upon them to make them confess the truth; but that they should persist in their testimony concerning their doctrine, and their mission to the last.

And that such wicked men as the persons I am now speaking of, the unbelievers, must suppose them to be, should with such an evil conscience set themselves to do the greatest good; I mean, deliver the most excellent doctrine to the world, that has the highest tendency to promote the honour of God, and the happiness of mankind. Certainly had they been knaves, they would have dealt in other matters, and have appeared in a different form; have flattered mankind, and have endeavoured to recommend themselves to their favour. In short, according to the fancy of our unbelievers, here are a company of the worst of men in the world, doing the greatest good in the world; and that with a certain prospect of bringing upon themselves the greatest present evils and sufferings. Can any believe this without infatuation?

Again, That these deceivers and cheats should be able without any human advantages of learning, subtilty or secular power to persuade so great a part of mankind to believe their fables; and upon terms of self-denial and sufferings, embrace the doctrines and stories they had invented on their own heads.

That all the experience that thousands and millions of sober, grave, and wise men have had of the truth and divinity of the Scripture; of its power to convince, reform, and change mankind; to comfort in their greatest distresses, to direct and guide in doubts and difficulties, &c. should all be mere delusion.

That there should be a sovereign, wise, and good God, the constant governor of this world, and inspector of human affairs; and that he should stand by and see so great, so plausible an imposture prevail among mankind, and never interpose for its defeat; but instead thereof, by strange, surprising providences, give open countenance to it.

I add, That the Bible should be false, and yet the discovery of this remain the special, peculiar attainment and priviledge of persons of our unbelievers character. This, I think unaccountable, and know not why I may not number it among the absurdities that affect their scheme. I would not aggravate matters here. But I think it evident, they do not reject the Bible because they approve of an higher and more excellent scheme of religion; because they have something better to advance in the room of the Bible. It is generally suspected concerning them, they had best see upon what principles they go that they quarrel with the Bible, because it quarrels with them, would disturb their pleasures, and abridge them of their liberties.

DISCOURSE X.

And that these should be the only men favoured with the judgment and taste to distinguish things, or that have the greatest share of honesty to profess and own the truth, is somewhat strange, and the belief of it, I presume, not a little absurd.

Well, these are some of the difficulties that clogg the unbeliever's scheme. Whether they do not amount to absurdities, I leave it to be considered. If they do, it will be allowed, they serve the purpose I mention them for, confirm the authority of the Bible, and assist and strengthen the conclusion I have been drawing from sundry topics and heads of argument, namely, that *the Scripture is given by inspiration of God.*

Thus I have not only shewn that the Scripture is true; but that it is inspired, and of divine original; which are two of the points I undertook to prove. It remains,

III. That I vindicate the canon of Scripture, or prove, that the present books of our Bible are the originally inspired books of Scripture. And for the clearer proceeding in this matter, I shall, 1. Premise a few things for stating the point about the canon of Scripture. 2. Prove that we have the original inspired books in our canon, or catalogue of sacred books of Scripture: and then, 3. Answer some questions, or objections, with reference hereto.

I. I shall premise a few things for stating the point about the canon of Scripture, and to give you some clear notions of the matter. And,

1. When I say the books of our present Bible are the original inspired books of Scripture, I do not mean they are the autographs, or the very books in the hand writing of the inspired authors. It may indeed be questioned, whether there were any great number of them together in this sense? whether Moses at first wrote the five books, that were

delivered to the Jews, with his own hand? or, whether the prophets and apostles wrote, with their own hands, all the sacred volumes, the church received from them, and in their name. They might employ amanuenses, some to write from their mouths. This seems particularly to have been the case of the apostle Paul, and it might be so of others; as appears from 2 Thess. iii. 17. *The salutation of me Paul with mine own hand, which is the token in every epistle, so I write:* intimating, that he used to employ others to write the epistles themselves, ordinarily, at least, that he sent to the churches: he dictated, and they wrote: and then he added with his own hand the salutation, which was a token and sign that the epistle was from him, and that he owned it. And this, I say, might be the case of the other sacred penmen. But however that be, whether they wrote themselves, or others from them, we do not now pretend to have the several first original volumes, or any of them. The individual ink and parchment, with, and on which they wrote, could not be preserved to our time without a miracle. As to the original book of Moses, or the Pentateuch, we find it was, by the special appointment of God, laid up by the side of the ark, Deut. xxxi. 25, 26. The text adds, *that it may be there for a witness against thee.* It was deposited there as a public authentic record, that if any should attempt to corrupt the law, this divine copy might be produced against them. Some think it remained by the ark till the destruction of Jerusalem, but after that, it is in vain to enquire further about it. As to the rest of the inspired books, I mean, in their first and original manuscripts, we know less of them; how long they were preserved, or when they perished. What we pretend to is, that they were wrote out for the use of the church in their respective ages, and communicated in faithful copies from one generation to another. But as to the original or first books, they are long since perished and lost. Nor could it be otherwise, as I said, without a miracle. Again,

2. I would premise, that I do not suppose the copies we have of the first original books are so absolutely perfect that there is not the least error therein. This is what can be said of no ancient book in the world. Tully complains of the Latin authors, that they were published with many blunders and mistakes in his time: and the same complaint has been made of all others, whether Latin or Greek historians, poets, and philosophers. And though more may be said in behalf of the sacred books, than of any of the rest; yet it would be extravagant to assert, they are brought down to us free of all mistakes. It is but about three hundred years since printing was found out: and before that time they were transcribed, I may say, almost an infinite number of times. And I think it not possible in an ordinary way, and without inspiration, that there should be no errors in the several copies. The ignorance, haste, carelesness, &c. of transcribers would probably betray them into mistakes. And we find in fact, that there is some difference, there are some various readings, even among the most ancient and authentic copies. But then I have two things to add, viz. that we have reason to conclude, that the mistakes would not be many, and that they would not be great. They would not be many. The high importance of the things themselves would excite more than common care. The church in every age received those writings as divine, and had a mighty veneration for the contents of them: and, consequently, would be watchful over them that they might not be corrupted and depraved. And as God designed them for the use

of the church in all ages, one cannot but expect a special superintendency of providence over them. So that we have reason, I say, to think the errors would not be many. And I subjoin, we may expect they would not be great. It is certain, they are not in matters of any great importance. All ancient copies agree in every article and doctrine of religion. And what various readings there are, are only in things of less weight, in which the christian faith and religion is not much concerned. And even here the skilful critic is able, by comparing the several copies, to discover which is the true and genuine reading. Often it may be done; and where it is otherwise, and it yet remains uncertain which copy is the true reading, which is most likely to be the original inspired text, it is in such minute matters that religion runs no hazards, suffers no damage: all copies agreeing not only in the essentials, but even in the substance and all important circumstances of divine doctrines and histories of fact.

3. I do not know that it is necessary to maintain, that all that was ever written by inspired men, is preserved and contained in our Bible. This, I am sensible, is a controversy of some difficulty. But as I do not think it proper for the auditory, I shall not trouble you with it. Some have thought the Bible mentions several sacred pieces, which we have not, as the *three thousand* parables or proverbs of Solomon, and the *thousand and five songs;* besides his books of natural philosophy; for we are told, that he *spake of trees, from the cedar-tree that is in Lebanon, even unto the hyssop that springeth out of the wall. He spake also of beasts, and of fowls, and of creeping things, and of fishes.* These they think might be inspired books, but now are lost. As also the books of Nathan the prophet, and of Gad the seer, mentioned 1 Chron. xxix. 29. The

DISCOURSE X.

prophecies of Ahijah the Shalonite, the visions of Iddo the seer, 2 Chron. ix. 29. The book of Jasher, Josh. x. 13. To which some have added several gospels whose names occur in the primitive writers: and the epistle to the Laodiceans, spoken of Col. iv. 16. as they would understand the text. These they think were the works of inspired men; but by some means or other now lost.

But others are of a different mind, and think none of these writings were inspired. However, I shall pass over this debate, and the arguments produced on the one side, or the other, for the establishing their different opinions. In the mean while, I do not think it any prejudice to religion to suppose, though we have no sufficient evidence of the fact, that there might be some divine writings, some narrations, or gospels, for instance, and some epistles, drawn up by inspired men that are not included in our canon, or catalogue of sacred books. The apostles had their distinct provinces, were dispersed through a great part of the world to spread the christian religion, they could not stay long in a place, and it is not improbable they might all of them, or most of them, leave abstracts of their doctrine behind them in the places where they had been; and when they took leave of the churches they had gathered, being called elsewhere. Now should it be granted, there might have been more of these than are now come to us, this is neither an argument against the authority of the books we have, nor against their sufficiency. There were many more things that Jesus did, than those the evangelists have written, as St. John tells us. And no doubt there were many discourses he delivered, many sermons of his apostles, which they delivered by inspiration, that were not recorded. And some that were occasionally written, which answered the end for which they were published; and yet not being intended for general and universal use, are not preserved and continued in the church. This may be granted without any disadvantage to the authority, or sufficiency of our Bible. Though, as I said, we have no certainty of it, and it is more than can be proved. Hereupon,

4. What I intend, when I say, that the books of our Bible are the original inspired books of Scripture, is in short this; that the books we now have and embrace as inspired, are those that the church of Christ has all along owned as such, and received into the canon, or catalogue of sacred Scriptures. It has received all these books as inspired, and received none else. And further, that they have come down to us in the main uncorrupt. None of those that were once admitted into the canon are lost; and none of them corrupted in any points of consequence, or importance. Let me add,

5. The sacred canon, or catalogue of inspired books, was not composed and finished at once; but gradually, and at different times. This may be affirmed with respect both to the Old Testament and the New. The books of the Old Testament were delivered to the church at diverse times; first the decalogue, or ten commandments; the two tables wrote by the finger of God, with the other laws revealed on mount Sinai; and afterwards the whole pentateuch, or five books of Moses. When and where Moses wrote these, with other questions of the like nature I pass over, and shall only observe, that the first and original book of the law was laid up in a chest or coffer, as is supposed, by the side of the ark, and kept there as the sacred standard of their religion under that dispensation: copies of it being dispersed among the people. And this was the first part of the scripture canon. The other books of the Old Testament were added afterwards, as they were occasionally written;

the perfons that tendered them to the church having firft given fatisfaction concerning their infpiration. How this was done, is a queftion of too great nicety, now to be confidered and refolved. Sometimes, it is likely, they came with the power of miracles; fometimes the perfons, that offered any revelation to be received by the church, were eftablifhed and known prophets; or they had the teftimony of allowed and approved prophets. They fpake in the name of God, and brought fufficient credentials with them: God giving teftimony to them in a fupernatural way that he fent them, and that their meffage was divine. Let me only obferve farther, with reference to the Old Teftament, that it is probable the canon of it was fettled; all the books of it reduced into one volume, and delivered to the church after the captivity. This is the common opinion of learned men, and they make it the work of the great fynagogue, as it is called, in which were prefent Ezra, Haggai, Zachary, Malachi, Nehemiah, and Zerubbabel. Thefe collected all the infpired books, fuch as were written during the captivity, as well as before, and committed them to the care of the church.

The like obfervations might be made concerning the canon of the New Teftament. It was at firft publifhed to the world, by Chrift and the apoftles in their fermons, before any part of it was committed to writing. Nor was it written all at once, but gradually fome at one time, and fome at another; in what order, and way, I am not now to enquire. I would only fuggeft, that as feveral perfons were extraordinarily called to preach the gofpel and publifh the doctrines of it to the world; fo fome of thofe were ftirred up to write for the ufe and fervice of the church, at different times, as it pleafed God by his fpirit to direct them. It is fuppofed the gofpels were written firft, and that in the order in which they now stand in our Bible: and the epistles occasionally, as the affairs of the church required, and the inspiring Spirit conducted. At last, before the age of inspiration ceased, and towards the close of it all the writings of the New Testament were collected into a volume, and left as a sacred trust to the church in future ages. This is supposed to have been done by St. John, who outlived all the other apostles.

I have given these hints in an hasty, superficial manner, the illustrating and confirming of which would require more time and discourse, than I doubt would be agreeable to some of my hearers, upon a subject so much out of their way. They may however, afford you an imperfect view of a very important subject. And so I proceed,

II. To prove, that the present books of our Bible, are the originally inspired Scriptures, that is, the books are the same that were at first given by inspiration of God. We have the same pentateuch that Moses delivered to the Jews. We have all the rest of the books both of the Old and New Testament, that the inspired writers left with the church. We have the same in number and kind, and they are not corrupted or depraved in matters of moment, much less, in points fundamental. I will evidence this with respect to both the Old and New Testament: yet very briefly, that I may not too long try your patience. Though methinks, if you would consider the matter, I might expect your attention, our faith and hope, our eternal all, depend upon the truth and divinity of the Bible, and to prove the books of it genuine, is the same thing with regard to your spiritual interests, as it is with regard to your temporal concerns, to prove your deeds and conveyances are genuine.

1. I will begin with the Old Testament, and prove that could not be changed, or corrupted;

but that we have the same original books, that Moses and the prophets delivered to the Jews.

To which purpose let it be considered, that it was morally impossible, that the books of the Old Testament should be changed or corrupted. The law was published and revealed in a very solemn and awful manner, at mount Sinai. The original book was laid up, as you have heard, in the sanctuary, to which they might have recourse upon occasion. Copies were delivered out for the use of the people, and dispersed among them, with a special charge that they should not add thereto, nor diminish from it, Deut. iv. 2. and again, xii. 32. *What things soever I command you observe to do it. Thou shalt not add thereto, nor diminish from it.* And as they had the law in their hands, so they were obliged to have it *in their hearts,* to teach it *diligently to* their *children,* and *talk of it when they sat in their houses,* when they *walked* by the *way,* when they *lay down,* and when they *rose up ; to write it upon the door-posts of* their *houses* and *upon their gates,* Deut. vi. 6, 7, 9. And Chap. xi. 18, 19, 20. And so conversant were they, and so expert in their law, that Josephus tells us they had it constantly in their mouths, and knew every thing in it as well as their own names.

And as the law was matter of every one's study, so the public reading of it was a constant part of their worship. We are told, *Moses had in old time them that preached him, being read in their synagogues every Sabbath day.* Add to this, that in the year of the release, at the end of every seventh year, the book of the law was produced, and solemnly read before all the people. They read their law every week by distinct portions in their synagogues, or places of religious worship. And on this occasion the whole volume was brought forth, and read before the people. Now these circumstances, and many more might be taken notice of, make it next to impossible, that the law should be changed, or corrupted. They had authentic copies of it among them. Some of the Jews tell us, Moses wrote thirteen copies thereof with his own hand, that he delivered one to the priests to be preserved in the holy place, and one to each of the twelve tribes to be kept by the elders of each tribe. The design of which, it is likely, was that the people of each tribe might have an authentic copy to have recourse to, if any thing was thought to be amiss in the more private copies; as the whole nation upon the like occasion might resort to the copy in the sanctuary. This being the case, it is, I say, morally impossible that a law thus promulgated, in which a whole nation had so great an interest, their government, polity, civil as well as religious interest depending upon it; a law so constantly read, so universally studied and known should be altered. None could attempt to do it without being discovered; nor would they escape the punishment due by the law to such a wickedness.

Again, as a farther argument, it is considerable, that they had the utmost veneration for their law. They reverenced it even to superstition, as might be shewn in many instances. Some have told us, that they thought every private man, that could, was obliged to write a copy of the law with his own hand. And they were strangely superstitious in the manner of their writing, which however let us see in what high esteem their law was with them, and that they thought they could not pay it reverence enough. But to omit other particulars, I will only take notice that they had an order of men among them, their Maforites, whose business it was to watch over the sacred text, and take care that not the least change should be made in it. And the pains they took to this purpose were very extraordinary. They numbered not only all the verses, but words and letters of the law; took an account how often any word occurred therein; criticifed upon the form of every letter, how differently it was written; and employed an induftry and art that was almoft incredible. Now was it likely, was it even poffible, that a book thus guarded fhould be corrupted?

I might farther urge to the fame purpofe, that our Saviour, who fo freely upon many occafions cenfures the Jews, particularly the Scribes and Pharifees for their faults, never once accufes them of corrupting their Scriptures, or of any defigns of that kind. He tells them of their hypocrify, their oppreffion and pride; of their making void the law by their traditions; but never charges them with changing it, or corrupting any of the books of it. But rather bears teftimony to them in this particular, whilft he directs to the fearching the Scripture, that is, the writings of the Old Teftament; for thefe were all the Scriptures extant at that time, and faith, that therein they had eternal life; which he would not have faid, had they either changed or corrupted it. And we find the apoftle mentions the Jews, as having the facred truft of the Scripture left in their hands, without hinting one word of their unfaithfulnefs, *unto them were committed the oracles of God.* Now as this crime, the corrupting the facred oracles, would have been the greateft of all crimes, we cannot imagine our Saviour and his apoftles would have paffed it over in filence, had they been guilty of it.

Farther, the New Teftament frequently intimates, that the text of the Old Teftament was not corrupted. This is implied in that our Lord and his apoftles fo often confirm their doctrine thereby, and appeal to the authority of Mofes and the prophets. The apoftle in the text declares, *all Scrip-*

ture, meaning the Scripture of the Old Testament, *was given by inspiration of God*. And speaking of Timothy's knowing the Scripture from his childhood, he says, they were *able to make wise unto salvation, through faith which is in Christ Jesus.* An argument that they were entire and not depraved. I might subjoin the testimony of their own writers, as Josephus, for instance, who, notwithstanding he upbraids them for their many crying iniquities, and imputes the dreadful judgments that came upon them to their sins and apostasies, yet clears them of any guilt in corrupting their law; and indeed, applauds their zeal in and about it. And, which is very much to our purpose, he gives us a catalogue of the divine books they had preserved; the very same that now we have. Philo, another of their learned writers, bears testimony concerning them; that from the going forth of the children of Israel out of Egypt, from the giving of the law, until his days, which was about two thousand years, there was not so much as a word changed or altered therein: and adds, that there was not any Jew but would rather die an hundred times over, than suffer his law to be changed in the least. And this I think sufficient to prove that the Old Testament is not changed; but that the same original inspired books are communicated to the christian church, that the church of the Jews received from Moses and the prophets. I must hasten through the other class of argument, viz.

2. To prove, that the books of the New-Testament remain the same and uncorrupted. I shall only mention the heads that might be insisted upon more fully.

It is a good argument that the books left by the evangelists and apostles were the very same we now have, in that we find in the most early writers of the christian church quotations out of them, in which the very same words are produced we now find in them. We have several of these quotations in the very first writers; which shews that the books, the christian church then made use of, and received as the writings of the inspired apostles, were the same and not different books, from those we have in our hands and receive as such. We have testimonies to this purpose above one thousand five hundred years old.

And then it is observable, that we have in the writers of the primitive church, even in the very first ages, lists of the sacred books of the New-Testament. They not only quote them, but number them; mention the four evangelists, Paul's epistles, and the rest as the works of such and such persons, whose names they bear. I cannot here produce the evidence of this; but dare be accountable for it at any time.

Again, Tertullian, one of the first of the fathers, who lived within a little more than an hundred years after the apostle John, takes notice of the original writings under the hands of the apostles; as what remained in some churches in his day. Now if this was so, the church at that time had a full opportunity of satisfying themselves concerning any book, or passage, by appealing to those churches as to such particular books, or passages.

Further, we have the canon of the New Testament owned and declared by an early council in the primitive church, which hath left it as it now is. They place the same books, and no more in it than what are now received in the protestant churches.

Some of the keenest enemies of the christian faith owned many of the books of the New Testament, that is, that they were written by such and such persons in whose names they appear. Thus Julian the apostate mentions the gospels of Matthew and Mark, of Luke and John. And others mention other books; an argument that nothing could be objected against the fact, that these books were wrote by such persons. They herein grant, that the christians did not forge their books, but received them from such authors.

I might add, that some of the fathers argue against the hereticks they oppose, that their doctrines did not agree with the unquestionable writings of the apostles.

In a word, it is not probable, nor indeed possible that these books should be forged, be changed or corrupted in any material points. For, 1. they could not be corrupted during the lives of the apostles, while the church was under the conduct of an infallible spirit, and under the authority of the prime ministers of Christ's kingdom. Should any then have attempted to impose spurious writings upon the church, there was an easy remedy at hand. We cannot suppose any books would then be admitted, but what were approved by the apostles and apostolic men. And consequently, for the first age the canon of Scripture must, I think, be allowed to be secure. 2. When the divine books were communicated to the church, they were received with great reverence and veneration, and esteemed as their glory and treasure. They looked upon them as a revelation from heaven, and charter for heaven; the rule of their life, and foundation of their hope. And we find that generally they would submit to any tortures and deaths rather than renounce or part with them. And can we imagine they would corrupt them themselves, or willingly suffer others to do it? No more than you would allow knavish men to tamper with the writings by which you hold your estates. 3. There were great numbers of copies spread abroad through the several churches of Christ, and in several nations. Now it cannot be thought all should agree in a design of changing or corrupting the original books. And if some only should endeavor it, the uncorrupted copies would remain to detect them. 4. They were very early and soon translated into different languages, and a multitude of learned men made it their business to teach, explain, and write comments upon them. Now supposing there was something wrong in one version, or in this or that copy, something changed, added, or taken away; there were many other copies, and other versions by help of which the neglect or fraud might be and would be corrected. 5. They were constantly read in their public assemblies. As the primitive christians used to be very conversant with them in private, so the reading of them was always a part of their solemn and joint worship. By which means, they could not but be well acquainted with them, and have them fixed in their minds and memories, which would be a security against any remarkable corruption of them. 6. Christians were soon unhappily divided into different parties and opinions, had many disputes among themselves about some articles of their faith; in all which they appealed to the holy Scripture as the standard of their faith, and the judge of their questions: and consequently no one party could corrupt the same, but the rest would complain of them, and expose them for it. 7. Add to all this, the watchfulness of divine providence, which we have reason to be satisfied would interest itself in this matter, and not suffer the word of God to be altered or corrupted in things of moment, that concern the salvation of mankind, or that would affect and destroy the design of his affording such a revelation to the world. In short, it is as reasonable to suppose, that a crafty lawyer could forge a new statute book, and a new body of laws for the people of England, and bring them into our courts, as that any men, whatever their designs were, could change or corrupt the books of the New Testament, which were received by all sorts of christians, as the rule of their religion, and charter of their happiness.

And thus, I hope, I have cleared in some measure the question relating to the canon of Scripture; have shewn you that the books of our present Bible are the original inspired books thereof. I promised to take notice of some objections: but must leave them to another discourse.

In the mean while, what has been said, is matter of no small satisfaction and comfort to the judicious and inquisitive christian. The Bible is his inheritance; its testimonies the rejoicing of his heart; and it cannot but give him a pleasure, the greatest pleasure, to see this well established, and its authority vindicated. And should we not value, study, and endeavor to improve our Bible, and the several books of it; when we have so good assurance that they are divine. The high importance of the things contained therein should recommend it. The blessed tendency of its doctrines, should recommend it. And methinks it should exceedingly raise our esteem of it, that it is a book sent from God. O learn to receive it, and reverence it as such; and to answer the apostles character of the Thessalonians, in which he so much rejoices, and with which I shall conclude, *For this cause thank we God without ceasing, because when ye received the word of God, which ye heard of us, ye received it not as the word of men, but (as it is in truth) the word of God.*

2 Tim. iii. 16.

All Scripture is given by inspiration of God, and is profitable for doctrine, for reproof, for correction, for instruction in righteousness.

I HAVE endeavored to clear and vindicate the canon of Scripture, have proved that the books of our Bible, are the Scriptures that were given by inspiration of God. I am sensible that several objections have been made to the account I have given. But as I am in haste to come to a conclusion, and cannot suppose many of my hearers so well acquainted with these matters, as to desire a full discussion and examination of them, or likely to receive it with advantage; I shall in a great measure pass them by, and only mention a few of the most considerable.

1. It is objected, that we know not when or by whom the canon of the Old or New Testament was settled and established. I answer, we have very probable evidence that the canon of the Old Testament was supervised and settled by Ezra after the return of the Jews from captivity: and that of the New Testament by the apostle John, as I observed before. However, it is sufficient if we can prove both were settled whilst the church was under the conduct of inspired men; who, we may be sure,

would admit no books into the canon, but such as were authentic and divine. Let us lay the scene among ourselves, and in our own nation : suppose we had had a succession of prophets, and several books of religion had been written among us, some in one age, some in another ; and offered to the church as inspired, at least, before all the prophets, or other inspired persons, were gone from among us, and that extraordinary order ceased, all the divine books were gathered into a volume, and delivered to the church, as the rule of religion. Supposing this the case : I cannot see we could reasonably doubt of our canon, though we knew not certainly when it was received in the church whilst it had inspired guides. And this is really the case with reference to the canon of Scripture. There were several prophets in the Jewish church, as Haggai, Zachary and Malachi, after the canon was finished, as we now have it. And we may conclude, that these men would neither suffer inspired books to be rejected, nor spurious ones to be obtruded on the church.

2. It is objected, that there are some books both of the Old and New Testament that we know not the writers of ; and had they been inspired, surely we should have them under the names of the inspired authors. To omit other instances, it is uncertain, say our objectors, by whom the epistle to the Hebrews was written, neither by the apostle Paul, by Luke, his constant companion, or by Clemens his fellow laborer, as he is called ; or by Barnabas. Some of the ancients ascribe it to one of these, and some to another. I answer, that though the writer of this or that book might for reasons, which then had their weight, be suppressed for a time ; yet at last it was generally known. Thus, for example, almost all antiquity agreed that the epistle to the Hebrews was wrote by the apostle

Paul. But I answer further, the character of the book itself is of far greater moment, than the name of the writer. If it brought evidence that it was a divine book, the question, who wrote it? is not very material. And if it was received as an inspired book in the age when it was wrote, and whilst the church was governed by inspired men, as I said before, this would be sufficient to satisfy the church in any after age concerning it.

3. It is pretended, there were many other books besides these we retain in our canon, that went abroad in the primitive church under the name of inspired authors; and how come those in our canon only to be admitted, and the rest rejected; when they claimed equal authority? I answer to this, I grant there was in the first ages of christianity a great number of apocryphal writings. It may well be supposed, that when so admirable an institution as that of the christian religion first took place in the world, its professors would be commenting upon it in a great variety of books, which they did under different titles, as acts, epistles, gospels, intineraries, recognitions, martyrdoms, and the like. And as these would be read by all sorts, so it is not improbable, but some of them might for a time pass for divine and inspired. But I add, when the church came to examine and try them, they were rejected, as being different from the genius, spirit, and manner of the apostles, as Eusebius gives the reason; they were not sufficiently recommended, were not approved by any apostle or apostolic men; were found destitute of internal characters, in some things contrary to the unquestionable writings of the apostles, &c. And therefore whatever esteem they might once have, they were upon good reason afterwards set aside, and of no authority, and became neglected.

4. It is farther objected, that some of the books in our canon, were not owned and received in the first age of the church. I answer, this may be granted without any prejudice to the authority of these books. The canon was not compleated at once, as I have already observed, but was a gradual thing. The books of the New Testament were written some at one time, some at another, upon different occasions. The apostles, you know, were sent forth to disciple all nations, to *preach the gospel to every creature*, and in their journies up and down, they wrote many of their epistles. And as the church was under persecution, and one part lay at a great distance from another, we need not wonder that some churches had inspired writings, which others at first knew nothing of; and hence might proceed the scruples that those had with reference to particular books. They were but lately come to their hands; they had not sufficient opportunity of examining them, and of receiving the testimony of their brethren concerning them. But then I add, after due examination, the books referred to in the objection, were universally received. So that in reality, this is so far from being an objection against the canon, that it is an argument in favor of it. The church first questioned some books, and doubted of them; which shews they were not credulous. But afterwards they admitted them as divine; which shews they had satisfaction concerning them. In a word, the first christians engaged in the profession of their religion, not with the looseness, indifference, and treachery of our times; but with an extraordinary warmth, zeal, and self-denial. Religion was the greatest thing in the world with them. They would not betray the christian church, part with any doctrine, or any rule of practice in the New Testament, much less any book of it, for all the world. The sacred vo-

lumes were dearer to them than their lives. No inducement, promises or threatnings, rewards or terrors, could prevail with them to give them up, or suffer them to be depraved. I might subjoin, that all the books of the New Testament seem very much of a piece; all written with the same spirit, and worthy of the same divine author. Not one of them has any internal character that disgraces it, or brings it under suspicion. So that as the books we at present have, are the same the first christians owned, after great caution, serious and strict examination, when there was any room for question, owned as divine, and gloried in as a treasure from heaven, we have abundant reason to own them as such too. Our Scripture is the same with theirs, both given by inspiration of God, both have that gospel, which, as the apostle expresses it, the *Holy Ghost sent down from heaven.*

And thus I have finished the third thing proposed under the head of vindicating the canon of Scripture. What remains in the course of the general method, is to answer objections against the inspiration thereof. A great deal has been offered to prove that the Scripture is given by inspiration of God. Many volumes formerly, and of late, have been filled with the argument. But notwithstanding all that has been said, or can be said, there are some that it seems are not, will not be satisfied. And I shall now consider what these persons have to alledge as the reason of their infidelity; if one may suppose they have any thing for it that deserves the name of reason. Was I here to defend the cause of religion at large, I should divide the objectors into different classes; for they seem to be of different thoughts, and act upon different principles in their opposition to the Bible. Some insinuate, that supernatural revelation is needless, and that natural religion, as they call it, is not only sufficient, but really preferable to that of the Scripture, which they reprefent as dull, abfurd, involved in difficulties, and unintelligible.

Others fpeak a little more modeftly. They allow the Bible has its excellencies: but then they think it wants evidence of its divinity. They would be willing, they pretend, to fee it well proved; but there are difficulties in their way that they cannot get over.

And fome of thofe that would be thought more in earneft, have collected from ancient and modern writers all the exceptions and cavils they can meet with againft particular paffages of the Bible. Thefe they fet off with fuch ornaments of language and oratory, as they are mafters of, and fend them abroad into the world as reafons againft the Scripture.

Others attack our arguments by which we fupport the authority of the Bible, and endeavor to raife difficulties, and fhew the weaknefs of them; fuch as are taken from miracles, prophecy, the fpreading of the chriftian religion, and the like.

But the main body of the antifcripturifts act a different, and even a meaner part. All their ftrength lies in a few quirks of wit, that they have picked up in common converfation, or in the clubs of their companions. They neither read, ftudy, nor underftand any part of the Bible, nor do they concern themfelves with the reafons that are offered in its behalf. They have received prejudices againft it, and thefe they run away with without ever examining matters. They get hold of a few topics of raillery, fingle out a few texts and phrafes, which they have learned in their manner to reprefent as ridiculous; and from the abufe of thefe, they condemn the whole, and even think they have gained a victory.

I am perfuaded, you do not expect that I fhould

DISCOURSE XI. 279

examine all their pleas, and lay open the cavils that each class of them bring against the authority of the Scripture. This would take up more time than I design to employ in the remaining part of the subject. And, as I would hope, I am not at present speaking to any of this unhappay character, it is less necessary to insist largely on these things. I shall however for the confirming your faith, take notice of, and endeavor to remove, some of the more plausible objections. I shall run through them briefly, and so pass on to what may be thought more useful.

1. Some of these persons take offence at the style of the Scripture: they pretend it is low, flat, and dull; has none of that vivacity and spirit that might be expected in an inspired book. I answer, this objection is not true with respect to the whole Bible. There is as true rhetoric, as strong figures, as much pomp and grandeur of style, in some parts of the holy Scripture, as in any book in the world. Job is thought to be not only the first, but the finest specimen of poetry that has yet been produced by any, either ancients or moderns. Several of the prophets deliver themselves in the sublimest strains of oratory. And it has been observed of the apostle Paul, that there is often not only a great purity in his language, but much art in his style; and that in his defence before Felix and Agrippa, he outsoars the highest flights of Cicero and Demosthenes.

But I grant, the main of the Bible doth not run in this strain of an orator. But then this is so far from being an objection against it, that it is rather an argument of its divinity. It speaks from God, teaches, commands, enacts, promises, and threatens in the name of the great Sovereign of the world. The importance of its matter, and the authority of its author, are its oratory. And indeed, these considered, human oratory would be an abasement to it. When a prince speaks from the throne, he doth not assume the style of a common declaimer, nor use arts of persuasion; his authority supersedes all the necessity of these things. And so it is in the case before us.

Others farther object, the difficulty and obscurity of Scripture. They think had it been a revelation from heaven, it would have been plain to all, and upon a level with every man's understanding; as every one is so much concerned in it. To this I answer, that what is absolutely necessary, is easy and obvious. None can misunderstand the Scripture in the great essential points of religion, without wilful and wicked neglect. In the mean time, I acknowledge there are difficulties, considerable difficulties in the Bible; and as it deserves, so it requires a good degree of pains and diligence rightly to understand it. So it has pleased God to order and state his revelation. Some things are exceeding plain and easy; some things profound, intricate and difficult; which demand the closest attention, and are fit to employ the strength of the greatest genius's and strongest capacities: a dispensation that, I doubt not, has a great deal of the wisdom and goodness of God in it. But this is a matter that needs farther explaining; and it would be for many reasons proper more fully to consider it. But I have not room here to make the necessary enlargement.

2. It is an objection against the Bible, that some who are fond of so unhappy, and one would think uncomfortable a cause, as that of infidelity, seem to triumph in that it contains doctrines, and relates facts, that are not only absurd and unreasonable, but downright impossible. And consequently, cannot be inspired, or a revelation from God. Many instances are given us under this head; as, the universal deluge, the preservation of such a number

of creatures, with proper food, in so small a vessel as the ark; that an ass should speak; that the sun should stand still, and yet the frame of nature not thrown into confusion; that Jonah should live in a whale's belly so long without respiration, and not be digested in the stomach of the fish, &c. And what difficulties they find in some doctrines of religion, is well known; as, the trinity, the incarnation, a virgin bringing forth a son, God and man united in one person, the resurrection of the dead, and the like. These, say they, are not only above our comprehension, but impossible; from whence they conclude, they are sufficient to sink and ruin the credit of any book that delivers them as true. To which I reply, 1. That many things appear incredible, and impossible for a time, that afterwards are well enough understood; appear impossible to some, yet are certain and easy to others. A multitude of instances may be produced to illustrate this from the discoveries that have been made in natural philosophy. It was once thought impossible there should be antipodes; and yet now no body questions it. The king of Siam, it is said, thought himself affronted by the Dutch ambassador, when he told him that in Holland the water would become so hard in cold weather, that men or elephants might walk upon it. 2. We believe a great many things we do not understand, cannot account for, and have reason to think as impossible as any of the things the objection refers to in Scripture. What notion have we of the infinite divisibility of matter, the union of soul and body, a vital union between spirit and matter. This every one believes, and yet no wise man will undertake to explain. Nothing is more universally agreed upon, as absolutely necessary, than the eternity of God; and yet the very notion is amazing, shocks the faculties, and almost overwhelms the mind; that any thing should exist without a cause of its existence, as God doth, is utterly inconceivable, and were we not constrained to say, it must be so; we should be ready to say, it is impossible. And the like difficulty might be observed of the divine omnipresence, or infinite extension. The thing itself is demonstrable, and yet the mode inexplicable. In short, we live in a world of mysteries: A multitude of things we see and believe are so; that they are, is plain and certain; yet how they are, we know not; and should be apt boldly to pronounce they could not be, but that we are sure they are. How unreasonable is it then to object against the Bible, because it delivers to us some things we do not understand; especially if they refer to the incomprehensible, unsearchable nature of God, or the extraordinary acts of infinite power. But 3. I would ask the objector, whether he believes God made the world? If so; all his cavils upon this head must be absurd. For nothing can seem more impossible, and can be more hard to be believed, than the doctrine of the creation; that something should be made out of nothing. The famous philosopher Aristotle laid it down as a maxim, against which there was no contesting, that nothing can be produced from nothing. Nor indeed can it be denied, without having recourse to infinite power. Now since it is granted by many, at least, that reject revelation, that God made all things out of nothing; or more properly, when there was nothing, did, by his sovereign word and command, bring all things into being. Since this is not thought impossible; nothing else certainly ought to be so; nothing, I am sure, related in the Bible. I proceed to another objection.

3. Some alledge contradictions in Scripture, and thence infer it cannot be inspired. I answer, the contradictions objected are only seeming, but not

real. Nor do I know one particular that is not capable of a rational solution. A little skill in criticism, in the Hebrew and Greek languages, their idioms and properties, and the antiquities and customs of those countries, where the scenes mentioned in Scripture lay, and the affairs were acted, will clear the main difficulties. A distinction of the different senses of words, of the different subjects and times, will often do it. Thus when it is said, *it is appointed for all men once to die.* And elsewhere, *if a man keep Christ's saying, he shall never see death.* There is no contradiction. The one place speaking of natural, the other of spiritual or eternal death. So when Moses says, *God rested on the seventh day from all his work.* And Christ saith, *my Father worketh hitherto.* There is no opposition or contradiction: Moses speaking of the works of creation, and Christ of the works of providence. Christ says, *John the baptist was Elias that was to come.* And yet John the baptist when he was asked, whether he was Elias? answered, *I am not.* He was not Elias in person, but was Elias in office and spirit, as I may say, and consequently, here is no contradiction. Samuel tells us, God *will not repent.* And yet elsewhere we read, that he did repent, that *he made man on the earth. That he made Saul king.* But here is no contradiction: repentence signifies in the one place a change of mind and council, from want of foresight of what would come to pass. And thus God cannot repent. But then he changes his course, as men do when they change their minds; and so he may be said to repent. And in the like method most of the rest of these appearing contradictions may be reconciled, viz. by distinguishing ambiguous words, distinguishing different times and respects, &c. Let me add, that considering the nature and quality of the Bible, that part of it is the most ancient book in the world; that it is written in a language but very imperfectly understood; that it contains a great variety of matters; treats of subjects of exceeding difficulty as well as importance, it is not to be wondered at, if some passages occur not easy to be understood, and that may appear at first sight inconsistent. In the mean time it must argue a base humour of cavilling, and a strong prejudice against the cause of the Bible to reject it on this account; when it comes recommended to us with such a torrent of Evidence.

4. It may be objected, that if the Bible be divinely inspired, and the subjects of it of that importance to mankind as is pretended; matters would not sure have been left under so much uncertainty, and so much in the dark: but a revelation intended for the good of all would have been accompanied with an evidence convincing to all. I answer, the evidence is sufficient. Had it been overpowering, there had been no virtue, no excellency in believing. God designed to try the tempers of men; that as is said in another case, *they that were approved might be made manifest.* But I answer further, this objection rudely arraigns the sovereignty of God, and prescribes to infinite wisdom. It is like the clay rising up against the potter, saying why hast thou formed me thus? indeed such cavils would be endless, should we indulge the vile temper. We might as decently ask, why did God make mankind liable to sin? why did he suffer him to sin? why did he not make every man an angel, and every angel a seraph? but as such a humour as this is utterly inconsistent with the subjection and reverence due from a creature to the author of his being, so it would undo him even in heaven could it find a place there. Presently cast him down, as the like it may be did the apostate angels, and lay

him in *chains of darkness*. We have abundant evidence of Scripture revelation, all that God saw fit to grant, and all that is necessary. He requires in order to believing, an humble, teachable disposition. If instead of this, we allow ourselves unreasonably to carp and find fault, the guilt of our Infidelity will lie at our own door, and our blood will be upon our own head.

5. It is objected, that notwithstanding all that is said in behalf of the Bible, and of christianity, mahometanism pretends to as glorious things, and has spread as much in the world, and yet is a vile imposture. But it would be easy to shew, that there is nothing in this objection, could I allow myself to stay upon it, and to shew that the case of christianity and the religion of Mahomet vastly differ. The one has all the marks of imposture imaginable in it, and the other none at all. Let me suggest a few things here.

Mahomet accommodated his religion to the humours of the Arabians, and therefore retained therein such rites and ceremonies as they were fond of, and had been accustomed to, and indulged them in such sins as he found them most addicted to. But nothing of this can be charged on christianity. Christ and his apostles strictly forbid all sin, required of all without exception the mortification of their most beloved lusts, cancelled the ancient ceremonies of the Jews, and all the foolish superstitions of the Heathens. Our Saviour made no allowance, granted no indulgence here. And yet his religion prevails against the strongest corruptions and most inveterate prejudices.

Mahomet changed his religion, altered his laws and ceremonies; as he found the humours of the people required. He sometimes established one law and manner of worship, and then superseded it; pretending divine revelation for both; though they were inconsistent. But Christ was always the same and his laws invariable.

Mahomet introduced his religion among a people of the most stupid ignorance, and consequently prepared to receive any delusions that should be artfully carried on. It is said, there was but one person in Mecca, where he began his forgeries, that could write or read. Whereas, on the other hand, Christ appeared among the most learned people in the world, and when learning was at the greatest height.

Mahomet never durst venture either upon prophecy or miracle, though urged and strongly pressed on that head; being conscious of his own inability. But you know how much of both these attended the ministry, and established the authority of the Lord Jesus.

Further, Mahomet forbad under pain of death all disputes about his religion. Whereas Christ submitted his to a free examination and enquiry.

Lastly, the religion of Mahomet owed its support to the power of the sword, and was by that means propagated. Whereas Christ and his apostles neither had, nor would accept of any such auxiliaries and helps. *The weapons* of their *warfare were not carnal, but spiritual, and mighty through God.*

So that though it must be granted, that mahometanism has prevailed in a great part of the world, God having in his just judgment given up a people to strong delusions, that had the christian religion among them, but wofully perverted, and grew weary of it. Though this must be acknowledged, it can be no diminution of the honor of the christian religion, or argument against its divinity, since it is so evidently of a different nature, and made its way through the world in a very different manner. Several nations believe and receive mahometanism, but such are subdued, and the conqueror may impose what laws he pleases upon the conquered. Once more,

6. It is objected, if the Bible be the word of God, if the christian religion be divine, if the Son of God came from heaven, as is related therein, and introduced and established his religion in the manner, as is there pretended, it is strange it has had no greater and better effects in the world. If it be so excellent an institution; how come they that profess it to live no better than other people? To this I answer in a word or two, and I have done with the objections. (1.) Multitudes profess themselves christians that are not so. And we must not judge of christianity from the conduct of such that only usurp the name. Suppose a company of men should enter themselves among the strictest sect of philosophers. Yet if they never acquainted themselves with their doctrines; never enquired into the precepts, nor regarded the rules of the profession; how excellent soever the institution was, it could have no influence upon such votaries. And this is the case of large numbers that are called christians. They profess the Bible, but they know little or nothing of it. They bear the name of Christ, and pretend to be his followers; but they never received his doctrine, nor his spirit. And, consequently, by measures ought to be taken from them in judging of the christian religion. I answer, (2.) Christianity has wrought a glorious reformation in the world. That body of men, that receive the Bible, differ as much from the rest of the world, as Jerusalem from Kedar. The church though it has great corruptions, yet has great excellencies; The Scripture, wherever it has come, ever has, in one degree or other, and with respect to some at least, brought a blessing along with it. But (3.) I confess, the christian religion has not

had that effect which might be expected; and I must own this is one of those providences, that appear to me dark and surprising; and, as much as any thing, inclines me to believe there will be a more glorious state of the church, than we have yet seen; when christianity will look more like itself, and shine forth in the lives of those that profess it with greater lustre. In the mean time the objection doth not conclude. The world is exceedingly the better for the Bible. I verily believe most of the virtue and religion, that remains in a corrupt degenerate world, is owing to it; and is to be found among those that embrace and profess it: and, I doubt not, a time will come when the beauty and power of the christian religion will appear more illustrious, than it has yet done; at least than now it doth.

Our duty, in the mean time, is to retrieve the credit of our profession by the purity, integrity, and holiness of our lives. The christian apologists in the primitive church (O that we could do it more universally now!) used to appeal to the professors of their religion for the excellency of it; intimating, that their enemies might there behold a beautiful idea of christianity. This argument is too much obscured and lost among us. Let us study every one of us to do our part towards recovering it, waiting for a more abundant effusion of the divine spirit to revive decayed religion, in our hearts and in our lives; *that others seeing our good works, may glorify* our *Father which is in heaven.*

I have now finished the first general observation from the text, viz. That all Scripture is given of God. And as I have treated the subject more at large than I intended, I shall endeavor to make some amends by a more quick dispatch of what remains. I hasten therefore to the next thing observed from the words,

II. That the inspired writings of the Old and New Testament are of great use to the church; *are profitable for doctrine, for reproof, for correction, and for instruction in righteousness.* As I design but a sermon or two more upon the subject, I shall not take any great compass; but shall, (1.) Consider the usefulness of the Scripture in general. And then, (2.) Consider the use of the several parts thereof. All Scripture, says the text, is useful; every particular, every book and portion of it.

I. I shall consider the usefulness of the Scripture in general; for what purposes it is useful. And I shall confine myself to the particulars the text speaks of and directs to. It is useful *for doctrine, for reproof, for correction,* and *for instruction in righteousness.* There is some difference among the critics about the sense of these words; though most I think agree in referring the two first to doctrines, or opinions; the two latter to manners. As thus the Scripture is useful or profitable for doctrine, that is, to teach us what to believe: for reproof, or conviction, namely of errors; it is useful for correction of faults in practice; and for *instruction in righteousness*; that is, in the whole compass of our duty both towards God and man. The meaning in short is, that the Scripture is a compleat rule both of faith and practice. It directs us what we are to believe, and leads us in the way of duty. Thus compleat is the Scripture. And therefore it is added, *that the man of God may be perfect, thoroughly furnished unto all good works.* I shall go over the particulars, and begin with the first.

1. The Scripture is profitable for doctrine. And here I shall hint what doctrines the Scripture teaches, and with what advantage it teaches such doctrines.

1. What doctrines the Scripture teaches. In general, I would suggest, that the Scripture being

inspired of God, must be a sufficient rule of faith, and contain all the necessary points of divine knowledge and belief. We cannot suppose that a God of infinite wisdom and goodness should indite a book on purpose to direct us in the way to heaven, and yet that book be defective in any necessary article of religion. No; *the Scripture is profitable for doctrine,* for all doctrine. How this is to be understood, I will let you see in a few propositions; therein comprising what I design upon the head.

1. I do not assert, that the Scripture teaches us arts, sciences, and philosophy. There is indeed a great deal of philosophy in Scripture, a great deal of rhetoric, and oratory; and many specimens of curious speculation and learning interspersed. But there is no system of any of these; much less a system of all of them. The Scripture was wrote for the use of all sorts of persons; the vulgar and ignorant as well as higher genious's; wrote to instruct us in the way to heaven, and not in the niceties of human learning. It is profitable for doctrine *that the man of God may be perfect, thoroughly furnished to all good words;* that the christian may be instructed in every thing that concerns religion, and may be a perfect christian; not the philosopher instructed in his theorems, at least, not in all of them, or in every problem, that may fall under his examination. Nor,

2. Do I suppose the Scripture teaches the doctrine of politics. I remark this, because I apprehend it a mistake in some that treat on this subject, and that it is attended with ill consequences, to found their doctrine of politics on the Bible. I grant it lays down general rules concerning civil government, and concerning the duty both of magistrates and subjects. As, that they, that rule over men, must be *just, ruling in the fear of God.*

DISCOURSE XI.

magistrates are the *ministers of God for good, a terror to them that do evil, and a praise to them that do well.* Such are the magistrates which God appoints and approves. And as those that are under them, enjoy the protection and many advantages of their administration, they are to be *subject not for wrath,* or merely through fear of punishment ; *but for conscience sake.* This the Scripture enjoins, and the obligation hereunto is evidently founded upon the nature and reason of things, and results from the very end of society. But it doth not determine the necessary form of civil polity, much less prescribe one and the same for all states, and all people in every age of the world.

Different forms of government are lawful in different places, or in the same place at different times. And, I apprehend, any form of government may be lawful, though not found in Scripture ; provided it be fitted to answer the general ends of government, and be managed consistently with Scripture rules. In short, as God has in nature, and by the ministry and help of human reason afforded sufficient means for human learning, so far as it is necessary in the world; the same may be said of civil government. It is included in the law of nature, the reason of mankind directs to it, furnishes rules for its management ; and it is left to the wisdom and prudence of every nation or community to choose the form, to specify and model it as they please. All that the Scripture doth here is only to superintend it, as I may say, and prescribe the duties of the several parts of society in general.

I will not affirm our text positively excludes the usefulness of Scripture in things of this kind. But I think, it directs us to expect and attend its teachings in things of a different kind. It is useful for doctrine, *that the man of God may be perfect,* not the politician; at least, that he may be perfect as a christian, not as a politician. The Scripture describes God's church, gives us the plan and form of that, and lays down rules for the management of it; teaches how to govern our hearts, and order our lives and converſations; that we may be fitted for the heavenly hierarchy, the city above. But it doth not meddle ſo much with the affairs of this world, as to lay down a ſyſtem of politics. Here human wiſdom, and human laws, have the chief intereſt.

3. When it is ſaid the Scripture is profitable for doctrine, we muſt not underſtand it, that it teaches us every thing about the doctrines of religion, that our curioſity may lead us to enquire after. There are a great many doctrines that men have brought into religion, which the Scripture ſaith nothing of. They are mere human figments, and framed out of their own heads. But as the Scripture is not profitable for theſe doctrines, I think we may with clearneſs and authority infer, the doctrines themſelves are not profitable. Of this ſort are a multitude of the doctrines the church of Rome would obtrude upon us under the notion of traditions. I may add, of this ſort are many ſpeculations, upon which no ſmall ſtreſs has been laid, in proteſtant churches, and which they borrowed from the ſchools.

Let me obſerve, that in the doctrines the Scripture doth reveal, even in the moſt important of them, there is a reſerve. It teaches us ſomething of them, but not every thing that belongs to this or that ſubject. It acquaints us with all that is neceſſary to ground our faith, and direct our practice; but not all we may deſire to gratify our curioſity. It gives us, for inſtance, the moſt excellent notion of the divine being. But as his nature is unſearchable, there are an hundred queſtions men indulge themselves in with reference to it, wherein it affords us no light and satisfaction.

It teaches us the doctrine of the trinity, that sublime and distinguishing doctrine of the christian religion. But then it doth not descend to all the particulars, the nice questions, and bold decisions, with which we have, if I mistake not, perplexed and obscured it. The Scripture is profitable for this doctrine. And the doctrine is a very profitable and comfortable one, if we will be content with what it teaches. But if we leave our guide here, and pretend to be wise above what is written, we shall soon find ourselves out of our depth, and to our own and others prejudices, *darken council with words without knowledge.*

The same may be said of many other doctrines of the Bible; as the doctrine of God's decrees, the state of future happiness, the resurrection, the nature, quality, and circumstances of the resurrection body, the condition of angels, their order, government, officers, and the like. ‛God has in great wisdom and goodness afforded us a revelation, in which he instructs us in all things he thought proper and convenient for us, and so far as they are so. He considers our occasions, necessities, and capacities; and accommodates himself thereunto. The best here, *know but in part, prophecy but in part;* and, indeed, how should it be otherwise, when God hath revealed things to us but in part.' Let us therefore confine ourselves within the limits God hath set us, be thankful he has revealed so much; be contented that he has revealed no more. The Scripture revelation is sufficient to employ our most diligent enquiries, at the same time that it must bound them. The apostle censures some for *intruding into things they had not seen;* referring to the doctrine of angels, into which it seems they pried and searched, as the word signifies; pretending to know what the Scripture has not taught concerning them. Let us be cautious and modest here; receive the doctrines the Scripture has delivered, and as they are delivered there; believe what the Scripture has told us of this or that doctrine; but not take upon us to know what it has not told us; proceeding in our assertions and decisions, where the Scripture does not go before us, with its light and instruction. This humor has occasioned no small mischief to the church; and indeed is the source of the most of those contentions that have disturbed its peace.

4. When it is said, the Scripture is profitable for doctrine, the least it can intend, is, that it contains all necessary doctrine for us to know and believe, in order to salvation. This may be concluded from its being inspired. Certainly if it be given by inspiration of God, and delivered to the church as a divine rule, it is not a defective and imperfect rule. Nor are we left to infer this, and make it out by reasoning. We find the Scripture often asserting its own sufficiency. Our apostle in this chapter, referring to the Scripture of the Old Testament, at least chiefly, says, they are *able to make wise to salvation*. And if so, they must include every necessary article of faith. And when in the text he affirms, *All Scripture is given by inspiration of God, and is profitable for doctrine*, &c. He adds, *that the man of God may be perfect, thoroughly furnished to all good works*. This, as I observed, is asserted of the Old Testament. And we have the same abundantly proved, with respect to the New. Christ told his disciples, that he had *made known all things*, he had *heard of the Father*. And when he was about to leave them, he assures them, he would *send the spirit, who* should *teach* them *all things, and bring all things* to their *remembrance, whatsoever* he had *said to* them. That the *spirit* should *guide* them *into all truth*. Now it must be considered, that as

the apoftles had a commiffion, being thus furnifhed and inftruƈted to go, and profelyte *all nations*, and *teach them all things whatſoever* their mafter had *commanded* them; fo they committed thefe things to writing, for the future ufe and fervice of the church. So that in the holy Scripture we have all neceffary doƈtrines of religion. What Chrift heard of the Father, that is, concerning the way and method of man's falvation, this he communicated to his apoftles. This the fpirit in them, revived, confirmed, and commented upon. This they preached to the world. The apoftle Paul tells the Ephefians, he had *not ſhunned to declare unto* them *all the council of God*. And this doƈtrine, the whole and entire doƈtrine, they communicated to the world in infpired writings, which I have proved are the very fame, that we, by the good providence of God, have in our poffeffion. The Scripture we enjoy is profitable for doƈtrine, and fufficient for all divine and faving doƈtrine: He that ftudies, underftands, and believes his Bible, and lives according to it, is *wiſe unto ſalvation*.

5. The Scripture is profitable not only for abfolutely neceffary doƈtrines, but it teaches us many other things for our greater improvement and comfort in religion, there is nó book, no chapter, no doƈtrine of the Bible, but what is ufeful in its place, and for its proper end and purpofe. But we muft not fay, that it is all neceffary; that if we had wanted any, we could not have been chriftians; the confequence of which would be, that if we are ignorant of any, we cannot be chriftians. And then how few would be approved? For who is acquainted with every part of the Bible; knows and underftands it all. As in the natural body, there are fome parts more effential, neceffary, and vital; others that have their proper office in the body, and highly ufeful, but not of equal neceffity with

the more noble parts. A man would be maimed, imperfect, and uncomfortable without them; but yet might live without them. Thus it is in the body of Scripture doctrines and revelations. It has its vital and essential points; and these are often inculcated, delivered over and over again, in one place and another; and indeed in a multitude of places: that as all are concerned in them, none that are competently attentive and inquisitive, may miss them, and overlook them. Beside these, there are a great many doctrines in the Bible that serve to enlarge and confirm our faith, to enrich our minds with a treasure of divine truths; to excite and employ our devotion. It delivers many doctrines of eminent use, which yet cannot be said to be absolutely necessary; that tend to adorn and perfect the christian's faith, to assist and conduct him in all the parts of the divine and spiritual life, and it highly concerns us to attend to these.

Some people, I have observed, notwithstanding the veneration they profess for the Bible; content themselves with a very scanty knowledge of it. They learn a short creed, or some of the general abridgments of duty contained in the Scripture; as, that it is required of us that we *do justice, love mercy, and walk humbly with God*: Or that of our Saviour, *Whatsoever* we *would that men should do to us*, we must *do* even *so to them;* that *he who believeth shall be saved*, and the like. These and such like maxims and general propositions they receive; and it is the stock of Scripture knowledge they set up with. All that is necessary, say they, lies in a little compass; is easy and plain; and as they persuade themselves they have sufficiently learned that, they enquire no farther. But these persons should consider that a little knowledge of the doctrines of the Bible is not sufficient, and all that is necessary to those that are capable and have opportunity for understanding more. Fundamentals are different according to the different state of persons. That ignorance which is excusable in one, I question not is destructive in another.

And then, a good measure of diligence and care is requisite to the understanding aright even those few plain and important doctrines of religion that these persons think sufficient. A man, it is granted, may soon learn the propositions that contain the essential doctrines of faith. But the doctrines themselves are not so easily learned as they may imagine. To instance in one of the propositions I mentioned before: *he that believeth shall be saved.* Before we can understand that, we must know what faith is; and in order to this we must be acquainted with the great objects thereof, as God, Christ, the Holy Spirit, the inspired Scriptures: we must know God in his nature, attributes, and relations to us; Christ in his mediation and offices; the Spirit in his work and office; the revelation that God has made of himself in his word. Faith respects all these; and no man can be said to believe that doth not in some degree know what he is to believe; I might add, and upon what grounds. Besides, we must understand the several acts of faith, its properties, and effects; the salvation promised to it; what it is, what it includes: and here is a large field, great scope for our enquiry and study, and which will necessarily lead the christian to a frequent, diligent conversation with his Bible. So that however easy, how few soever, the essential, necessary doctrines of religion are, it is certain they cannot be learned without the Bible, nor without a faithful, and diligent use of it. They do not require indeed a great capacity, and strength of genius in every one to understand them; but they require an humble, teachable disposition, an honest heart, and a diligent serious search, according to every one's ability.

Again, according to the principle the persons, I am now concerned with, act upon, I cannot see but the greatest part of Scripture is rendered useless. If no more be necessary than a few short, general propositions ; why did God indict a book so copious, and full of divine matter ? Commit it as a favor and trust to the care of his church ? if a few short sentences and propositions, be all that are needful and useful, what serves the rest of the Bible for ? why was it given? and how will these persons reconcile their notion with the reverence they pretend to of the holy Scripture and its author.

However, if but a little of the Bible be absolutely necessary ; the rest is highly useful and valuable, and therefore should not be neglected. And it must argue a vile contempt of sacred truths to despise any of them under a pretence they are not necessary ; that we may be christians without them ; be saved without them. We do not act at this rate in secular concerns, are not content with just so much food as is necessary to support life ; with such attire as is barely necessary to answer the end of cloathing ; nor with so much estate as is absolutely necessary to subsist us. And why should we act so in the affairs of religion ? I am afraid this moderation doth not proceed from a nicer head in distinguishing what is most important in sacred things ; but from a distemper of heart that leads us to despise them. David no doubt understood, as well as most others, the essential and necessary doctrines of religion ; had well digested them, and was in full possession of them ; and yet how vigorous was his desire after divine knowledge? how diligently did he pursue the study of divine subjects? that part of sacred revelation, which God had then favored the church with, was his constant meditation and delight. Read cxix Psal, and you will see the temper of that great and good man with respect to the law of God, or that system of revelation the church then had. And if you rightly compare his spirit and your own, I am persuaded you must either censure David or yourselves; and I leave you to consider which is most reasonable. I have staid the longer upon this matter, though it may look like a digression, because I apprehend the discourse seasonable to some, and that there may be occasion for admonition and caution here.

But to return, the Bible, I say, teaches us not only all that is necessary, absolutely necessary, but many other things for our greater improvement and comfort. It gives us an entire system of divine truths. You cannot expect I should enumerate them; though it may be proper to offer a few general hints.

The Scripture delivers to us the great doctrines concerning God; his nature and attributes; his relations to us, and government over us; concerning the trinity of persons in the godhead; concerning providence and the properties of it; that it is constant, sovereign, universal, reaches to all persons and things, and circumstances of things. It delivers to us, the doctrine of the creation: that the world was made, by whom, when, in what time, order, and the like: the state and circumstances of man in innocence; his fall, sentence, and condemnation. It acquaints us with the provision God made for the relief of apostate man, by the promised seed. It teaches us the great doctrines of morality; which we have abridged in the decalouge, commented upon in the Old Testament, and more fully in the New. It acquaints us with the great and glorious transactions of the Mediator; lays before us the plan and scheme of our redemption, as it was accomplished by him; gives us an account of his incarnation, life, doctrine and miracles, his death, resurrection, ascension, and sitting at the right hand of God; with the beneficial offices he sustains and executes. It acquaints us with the new covenant in the last edition of it; its duties and privileges; the office of the Spirit; his gifts, graces, and consolations, with all the sublime and excellent rules and laws delivered to the church, by the Son of God incarnate; and by his ministers. It makes known a future heaven, and in some measure unvails the glories of it. Thus the Scripture is profitable for doctrine. It delivers all the great important doctrines of religion; and that so fully and particularly, that if we receive its instruction; we cannot be ignorant of any thing necessary for us to know.

I would here observe, that these things are contained in several parts of the Bible, and often repeated there. The Old Testament has the same doctrines with the New; that more obscurely, this with greater clearness and explication. Moses speaks of Christ though with a vail on his face. The one was a preparatory dispensation, and included very much the same things with our gospel, but under types, and symbolical representations. In short both had the same religion. But we have it in a more perfect state, and in a clearer light.

I might farther take notice that whatever some may object to the contrary; there is a great deal of method and order in Scripture. It begins with an account of the original of all things; with the state of innocency, the fall of man, the early discovery of God's purpose of grace. It proceeds to acquaint us how the world was peopled; with its degeneracy; with the choice of a family, that of Abraham, which God inclosed as his church; and the progenitors of the Messiah. It gives an account

DISCOURSE XI.

of the particular revelations God made to this family from time to time, gradually; and of the laws and ordinances established among them, of the many additional hints concerning the Messiah; the types and prophecies that insured him till the *fulness of time* came, and *God sent forth his Son made of a woman*. The New Testament begins with his pedigree, genealogy and birth; carries us through all the circumstances of his life, his death and resurrection; gives us the history of the church in the first age of it; its constitution, laws, and administration; and foretells the state thereof in after ages.

In a word, though the doctrine of Scripture be not delivered in the method of our systems, there is a great deal of beauty even in the method of it. And I dare say, whoever will study it with competent helps, and with humility, diligence, and a suitable reverence of God; with that deference a worm owes to infinite wisdom; will find himself not a little instructed and entertained, and his faith confirmed and established: will see cause to admire even the method of Scripture doctrines, which the proud and censorious so much carp at.

You will allow me to make a remark or two under the other head, and I have done, viz.

2. With what advantage the Scripture teaches us these things; it is *profitable for doctrine*: and it is in a special manner so; more so than any other book, exceeds all other revelations; and no wonder, when it is *given by inspiration of God*. It may be expected a book from heaven should appear with bright and distinguishing characters upon it; and that it should teach in a way worthy of its author. And thus doth the holy Scripture. This has been shewn in part already in the foregoing discourses. I shall only touch a few things here just to let you into my meaning.

The Scripture teaches us many doctrine that we could not otherwife have known: as the fall of man, the original of fin, the trinity of divine perfons in the godhead, the incarnation, and whole doctrine of the mediator, the offices of Chrift, and of the fpirit, and indeed every thing that is properly gofpel: the entire method of our intercourfe with God through a redeemer. All this, with all its particulars, we owe to Scripture revelation. And then,

The things that we might otherwife have underftood fomething of, the Scripture teaches more fully and certainly. I might inftance in the creation and whole fcheme of providence. It is known and I took notice of it before; how darkly and confufedly the greateft philofophers talked upon thefe fubjects. Some thought the world was made by chance; others thought it was not made at all, but was eternal. Some denied all providence; others confined it to the heavens, leaving this lower world to its own care and government. And all of them fo diftinguifhed providence and limited it, as to make it a very ufelefs and uncomfortable doctrine at beft, if indeed it imported any thing. I might carry the like remark through a great many other inftances; as the attributes of God, the immortality of the foul, and a future ftate of rewards and punifhments. Thefe fubjects the philofophers, who cultivated natural religion, talked of; but plainly difcovered they knew very little of them. They talked backward and forward, as men in the dark, that could not tell what to fay, or what to believe.

But the Scripture is profitable for doctrine. It comes in here for our relief, and in a few texts fcatters all thefe mifts, and gives a fatisfaction in thefe great points, that in vain we feek for in all the books of the philofophers. ' One of the ancient fathers triumphs on this head in behalf of the Bible.

"By virtue, *says he*, of faith, and the knowledge
"of the holy Scriptures, rustics and mechanics
"exceed the deepest philosophers. Ask a boy
"educated in the christian religion, who made him?
"he will tell you God, which is more than Aristo-
"tle or Democritus would have told. Demand of
"him, why he was made? he will answer to glori-
"fy God. And hardly would Plato or Pythago-
"ras have replied so wisely. Ask him concerning
"his soul, he will tell you, it is immortal, must be
"judged according to the deeds done in the body,
"and be happy or miserable forever. About
"which points such great men as Socrates and Se-
"neca could say nothing positively. So much are
"we beholden to the Bible, and so great the ad-
"vantages we receive by it. It clears difficulties
"in such doctrines, that the greatest men in the
"world, destitute of its light, were puzzled with,
"and delivers the great things of religion to us
"with extraordinary clearness and certainty."

I might add, it teaches with great ease. The philosophers scheme of natural religion, as it was very imperfect, and uncertain to themselves generally; so it was hammered out with much pains and labor. But divine doctrine distills as the dew; and the Scripture comment makes all the rules and principles, they disputed so much, plain and easy.

In short, it teaches with authority. God's spirit is promised to accompany the Scripture revelation. It did so, in some degree, under the former part of it, the Old Testament: It does so more eminently under the New; which is therefore called, *the dispensation of the Spirit*. And his office is not only to reveal the object, but to assist the eye, to remove prejudices, open the heart, enlighten the mind, and carry home divine truths to the consciences of men. And indeed the more glorious effects of Scripture, are owing to the concurrence and influence of the Holy Spirit. The Bible is his book, and allow me to say, he continues to be the teacher of it. O let us wait for, and depend on his instruction. You have heard how much you owe to the Bible, and what use you are to make of it. Be thankful for it, improve it for the purposes it was given; read it often, and diligently acquaint yourselves with all its doctrines; and while you do so, beg for divine instruction, that the Holy Spirit may unvail your eyes, that you *may behold wondrous things out of God's law.*

DISCOURSE XII.

The Scripture shewn to be profitable.

2 Tim. iii. 16.

All Scripture is given by inspiration of God, and is profitable for doctrine, for reproof, for correction, for instruction in righteousness.

TWO things I observed in these words, namely, the divine inspiration, and great usefulness of the Scriptures; and having treated somewhat largely concerning the first of these, I proceeded to consider the other, which I entered upon in my last discourse. The proposition I laid down, is, *that the holy Scriptures, or the inspired writings of the Old and New Testament, are of great use to the church.* Where I proposed to speak of the usefulness of the Scripture in general, and then to shew the use of the several parts thereof. In considering the former point, I told you, I would confine myself to the particulars specified in the text, and make it appear that it is *profitable*, or useful, *for doctrine, for reproof, for correction, for instruction in righteousness.*

I. The Scripture is *profitable for doctrine.* This I have already shewn you, suggesting what doctrines the Scripture teaches, and with what advantage it teaches such doctrines. And now I go on to the next particular.

II. The Scripture is *profitable for reproof,* for

conviction of errors, as I before took notice. The word is understood by many in this place. And, indeed, this does not seem so much a new and another property of the Scripture, as a necessary consequence of the former. As the Scripture is the rule and measure of truth, teaches us all necessary truth; what we are to believe and know in order to salvation; it doth in consequence hereof, detect error, and shew us what we are to reject; what is contrary to this rule, is false; what is beyond it, is superfluous; and what is short of it, is defective.

So that here I have a fit occasion to discourse upon the sufficiency and perfection of the holy Scriptures. But as I have detained you too long in speculation already, I shall not handle the subject in a controversial way, nor trouble you with the arguments or cavils of the church of Rome upon this head, who, as they set up another rule besides, and contrary to the Scriptures; so they advance a great many things highly derogatory and dishonorable thereto. But that I may dispatch what remains in a discourse or two, as is my intention, I shall not enter upon a debate with them; only offer a few remarks for clearing the proposition before us. The Scripture *is profitable for reproof*, or useful to detect and discover errors, doctrinal errors. And,

1. Let me observe, that we must not extend it too far. It is not profitable for reproof and conviction of error in all cases, as in philosophy, politics, and the like. It is no argument that this or that problem in philosophy, this or that theorem in mathematics, is false, because not taught in Scripture; or that this or that system of politics is wrong, because we do not find it there. The reason is, the Scripture was not wrote to instruct us in these things, nor doth it deliver all the doctrines that concern them. The usefulness of Scripture

for reproof, is parallel to its usefulness for doctrine. It extends as far in the one case as in the other; but no further. In short, it teaches the doctrines of religion, and convinces of errors in religion, but not in human sciences.

2. As the Scripture is a divine rule given by inspiration of God, all those doctrines that are contrary thereto, or inconsistent therewith, are condemned by it, they fall under its reproof and censure. We must have recourse *to the law and to the testimony, whoever speaketh not according to this rule, it is because there is no light in them.* The Scripture is the standard of divine doctrines, and whatever is advanced in religion, by whomsoever, or by what authority soever, if it doth not consist therewith, it is to be rejected; it is an error, the Scripture reproves and convicts it as such.

Thus the doctrine of Polytheism, or of many gods, with the worship and service paid them, which overspread the heathen world, is reproved in Scripture, which teaches us that there is but one God. The doctrine of the unitarians, that deny three divine persons in the godhead, is reproved there also. The same may be said of the doctrine of the Pelagians, that deny original sin, contrary to that of the apostle, *by one man sin entered into the world, and death by sin; and so death passed upon all men, for that all have sinned.* And again, *by the offence of one, judgment came upon all men to condemnation.* And *by one man's disobedience, many were made sinners.* The Scripture is profitable for reproof here. If any shall (as many have both formerly, and at this day) question this doctrine on account of the difficulties of it, they stand convicted and reproved by the holy Scripture. Thus God has taught in his word, and we are not to oppose our reasoning to our rule. The doctrine of the Antinomians, that discharge men from any obligation to the moral law, making it void as a rule of life, and substituting, what they call faith, instead of obedience; this also is reproved in Scripture, not only in a few texs, but it is indeed contrary to the scope and design of the whole of it. The doctrine of the Semi-Pelagians, or more rigid Arminians, that deny special grace, the immediate concurrence, operation, and influence of the Holy Spirit, is reproved there likewise. The apostle, I think, understood nothing of their doctrine, if he understood his own motto, as I may call it, *by the grace of God I am what I am.* He adds, *I labored more abundantly than they all; yet not I, but the grace of God which was with me.* And again, *it is God which worketh in you, both to will and to do of his good pleasure.* If it be suggested, that we are reasoning creatures, capable of judging what is right, and chusing what is best. I grant all this: but then, I say, we are sinful, depraved creatures, and stand in need of the grace of God, of supernatural help and influences; this the Scripture teaches, and this, I think, every good man's experience confirms.

I might instance in a multitude of doctrines, that the Romanists brought into the church, and by which they have in the grossest manner corrupted the christian religion; as the doctrine of transubstantiation, expresly confuted by our Saviour, who calls the bread in the sacrament bread several times, even after consecration. They say, no bread remains, but that it is turned into the body of Christ. Now if the Scripture be true, this doctrine is false. So their doctrine concerning worshipping saints and angels, concerning many mediators, to whom they make application for succour and relief, the Scripture reproves, when it commands us to *worship the Lord our God;* telling us, that *him only* must we *serve.* And assures us, there is but *one mediator between God and man, the man Christ Jesus.* I might mention several other doctrines, as the sacrifice of the mass, their doctrine of merit, indulgence, communion in one kind, denying the cup to the laity, and the like. All which are contrary to Scripture, and cannot be received without intrenching upon, and indeed destroying its authority as a rule of faith and practice. And, to mention no more, what shall we say of their Latin service, or praying in an unknown tongue, which is a direct contradiction to what the apostle teaches and enjoins, 1. Cor. xiv. If the apostle was herein inspired, we may be sure these new teachers are far from infallible, whatever they pretend, and that their doctrine is false and erroneous.

In a word, the Scripture being given by inspiration of God, is a sacred rule, a divine standard and measure of doctrines; and whoever would impose upon us any articles of faith, or rules of worship, that cannot bear an examination thereby, or that contradicts our rule, are to be rejected.

3. As the Scripture is a complete and perfect rule, so all doctrines that are besides this rule, and not included in it, come under reproof. It is argument enough against them that they are not taught there. Of this nature are many circumstances of divine doctrines, in which we are apt to add to the word of God, under a pretence of explaining it. I might instance in the free and too bold, as I apprehend it, explications of the doctrine of the trinity, the incarnation, the personal union of the word, with the man Christ Jesus, the reasons and ends of infinite wisdom in the mediation of Christ and attonement made by him, the manner of the spirit's operations upon the souls of men, the nature and several ingredients of future blessedness, the manner and quality of the resurrection of the body. I am mistaken if the Scripture be not profitable for

reproof here, if we would harken to it. It reveals these doctrines, but it doth not reveal all we may be inqisitive to know about them, and if we insert in our explications what the Scripture doth not warrant, insert as necessary parts of these doctrines, we are exposed to the reproof and censure thereof. For if that be a perfect rule, it needs not our supplements, and when we go beyond it in our doctrines we offend as well as when we go contrary to it.

I add, as some transgress by supplying circumstances of divine doctrines, so others by inventing new doctrines, about which the Scripture says nothing at all. In which respect the Romanists are notoriously guilty. They *teach for doctrines the commandments of men.* As in their doctrine concerning the headship and sovereignty of the Pope, infallibility, the seven sacraments, and the rest of the twelve additional articles of their Trent creed. The Scripture reproves these doctrines and convinces them of error. They ask sometimes, where doth the Scripture condemn them? but supposing we could not shew them where they are condemned, as often we can; it is sufficient that it doth not command them, hath not revealed them. *The Scripture is given by inspiration of God, and is profitable for doctrine, for reproof, &c.* The apostle adds, *that the man of God might be perfect, thoroughly furnished to all good works,* Now, how should *the man of God be perfect* by the help of Scripture, if any thing necessary for his knowledge and belief, was wanting therein. It cannot be a rule to us, nor can we conclude it given by inspiration of God, if it doth not teach us all that is necessary to salvation.

4. As the Scripture is a divine and perfect rule, so it is a necessary rule. We are not to receive doctrines contrary to it, nor ingraft doctrines upon

it, and add them thereto; no more must we neglect the doctrines it teaches. *Go forth*, says Christ to his apostles in their commission, *and disciple all nations, teaching them to observe all things whatsoever I have commanded you.* We must not make any thing necessary, which the Scripture has not taught and made necessary; neither must we overlook and dispense with any thing it has taught and made necessary. A great many are reproved here by the authority of the Scripture, as well as in the other particulars mentioned before. We have gross instances of this with reference to the sacraments. Some, you know, deny both of them, water-baptism as they call it, and the Lord's supper? though we have the institution of both in Scripture, and that in most express terms; and have both recommended to us by the constant practice of the apostles and primitive church. Others, though they own the sacraments, yet take a liberty with them to change and model them at pleasure. Thus, when Christ in the institution of his supper delivered the cup as well as the bread, and said, *drink ye all of it*, they with a strange presumption interpose here, and forbid the cup to the laity. These errors the Scripture condemns and reproves. Nor can I see it is consistent with the veneration we owe to it as an inspired writing to assume this liberty to ourselves of dispensing with its rules. If it be a divine revelation we must neither add to it, nor take from it. I may add,

5. The Scripture is profitable for reproof and confutation of practical errors, as well as such as are doctrinal, as we call them, and such as are more speculative. It delivers a great many divine maxims for the government of the hearts and lives of men, and consequently lays open such errors as are contrary thereto. Thus that fatal error of covetousness, or dividing our affections between God

and the creature, is condemned by that paſſage, *thou ſhalt love the Lord thy God with all thy heart, and with all thy ſoul, with all thy might, and with all thy mind;* by that of the apoſtle, *love not the world neither the things that are in the world; for if any man love the world, the love of the Father is not in him.* An indifference and coolneſs in religion, preferring any preſent little intereſt to that of our ſouls, is reproved by that Scripture, that bids us, *ſeek firſt the kingdom of God and his righteouſneſs, and all other things ſhall be added to us,* by that which bids us, *labor not for the meat which periſhes, but for that which endures to everlaſting life.* And by that which cenſures the unreaſonable ſolicitude of Martha, even when ſhe was miniſtering to the Lord Jeſus himſelf, *Martha, Martha, thou art careful and troubled about many things, but one thing is needful.*

There are certain divine principles of wiſdom and religion recommended in the word of God, by which it not only directs us in our choice and conduct, but reproves and cenſures us when we act contrary thereto. O endeavor to attend to the admonition and reproof of the Scripture, bring your hearts under the authority of God's word; believe, chooſe, and act according to the precepts and rules of it. Admit nothing contrary to it as a doctrine of religion, nothing beſides it, nor neglect any thing in it. We are to receive it as a divine, perfect and neceſſary rule; and ſubmit to its reproof in all things as we ſtand obnoxious thereto. It follows,

III. The Scripture is *profitable for correction.* This, as I obſerved before, refers to manners: it corrects the diſorders in the converſation. Concerning which let me obſerve a few things briefly.

It condemns all ſin without exception, and grants no indulgence to any iniquity. *The law of God is perfect, converting the ſoul,* Pſal. xix. 7. It is perfect in this reſpect, as it ſearches out all iniquity, points it out and censures it, and if we harken to its admonitions and teachings, converts the soul from it. Hence it follows, ver. 11. that the Psalmist, speaking of the judgments or statutes of the Lord, adds: *Moreover by them is thy servant warned;* warned of sin, and warned of danger. This property is often ascribed to the holy Scripture, or word of God, particularly in Ps. cxix. *Thy word, saith he, have I hid in my heart, that I might not sin against thee,* ver. 11. And again, ver. 9. *Wherewith shall a young man cleanse his way? by taking heed thereto according to thy word.* The word of God is a sovereign remedy against sin, when it is received with faith and treasured up in the heart, as a governing principle there. It helps to cleanse the way and course both of young and old. The rules and maxims of the moral philosophers were in some things *profitable for correction.* They laid down many excellent rules for the government of the passions; but with such a mixture and alloy of sinful tolerations, that their best systems were altogether insufficient to accomplish a thorough reformation. Pride and vanity were virtues with them; revenge allowed, when a provocation was given and an injury received; and some very gross vices were pleaded for by many of them, as I had occasion to observe before. But the correction, the holy Scripture is profitable for, is more entire and complete. It extends to every corruption, and is levelled against every sin, against the whole old man. It teaches to *deny all ungodliness and worldly lusts,* Tit. ii. 12.

Farther, it strikes at the root of sin in the heart and affections. Never did any institution of religion proceed with so much purity and divine authority, as the Scripture does in this respect. *Beware that there be not a thought in thy wicked heart,* says the law of God, Deut. xv. 9. It lays restraints upon the inward defires, the firſt motions of the heart, difcerns and condemns fin there. Hence, according to the doctrine of our Saviour, rafh anger is murder, and a wanton glance adultery, Matt. v. 22, 28. It purifies the fountain, and mends the principles from whence our actions flow.

Again, it furnifhes the ſtrongeſt motives againſt fin, oppofes it with all the force of argument and perfuafion. It reprefents, how much it is againſt our prefent intereſt, our peace and comfort, our honor, and even our profit in moſt cafes; and how utterly inconfiſtent with our future and eternal intereſt. *He that finneth againſt God wrongeth his own foul. The wages of fin is death,* everlaſting death. In fhort, *the wrath of God is revealed from heaven* in Scripture *againſt all ungodlineſs of men.* It fets a flaming fword, as it were, to difcourage finners, and throws terrors and deaths in their way. No book in the world doth or can appear againſt fin with fo much authority as the Bible doth. Did we believe its reports and confider its threatnings in their utmoſt extent, view fin in its connection with death and hell, according to the Scripture account of the matter, we ſhould not make fo light a thing of it, as we are many times too apt to do: the very appearance of it would give us a fort of horror. In a word, the account the Scripture gives of fin, of its original, nature, tendency, prefent miferies and torments, and future punifhments is a very proper means to keep us from it. Herein it is *profitable for correction.*

I will only add, that the Scripture *is profitable for correction,* as it is attended with an inward efficacy and force. *The word of God is quick and powerful, and fharper than any two-edged fword, piercing even to the dividing afunder of foul and fpirit, and of the joints and marrow, and is a difcerner of the thoughts and intents of the heart.* It not only speaks against sin and condemns it, but ransacks the heart, penetrates the conscience, and rises against it with a majesty and authority that is peculiar to itself. Good men find this divine efficacy in the word. A text of Scripture will have more force to check and controul an unruly passion, than an hundred smooth harrangues of human composure. David experienced this sovereignty and mark of divinity in the Scriptures, and celebrates it throughout Psalm cxix, and in other places. And sometimes it pleases God to give it the like efficacy towards sinners. *The weapons of our warfare,* says the apostle, *are not carnal, but mighty through God.* The word of God discovers vice and dethrones it. It has done so in a thousand instances. Particularly at the first preaching of the gospel, which made one of the fathers glory of it in this respect. Shew me a passionate man, *says he*, and with a few words of God I will render him mild as a lamb, and the like with respect to the unclean, &c. Thus *profitable* is the Scripture for correction and reformation.

IV. The only head that remains to be touched is, that it is *profitable for instruction in righteousness*, that is, for instruction in all the parts of our duty towards God, towards our neighbor, and towards ourselves. It teaches us, as is said more particularly of the gospel, *to live soberly, righteously, and godly in this present world.* We have there rules of perfect holiness set before us, directing how to govern our appetites, senses, desires, affections, and passions; rules of temperance and chastity in thought, speech, and behaviour; of meekness, humility, and the like: rules of justice towards men, in all our commerce or intercourse with them. Our Saviour comprises the substance of all in two maxims, that we *love our neighbor as ourselves,* and that *whatever we would that men should do unto us, we should do even so unto them.* These are enlarged and commented upon in a variety of particulars, all tending to exclude injuries, oppression, and every thing that is hurtful, and to establish an exact decorum and equity in our mutual correspondence. And with equal beauty and perfection, it prescribes to us the scheme and method of converse with God. It directs us to *love* him *with all* our *hearts,* to *fear* him, to *trust* him, to *delight* in him, to *worship* him, to devote ourselves to him, to choose him and rest in him, as the only felicity and happiness of our souls, to make him the Alpha and Omega, the first and the last, the beginning and the end of our actions, and indeed the all in all.

This is the general use of the holy Scripture. It was *given by inspiration of God, and is profitable* for these high and noble purposes, *for doctrine, for reproof, for correction, for instruction in righteousness.*

A reflection or two upon what has been said shall conclude this point. And,

1. We may see hence the vanity of that plea the church of Rome advances in behalf of oral tradition. They own with us, that the Scripture is given by inspiration of God; but they pretend, that there are several divine doctrines, necessary truths not contained in the Scripture, which the apostles delivered to the churches by word of mouth. To this we have to answer, that it is not to be supposed God should indite a book, for the use of his church, and that book should be defective in any necessary point. That the Scripture every where witnesses to its own perfection. The text tells us, it *is given by inspiration of God, and is profitable for doctrine, &c. that the man of God may be perfect, thoroughly furnished unto all good works.* And in the foregoing verse, it is said, that the holy *Scriptures are able to make wise to salvation.* Farther, we have

express caution against these unwritten traditions. Thus in the Old Testament, *You shall not add to the word that I command you, neither shall you diminish from it.* And we find the whole Bible has a seal set to it, is shut up with this awful saying, that *if any man shall add unto these things, God shall add unto him the plagues written in this book. And if any man shall take away from the words of this book, God shall take away his part out of the book of life.* It is an inspired book, *is profitable for doctrine, for reproof,* and for all the purposes of religion, is able to make the man of God, the minister, the christian, perfect; perfect in faith, and perfect in all duties and offices. God has not left it to the caprice and humor of men to add to it, and change it at pleasure. If he had, it would be no complete rule, and would soon cease to be any rule at all. I might subjoin a multitude of arguments against this sorry pretence of the Romanists, was this a place to debate that matter. I shall only take notice farther, that the tradition they boast of has always disgraced itself, and proved itself an imposture. Their most early traditions have the most palpable marks of fable in them. As that of Papias concerning the Millennium; that of the primitive church, which occasioned so scandalous a division among them, relating to the time of keeping Easter. Had tradition been any good rule, surely we might have expected it would have run clear, and not been so muddy at the very fountain head, as we find it was.

Nor has their tradition only failed them, but betrayed them into a direct opposition to the holy Scripture. For upon this stock they have grafted several doctrines contrary to the inspired writings, as purgatory, indulgences, their Latin service, the sacrifice of the mass, &c. Not to say, that they have among them traditions inconsistent one with another. In one age they establish doctrines, as sacred and divine, by virtue of a pretended tradition, which in another age are condemned as heresy and loaded with an anathema: as, the eating of things strangled, and blood, the immaculate conception of the virgin Mary, and the like.

But I shall not enlarge on these things. You have your Bible, christians, and there you have a perfect rule of faith and practice. Study that, and you will find it profitable for you in all respects. It will *make the man of God perfect*. If you neglect that, you will lose yourself in the labyrinth of human fictions, and neither know what to believe, nor what to practice.

2. Is the *Scripture given by inspiration of God, and profitable for doctrine, for reproof, for correction, and for instruction in righteousness;* let us use it for all these purposes, receive its doctrines, receive all its doctrines, acquaint yourselves with what it teaches, and resign to its authority therein. This is a matter of no small importance, and will require no small industry and humility. Do not object against any of the doctrines of the Bible, because they do not seem to stand upon a level with your understanding. Whatever God teaches is true; and it is enough, should be enough to us, that he teaches it, whatever difficulties there may seem to be in it. We should learn to reverence infinite wisdom, and submit our narrow faculties to the conduct thereof. And then endeavor to receive all the doctrines of Scripture. It *is profitable for doctrine*, and there is no doctrine of the Scripture that we should esteem unprofitable. Such a temper is profane, and includes in it a sort of blasphemy against the divine wisdom. God knows better than we do what is necessary and good for us, and wherein he has condescended to be a teacher, we should be cheerful and humble learners. Study therefore your Bible, and endeavor to be complete in all the will of God.

DISCOURSE XII.

Whatever God speaks, we should be ready to hear. All *Scripture is profitable for doctrine*, and it very ill becomes us to neglect the greatest part of it under a pretence that it is not necessary.

Farther, use it *for reproof*. Reject every doctrine contrary to it, and that is against what it doth reveal, and every thing that is besides and above what it doth reveal. Let it be the measure and boundary of your faith. Endeavor to come up to it, and not go beyond it.

Use it *for correction*. Mind its admonitions, and allow yourselves in no thoughts, desires, words or acts the Scripture sets a mark upon as sinful or unlawful. This is to be christians indeed. And according to our care and exactness herein, we are more or less christians. Hearken to it, and let it correct every sinful motion and disorder in the soul, and every wry step in your course of life.

Once more, use it for your *instruction in righteousness*. As it prescribes to you in every part of your conversation, teaches you how to conduct yourselves in your whole converse in the world. To which purpose, it will be of exceeding advantage to you, if you collected and wrote down the principal rules that refer thereto both under this and the former head. For instance, the Scripture rules for correcting the iniquity of our thoughts, desires affections and actions, and the rules for the conduct of all these, write down the most pertinent Scriptures that refer thereto. Frequently peruse them, commit them to your memories. Set them before you as matter of daily duty. Look upon it as your great business to practice according to these rules. Endeavor to be good proficients herein. And in proportion to your attainments in this matter, so is your stature in religion. O that I could prevail with you to do this. Nothing in the world would be more your interest. And indeed without some attention and care this way, you lose the main advantage of the Bible; you only profess religion in a general confused manner; all you hear, and all you read in the Scripture will turn to little account. Take this method, christians. God has given you a book full of glorious excellencies. Use it for its proper end. And consider for your encouragement, that if you believe it, study it, live it, it will be in every respect profitable to you: it will be *a light to your feet, and a lamp to your paths;* will support you under your difficulties, fortify you against temptations, guide you in your duties, and carry you safe to heaven. Therefore make the holy, inspired Scripture your rule, live under its conduct and influence, and you shall die with its comforts.

II. I come now to consider the usefulness of the several parts of Scripture. It is *all profitable*, says the text, every book and part of the Bible has its use, and is of service to the church. What its usefulness is, I am now to enquire. The subject is copious, and of no small importance; and yet I must very much pass it over. Though I own it was one thing I had principally in view in the choice of my text. If nothing prevent, I may endeavor the satisfaction of those that desire it another way, and upon other occasions. What I have before me, is, to shew the usefulness of the several parts of the Bible. Concerning which I shall, first premise a few things, and then speak to the subject more directly in another discourse.

I shall at present only premise a few things concerning this matter. As,

1. That we have great reason to conclude that all Scripture is profitable and useful, in that it is given by inspiration of God. Since he is the author of it, we may suppose it is useful and pertinent, even though there were some parts and passa-

ges of it that we could not understand. A wise man will not write a book of no use and value; much less, the only wise God. We find the prophet celebrating God in his common providence, as instructing the husbandman in the management of his affairs, and inferring, that there must be wisdom in the management since it was from God. *This cometh forth from the Lord of Hosts, who is wonderful in council, and excellent in working.* What cometh forth from God, who is wonderful in council, and excellent in working, cannot be worthless and insignificant. And thus doth the Scripture, all Scripture, every part of it. And yet,

2. Though all Scripture is profitable, it is not alike so, nor all useful for the same purposes. Some part of Scripture was written for one, other parts for a different end. It is not all useful for one and the same end: but all excellent and useful for its proper end. As in the work of creation God pronounced all things good, very good: not that every creature or species of creatures have the same degree of excellency, or answer the same purpose; but all are good in their place, and answer the particular end God designed them to serve. There is a mighty difference between a man and a brute, a seraph or an insect; and yet both are good. So it is with respect to the holy Scripture, it is all divine, excellent, and good; but it is not all alike important and excellent, nor doth every part of it afford the like instruction. I cannot therefore understand the humor of some devout men, that when they have read a chapter of the Bible, think themselves obliged to enquire what they can find of Christ there. We have a great deal of Christ in the Bible, but not in every chapter of it. And we should not look for him where he is not to be found. The Scripture is useful for many purposes. Some parts for one, some for another purpose. And we

then make the truest and best use of it when we refer every part to its proper purpose, what God intended in it.

3. Let me observe, that the Bible was not delivered at once, as a complete system of divinity, and body of religion, but contains various, successive revelations, gradually made, as seemed good to infinite wisdom. *God, who at sundry times, and in diverse manners, spake to the fathers by the prophets, at last spake to us by his Son.*

Was I to illustrate this, I should give you a short view of the different dispensations of religion, the different states of revelation in the several ages and periods thereof; as, under Adam, Noah, Abraham, Moses, and the Son of God incarnate. Adam had a revelation from God both before his fall and after, a plan of religion delivered to him, upon which his intercourse and acceptance with God was founded. This was continued among the patriarchs with enlargements at several times; as under Noah and Abraham. And under Moses a new peculiar dispensation, a theocracy was introduced; not to set aside any former revelations, laws, and methods of religion; but to serve the wise design of providence at that time, and to prepare for a fuller and more glorious state of religion under Christ. These several dispensations make up the Bible, and the survey of them would shew you the progress of divine revelation, the usefulness thereof, and, I reckon, would direct to the best method of explaining it. But this is what I must not now pretend to.

4. Every revelation God made to the world was designed for the use of the church, not only in the age when it was given, but in all future ages. The apostle tells us, that the *things which happened* to the *Jews* were *written for our admonition, on whom the ends of the world are come.* Indeed the church of

God, strictly speaking, is but one body, subsisting at different times, and in different forms. First in its infancy, then in a more improved state, till it was brought to a state of maturity under the gospel, and at last shall be brought to a state of full perfection in heaven. Now the revelation vouchsafed to the church, at any time, was for the service of the whole body at all times. When any new revelation was given forth, it did not make void any thing that went before, but supposed it was built upon it, and was supplemental to it, except in the case of the gospels vacating the typical and temporary dispensation of Moses. And consequently those that live under the last dispensation of religion, when revelation is finished and compleated are distinguished by special advantages, which is our case that enjoy the gospel. We have the benefit of all foregoing revelations, the light, instruction, admonition, and examples of former ages, the whole treasure of the holy inspired Scripture, all the glories and excellencies of the Bible are committed to us and lodged in our hands. Let us be thankful for our privileges, and endeavor to improve them. If every part of Scripture be profitable and useful, to be sure the entire Scripture must be so. But I must leave what remains on this subject to another opportunity.

DISCOURSE XIII.

The usefulness of the several parts of Scripture.

2 TIM. iii. 16.

All Scripture is given by inspiration of God, and is profitable for doctrine, for reproof, for correction, for instruction in righteousness.

I PROCEED now to enquire into the particular usefulness of the several parts of Scripture. It cannot be expected, that I should examine the usefulness of every book. That would require a volume rather than a sermon. Nor can I go through the several dispensations of religion and distinct periods of revelation, and give an account of those parts of the Bible that fall under each. How much advantages soever there might be in such a method, I must here decline it. All I can do, is to make some observations upon the Bible, as divided into the several subjects of it. And I shall consider it under the following heads, as containing histories, prophecies, ceremonies, matters of morality, and doctrines.

1. Let us consider the historical part of the Bible. This is highly useful to the church. A great deal of it you know is wrote by way of history, and there is scarce any history in the Scripture but what affords abundance of divine instruction. Reflect a little on the first book in the Bible, Genesis. A few chapters of that sacred history are of greater

use to the church than any large volumes of common writers. I will only take notice of three or four things of which we have an account in this book, and, I may add, in no other book in the world, but what borrows from it. As

1. The creation of the world. The philosophers, that wanted the conduct of revelation, were utterly at a loss and in confusion about this matter, and run into wild and absurd hypotheses, as I had occasion to observe before. Some of the best of them, that believed and acknowledged one God, supreme and eternal, and that he was infinitely good, thought his goodness must necessarily communicate itself, and thereupon concluded it did so from eternity, and consequently that the world must be eternal. Now this history removes all scruples here, and satisfies all questions in a few words, tells us the world was made, made in time, and made by God, by a free, and yet powerful act of his will. *Let there be,* saith God, *and there was.* His *fiat* or sovereign word brought all things into being. This clears all difficulties, and at the same time has such a grandeur and majesty in it, that Longinus allows it to be an instance of the true sublime. *In the beginning God created the heaven and the earth, and God said, let there be light, and there was light. Let there be a firmament, &c. and it was so.* With how much majesty is this spoken, and how fit to convey to the mind an idea of God's greatness, his infinite greatness. *By the word of the Lord were the heavens made, and all the hosts thereof by the breath of his mouth.* How glorious a being is the author of this amazing work? how justly may we say of him as Job does, *I know that thou canst do every thing.*

We have here also an account of the degeneracy of the human nature, that lapse or fall of mankind: a point about which all the philosophers were puzzled and nonplused. They found in themselves, and observed in the world, a strange disorder in the human mind, that the passions and affections were become headstrong and impetuous, and that reason was not strong enough to curb and master them. And hence some of the wisest of them inferred, that reason had been some how weakened and hurt, and thereby lost the dominion they supposed it originally had; though how to account for it they knew not. But this the Scripture history clears up. It tells us that man fell, and how he came to fall. In which it represents two things among others that suggest matter of admiration and caution to us, viz. The danger of pride and sensuality, the devil making use of the body of a seraph, or bright shining serpent, insinuated to the woman, that if they eat they should be advanced to an higher station, be as God in wisdom and independency, and thus flattered their ambition and took with them, and then the fruit appeared pleasant to the eye, as well as desirable to make wise; both their rational and sensitive appetites were flattered at once, and this hurried them into the transgression, and occasioned their fall. See here the danger of pride, and of pleasing the senses. It undid man in paradise, man in innocency, and continues the great danger of mankind to this day. Another thing suggested in this history of the fall is, the shame and cowardise consequent upon sin. No sooner had Adam sinned, but he hid himself among the trees of the garden. Before the presence of God was his life and his joy, but now he runs away from it. *I heard thy voice,* says he, *and hid myself, for I was afraid because I was naked.* Sin had stripped him of his innocency and his ornaments, and now the presence and voice of his maker fills him with terror. And this is the natural fruit of sin. However it appears during the temptation, when the pleasure is over and the mask is thrown off, it issues in bitterness, shame and horror. It is said of our first parents, that *the eyes of them both were opened and they saw that they were naked*, they saw their guilt and were filled with confusion upon it. And thus it still is with sinners when conscience is awakened.

I might take notice of the institution of marriage between one man and one woman, in opposition to polygamy. That practice which generally obtained in the world, and is attended with so much mischief, stands here condemned by the original appointment of God. And of the institution of the sabbath, or a seventh day of sacred rest and religion, after six days of labor. This was set apart by the example, benediction, and command of God immediately upon finishing the creation. It was instituted before the ceremonial law was in being, and consequently, is of a moral nature, and of perpetual obligation.

I might add the original of the soul. It was not created with the body, and out of the dust, as the body was, but created immediately by God, *He breathed into him the breath of life, and man became a living soul.* Plainly intimating, that it is distinct from the body, and consequently can subsist without it.

Now these are points of such high importance, that the little order and religion there is among mankind very much depends on them ; and they are wholly owing to the history of the Bible. The three first chapters of it give more satisfaction in these, and the like great principles and doctrines of religion, than all the philosophers in the world, that are destitute of Scripture light.

I mention these things, not only as an argument of the great worth and usefulness of the Scripture ; but with design they may recommend and endear the Bible to you. Read the first, second, and third of Genesis, and there you may learn, what you may travel the world round in quest of, and never learn unless you find a Bible, or converse with those that have lighted their lamps at this torch.

And how valuable an hint is that, Gen. iii. 15. concerning the promised seed. When God was proceeding against the several criminals, in the midst of that more awful scene he discovers the purposes of his grace, *The seed of the woman*, says he, *shall bruise the serpent's head*. The purport of which is, that an eminent and extraordinary person, who should be the seed of the woman alone, should appear in the world, destroy Satan's kingdom, rescue and deliver fallen man. This the apostle four thousand years after refers to and owns the accomplishment of ; *When the fulness of time was come, God sent forth his Son made of a woman, made under the law, to redeem them that were under the law, that we might receive the adoption of sons.* A glorious sentence ! of more consequence to mankind than all the victories and triumphs recorded by the Greek and Roman historians.

I might take notice of the universal deluge, the destruction of Sodom and Gomorrha, with many particulars relating to the patriarchs and their religion, in which we have not only several wonderful and important events described, with a certainty and clearness, that in vain we seek for in other histories ; but the divine providence set forth in the government of the world, the divine attributes displayed, his knowledge, wisdom, justice, holiness, and hatred of sin manifested in such a manner as is most fit to strike the minds of men and beget in them a fear and reverence of God, and lay the foundation of divine worship and religion.

You see I can only give you a taste of things, and of the great usefulness of the Scripture under this head. Should I pursue the subject, even in this superficial manner, it would require many sermons.

I will therefore only observe farther, that besides the instruction the sacred history affords from the matter of it, its several narratives are generally so many confirmations of its predictions and prophecies. The history of Abraham and his posterity, for instance, their sojourning in Egypt, their deliverance from thence, their settling in Goshen, their apostacies, captivities, and restoration afterwards, are the fulfilling of the promise made to Abraham, of the prophecies uttered by Jacob when he was leaving the world, and the predictions of Moses. So that this part of the Bible, which indeed is a considerable part of the Old Testament, is exceeding useful to the church; it shews the divine providence governing the world in a sovereign manner, shews the divine knowledge in all events, and the truth of all his promises, and confirms our faith in the belief of the Scripture.

As to the New Testament history, it is full of glorious events; your own knowledge will furnish you with the particulars, and a little reflection convince you of the usefulness of them. It relates the incarnation, life, miracles, sufferings, crucifixion, resurrection and ascension of the Son of God; the pouring out of the spirit, the ministry of the apostles, and the surprising success that attended it, and herein lays the foundation of the christian faith and religion, strictly such, and at the same time confirms and establishes a great part of the Old Testament.

But I must not enlarge, you see by these hints, that the history of Scripture is profitable. Was it not besides my present purpose, I might shew it was *profitable for doctrine, for reproof, for correction, and for instruction in righteousness.* But I rather choose to take notice of its usefulness more in general.

2. As the historical, so the prophetical part of

the Bible is profitable and useful. You must not expect, and I dare say, do not desire, I should make a collection of the prophecies, and go through every one of them, to shew their meaning and usefulness. But as you have a good deal of the Bible in this strain, it cannot be improper, I am sure not impertinent to the subject, to touch upon the general uses of the prophecies.

And it may be affirmed of them, as is said of all Scripture in the text, that they are *profitable for doctrine, for reproof, for correction, for instruction in righteousness.* The prophets though they insisted much upon predictions, denouncing judgments, foretelling deliverances, salvations and the like; yet they did not confine themselves to these subjects. They were a sort of divine and extraordinary preachers to the people; one design of whose ministry was to preserve a sense of providence and religion among them; accordingly, we find their sermons full of instruction, admonition and reproof.

They give us noble ideas of God and providence, and call upon those to whom they were sent, to consider their ways, to repent and reform. The Jews had a large body of ceremonial laws, in which they were very much employed, and we find they were apt wholly to place their religion therein. This the prophets take notice of, and frequently censure, calling them to mind the weightier matters of the moral law, justice, mercy, and the love of God, letting them know all their ritual services would signify nothing, whilst they neglected the great moral duties of religion. We have a multitude of instances to this purpose in the discourses of the prophets; particularly, Isa. xiii. 14. *Bring no more vain oblations,* saith he, in the name of God, *incense is an abomination to me, the new moons and sabbaths, the calling of assemblies I cannot away with;*

it is iniquity even the solemn meeting ; your new moons and your appointed feasts my soul hateth, they are a trouble to me, I am weary to bear them. He adds, ver. 16. *Wash you, make you clean, put away the evil of your doings from before mine eyes, cease to do evil, learn to do well, seek judgment, relieve the oppressed, judge the fatherless, plead for the widow.*

And in the like strain many of their discourses run. Their office, in short, was to guard and reform religion, to teach just notions of God and providence, and to inculcate the important duties of the moral law. And for this purpose their writings are of lasting and constant use. The sermons of the prophets concern us, as well as the people to whom they were immediately sent, and we shall find no small advantage in a diligent perusal of them. Here we meet with the most lively representations of God in his nature, attributes, providence, and government. What an awful description is that of the Supreme Being, Isa. xl. 12, 15, 16. *Who hath measured the waters in the hollow of his hand? meted out the heaven with the span, comprehended the dust of the earth in a measure, weighed the mountains in scales, and the hills in a balance ? behold the nations are as a drop of a bucket, and are counted as the small dust of the balance: behold, he taketh up the Isles as a very little thing. Lebanon itself is not sufficient to burn, nor the beasts thereof sufficient for a burnt offering. All nations before him are as nothing, and they are counted to him as less than nothing and vanity.* And how majestic and yet comfortable is that representation of him, Isa. lvii. 15. *Thus saith the high and lofty One, that inhabiteth eternity, whose name is holy, I dwell in the high and holy place; with him also, that is of a contrite and humble spirit, to revive the spirit of the humble, and to revive the hearts of the contrite ones.*

And as we are furnished with suitable apprehen-

DISCOURSE XIII. 333

sions of God, so we are instructed in our duty in an admirable manner; our duty towards God, our neighbor, and ourselves. Micha sums up all in a few words, chap. vi. 8. *What doth the Lord thy God require of thee, but to do justly, to love mercy, and to walk humbly with thy God.* These great branches of our religion are here enlarged upon, the contrary sins pointed out in a way that is very proper to awe the consciences and strike the passions. Glorious is the advantage of the prophetic writings in this respect. Nor, it may be, can the man of God, the believer, the christian be better furnished any where for every good work than from hence. This part of Scripture is profitable, and it is well worth our while to study it diligently, to acquaint ourselves with the doctrine, the language, style and phrase of the prophets, hereby our minds will be enriched with excellent divine notions, armed against sin, and not a little assisted in devotion.

Again, the prophetic part of Scripture, as consisting in predictions, is of mighty use, particularly, as it manifests the infinite knowledge of God, and his sovereign providence over the world. We find there a multitude of surprising events at a vast distance foretold, which accordingly took place in the very time and manner signified in the prophecy. Now this shews, that all things, even future, as well as present *are naked and open to the eyes of him with whom we have to do;* that known unto the Lord are all his works from the beginning unto the end; that his eyes run to and fro throughout the earth, conducting with a steady sovereign hand all things to such issues, as he has foreseen and appointed. With what sovereignty, how becoming is that spoken, Isa. xlvi. 9, 10. *I am God, and there is none like me; declaring the end from the beginning, and from ancient times the things that are not yet done, saying my council shall stand, and I will do all my pleasure*. And when we see this done in the accomplishment of numerous prophecies, it serves to give us high and exalted thoughts of the Deity, a reverence of his providence, and should teach us to commit all affairs with faith, dependance and full resignation into his hands, the affair of the church, and our own particular affairs.

Farther, the prophetic part of Scripture is useful as it affords a strong argument against sin, and unto obedience. Some of the prophecies are declarations of God's free and gracious purposes towards his people in this or that event; many of them denunciations of judgments against transgressors; or assurances of deliverance and salvation to the penitent or obedient. Now, if we consider these prophecies aright, consider the design of them and their accomplishment, we cannot but look upon them as so many standing testimonies against sin; of the evil and danger of it, of the good of obedience, and the like. He has destroyed kingdoms, families, persons, for their iniquities, he has published his purpose before hand, and at last accomplished it in terrible vengeance. Stand in awe, O my soul, and sin not, says the believer. This use we should make of the prophecies of Scripture, and shall make of them, if we read them with attention, understanding and faith.

I might add, though I cannot stay to enlarge upon it, that the prophecies were to those that first received them, insurances of future events. They brought distant things as it were before their eyes, and into present view. And consequently, were a trial and exercise of their faith, their hope and trust, and a direction in many particulars of duty.

Besides, the prophecies accomplished, and so viewed by the church in after-ages, are a glorious confirmation of faith. They shew us not only that the Lord is God, *Elohim*, governor of the world, that he rules in the armies of heaven, and among the inhabitants of the earth; but they shew us also the truth of his word, the infpiration and authority of thofe that were employed to deliver it. We cannot have a greater evidence of the divine commiffion of the penmen of Scripture than the fpirit of prophecy that attended them; efpecially when we fee their predictions come to pafs. No man could fay and declare fuch things fo long before hand, unlefs God was with him. So that when we are reading the prophecies we are reading the credentials of thofe divine minifters from whom we receive our religion, who have fpoken to us by the word of the Lord, and in the name of the Lord. On which account, as well as others, we fhould exceedingly value them, and delight in them.

Once more, the prophecies are highly ufeful as they are a pledge and earneft of the accomplifhment of fuch events as are yet future and waited for. *There failed not ought of any good thing,* fays Jofhua, *which the Lord had fpoken to the houfe of Ifrael, all came to pafs.* Now when we fee all come to pafs which God hath fpoken, in fo many inftances heretofore, we may reft fecure that all which yet remains to be fulfilled, fhall come to pafs alfo. God fpeaks of our deliverance by Chrift four thoufand years before the event, and this wonderful thing was accordingly made good. He has fpoken of the revolutions of kingdoms and nations, their rife and fall long before they were in the world, and all has come to pafs. Hence our faith may argue and conclude, even with a fort of triumph, that all God's promifes and predictions in behalf of his church, fhall have their accomplifhment in the time and manner he has appointed. For inftance, antichrift fhall be deftroyed, all rule, authority, and power be put down under the feet of the Lord Jefus; Chrift's little flock fhall be preferved, and receive a kingdom ; the dead shall be raised incorruptible, and the living saints changed. This a christian may look for, and conclude upon with as much assurance as if he had heard the voice of the archangel, the trump of God, and saw the Lord Jesus descend from heaven in his Schekina and glory. So many wonderful things foretold in Scripture have been already wonderfully accomplished, that we cannot reasonably question any thing that remains to be accomplished. No, heaven and earth shall pass away, but not one iota of the divine word shall fail. O be thankful for every part of Scripture, particularly for the prophetic part of it, and when you peruse these glorious testimonies of God's wisdom, knowledge, power and providence, endeavor to make a useful improvement thereof: celebrating and adoring God in what is past, depending upon him for what is future ; remembering that of the apostle, *Whatsoever things were written aforetime, were written for our learning, that we through patience, and comfort of the Scriptures might have hope.*

3. The ceremonial or ritual part of the Bible, is of use to the church. The Old Testament religion was much concerned in these things, in sacrifices, washings, meats, drinks, the observation of days, &c. and so large a portion of the Bible is employed about them, that it cannot but be worth while for a man that hath a reverence for it, to enquire into the meaning of such institutions, *All Scripture is profitable*, and surely this. Otherwise it had not been given *by inspiration of God*. What the use and profit of it is, I am briefly to represent. You cannot expect I should descend to particulars, and consider the several rites of the Levitical law. All that comes within the compass of my design, is, to offer a few general remarks upon the subject.

The ceremonial or ritual part of Scripture, was

of use to the church, when the particulars thereof were in force, as they were the matter of their obedience; tokens of God's sovereignty and dominion over them, and expressions of their subjection. Though neither we, nor they that received the ceremonial services, should be able to account for all of them, the will and appointment of God was reason enough to determine the obedience of those that were enjoined to observe them. The church was then in its non-age and infancy. And as parents sometimes prescribe to their children such and such services, the design and end of which they do not understand, why might not God deal thus with his people at that time: and as the compliance of children in this case is acceptable and pleasing, and of use to train them up to subjection, so, no question, it was in these institutions of religion. Though the Jews knew not what God intended by some of the ordinances established among them, they knew they were the laws and prescriptions of their sovereign and wise creator and governor, and consequently that their obedience would be acceptable to him and profitable to themselves. And if we consider the ceremonial law in this view, it is still useful even to us, as it affords us an important admonition and instruction, viz. to be subject to the will of God in all things, even when we do not clearly apprehend his particular design therein. There was a great deal of this in Abraham's faith and obedience; for which he is so justly celebrated, and mentioned with so much honor in the Scriptures, and in the church of God to this day. *Take now thy son,* says God to him, *thy only son, Isaac, whom thou lovest, and get thee into the land of Moriah, and offer him there for a burnt-offering, upon one of the mountains which I will tell thee of.* Strange! what can this mean? was he not the son of his hopes? the root of that glorious seed in whom all the families of the earth should be blessed? and must he now be cut off by the hands of his own father? what then would become of the promise? and yet Abraham makes no objection, but addresses himself to this difficult amazing duty; and for this he had an honor put upon him, by which he has been distinguished ever since. God has a right to command, and it is our place to obey. And though his laws carry with them generally sufficient evidence of their reasonableness, and we are convinced of their benificial, comfortable tendency; yet when it is otherwise, as it might be often in the case of the Jews, his will is reason enough. And indeed the more we are disposed even to an implicit subjection to the will of God, the more excellency there is in our faith and obedience. And when we find a people so long trained up in such a course of obedience, it should teach us to bow our understandings and wills to the divine revelation and will, even when we have not a clear understanding of the intention of the lawgiver.

Again, the ceremonies and ritual services of the law were useful to the church, as they were a means of absolution, and of obtaining pardon of sin. There were indeed some exceptions; presumptuous sinners had not the indulgence of a sacrifice, were not allowed to bring their offerings, but were to be cut off. Nor could the blood of bulls and goats take away sin, purge the conscience, and make the comers thereunto perfect. They were not in themselves of sufficient efficacy for this purpose. But, as they were of divine appointment, and had a respect to the atonement of the Son of God, they were tokens and assurances of God's pardoning mercy and grace to them, and to the penitent and sincere available, no doubt, for their real absolution.

Farther, they were useful as types of the Messiah;

as so many sensible assurances of the accomplishment of the promises concerning redemption by Christ; *The seed of the woman shall bruise the serpent's head.* This was the foundation of all that friendly intercourse between God and man after the apostacy. Now every sacrifice they brought and slew, was a sort of a representation of this great and glorious event. And hence, it may be, he is called the *Lamb slain from the foundation of the world.* He died, as it were, in a figure, and hung upon the cross as often as the sacrifice died and was laid upon the altar. So that here was a glorious institution to exhibit Christ. And when we look back upon these ancient records, as we see the venerable monuments of divine wisdom; so comparing them with the event, we have our faith not a little confirmed and established. Christ was to come, to die, to justify us by his blood. The Jews had the earnest of this in their hands, in their sacrifices and other services: and many hundred years after we have the thing itself; have seen the salvation of God. The same rites and shadows that directed their faith to Christ, confirm our faith in him.

And then, these rites and ceremonies were designed as a distinction of that nation, to which they were given, from the rest of the world. God chose Abraham, and called him from among idolators to be the head of a peculiar people. His family was to be the seat of God's worship in a special manner: of them the Messiah was to be born, and that his birth and descent might certainly be known, it pleased God to inclose this family and people, and by peculiar laws and rites to divide between them and the rest of mankind. They were not to intermix with the world about them, intermarry with other nations, worship, or freely converse with them.

And to keep up this diſtinction, the law of ceremonies was *a wall of partition*, as the apoſtle calls it, Epheſ. ii. 14. which was broken down when Chriſt came, the end, one end, of the incloſure being attained. So that whilſt we peruſe this part of Scripture, we may entertain ourſelves with the contemplation of this great deſign of divine wiſdom and grace towards the church. God ſet apart that people and ſet a mark upon them from whom the redeemer was to deſcend. He was to be the ſon of Abraham, of the tribe of Judah, of the family of David; and thus the Scripture aſſures us he was. *It is evident*, ſays the apoſtle, *our Lord ſprung out of Judah.* It was a matter of the laſt importance to know the Meſſiah when he appeared, that this was he that was to come, and that we muſt not look for another. Now that this might be manifeſt to the church, God thus ſeparated the family and nation from whence he ſprung.

Again, this part of Scripture revelation is uſeful, as it tends to give us high notions and an auguſt idea of Chriſt and the chriſtian religion. All this glorious apparatus, all the laws and ſervices of that diſpenſation, which were the ſtudy and employment of the church for ſo many hundred years, were deſigned to introduce the goſpel ſtate. And with what ſolemnity do they introduce it! the incarnation of Chriſt, his ſacrifice, and our redemption by him, are among the chief of the works of God; the greateſt myſteries of his grace. And methinks, when it is conſidered that the glory of the Jewiſh temple, and all the ſervices thereof, all the ceremonies and rites of a law revealed from heaven, referred to this, and were to iſſue and terminate in it; and indeed were contrived on purpoſe to give notice of the goſpel, to proclaim Chriſt, and to uſher him into the world; when we conſider this, and ſeriouſly reflect upon the providence of God therein,

DISCOURSE XIII.

we cannot but infer the glory of the gospel state. Let us make this use of that part of the Bible, that to many appears useless. We may judge of a building in some measure, by the greatness of the scaffolding. Certainly such a vast preparation was never designed to introduce a thing of little moment.

I add, this part of revelation and state of religion is of use, as it may administer cause of thankfulness to us, that we are under an higher and more excellent dispensation. The apostle often speaks of the Jewish law in terms of great diminution. He calls the ceremonies thereof, the *elements of this world*, *beggarly elements*, speaks of the law as *a school-master to bring us to Christ*; as insufficient; *a shadow of good things to come*, and represents the services and laborious performances of it, as a yoke, that neither the Jews of that age, nor their *fathers were able to bear*. Now among other advantages we have by the levitical law, this is one, the exciting our thankfulness for the more manly, spiritual, rational religion of the gospel. Not but that there was an excellency in their religion, and a reverence due to it, as it was the appointment of God. No doubt, serious upright persons enjoyed acceptance with God, and intercourse with him in it. But that glory was nothing, compared with the glory of the gospel which excells. Now when we find in what low services, comparitively, their religion consisted, we should rejoice and be thankful that we are called to more noble and divine work.

Once more, the ceremonies and rites of Moses were useful to the church at that time, and are still useful to us, as they contain many moral documents and instructions. I might go through a great number of particulars, and at large illustrate this; but can only hint at things in a general way. Circumcision refers to the inward mortification of sin, and was designed to teach the necessity of it. *Circumcise*, says Moses, *the foreskin of your hearts, and be no more stiff-necked*. And the apostle plainly intimates the same, when he makes the true *circumcision of the heart, in the spirit, and not in the letter, whose praise is not of men, but of God*. Their various washings and purgations preached to them their defilement by sin, and the necessity of inward and outward sanctification. Their thank offerings were an acknowledgment of their dependance on God, teaching them and us how reasonable it is we should daily own our daily benefactor. Every offering for sin represented the evil and demerit of it, and was a signal that the sinner deserved to die, that his life was forfeited to the justice of God. Accordingly, there was a confession of sin constantly accompanied such sacrifices, by which the necessity of repentance and reformation was urged upon the offenders, and was owned by them. In short, the law was an emblem of the gospel and the religion thereof. It held forth in a figure the death and sacrifice of Christ, the purity, holiness, and obedience of christians, their separation from the world, and from all uncleanness. All the sacrifices that referred to sin, all the laws about uncleanness, and means appointed for purifying, were public significations of the necessity of holiness and purity both in heart and life. And we should now read them as so many admonitions thereto, and cannot better improve them, than by a thorough compliance with the rules of the gospel, which are the moral of those institutions. In this sense, *Christ is the end of the law for righteousness to every one that believeth*.

Thus it appears, that even this part of Scripture, which may be looked upon of least value and use, and that some have very rudely objected against as absurd, and unworthy of a divine lawgiver; that this is profitable to the church. It answered wise

DISCOURSE XIII.

and great purposes at the time it was given, and was in force, and continues still highly useful. Let me add,

4. The moral parts of Scripture are profitable. By which, I mean, those books that concern the direction of our faith, the furnishing us with good principles, and especially that concern the conduct of our lives.

The book of Job represents a surprising scene of providence, full of great and excellent instruction. Particularly it represents the malice and industry of Satan in prosecuting his designs against us; how watchful he is to gain and improve occasions to our hurt. This appears in his management against Job. He waits and seeks for a commission against him, which he no sooner obtains, than he improves it to its utmost extent, and as far as he could go. Here we are taught what the apostle long after takes notice of, that *we wrestle not against flesh and blood, but against principalities, against powers, against the rulers of the darkness of this world, against spiritual wickedness in high places.*

This book also represents the safety of good men under the divine protection. *Hast thou not made an hedge about him,* says Satan concerning Job, *and about his house, and about all that he has on every side?* Our families, persons, I may add, our names, reputations, our bodies, and souls, all are in the hands of God: neither men nor devils can hurt us without permission from heaven. This we learn from that ancient book, it may be, the most ancient in the world, written many thousand years ago. And how comfortable is it to find it there,? Good men are still encircled by the same divine arm. God makes *an hedge about them, and about all that they have. Lord, how are they increased that trouble me?* says David, *many there be which say of my soul, there is no help for him in God.* He adds, *But thou,*

O Lord, art a shield for me, my glory, and the lifter up of my head. And says our Saviour, *fear not, the hairs of your head are all numbered.*

Again, It represents the sovereignty of divine providence in the government of the world, and in the disposal of the affairs of particular persons. The devil could do nothing against Job without a commission from heaven. And that which I would here more especially observe, is, that this upright, good, and perfect Man, as he is called, is by the providence of God brought under a course of exercises and trials, a severity of discipline, the greatest that, it may be, any ever met with. God is righteous in all his works, but he is sovereign in all his providences; and we should learn by this instance, to submit to him an any, in all his rebukes how heavy soever. He has wise ends in all he doth; will be faithful to his word, and take care of his upright, sincere servants. But this does not exempt them from trials and sufferings. When you see Job, so eminent and holy a man, pass through such a series of afflictions, amazing afflictions; learn to reverence the divine sovereignty. Do not think much at any of the trials that may be your lot and whatever God doth, own his authority; *Be still, and know that he is God.*

Farther, this book represents to us an example of patience truly glorious, not without flaws and imperfections, but yet truly excellent and glorious. God smote Job, lies in the dust, and when he was stripped of all, submits and adores. *The Lord hath given,* says he, *the Lord hath taken, blessed be the name of the Lord.* And even after a most dismal train of calamities, it is remarked of him, that *in all this Job sinned not, nor charged God foolishly.* We have heard of the patience of Job, as the apostle expresses it. We here read the history of it, and we

DISCOURSE XIII.

should set it before us for our admonition in our adversities.

And then, this divine book represents God in his sovereignty, majesty and greatness, and that with more life and advantage than perhaps any other book in the world. It gives us such a view of him in his works and providence, and his excellencies, and should awe and impress our minds, and silence our complaints. Even Job forgot himself, and was too bold, till God came forth and displayed his glory; and this reduced and humbled him. *I have heard of thee by the hearing of the ear*, says he, *but now mine eye seeth thee, wherefore I abhor myself, and repent in dust and ashes.*

Here is represented the weakness and infirmity of good men, even the best of men. It was one design of God in this dispensation towards Job, to exercise and manifest the integrity, and uprightness of his servant, to confute Satan, and shew that Job was not an hypocrite, as he insinuated. But though Job shewed his integrity he shewed also his infirmity; though Satan was baffled, Job was humbled. And, it may be, had he stood his ground under such shocking trials, without discovering any frailties, it might have been more dangerous to him than his miscarriages. God hereby humbled him, taught him dependance, let him see his meanness and insufficiency. Good men, the greatest men in this life can go through no difficult work, no difficult trials, but it will many ways appear they are men, but men, sinful, frail creatures. And though they are owned, accepted and honored of God, it is still upon terms of humility and repentance, and in such a way as leaves the success of all, and the glory of all, to God, and to the praise of his grace.

I add, here is represented the care of God towards his faithful servants, and the comfortable issue of all their trials and conflicts. We do not,

I grant, always see this at present, and in the manner, as in Job's case: But *it shall be well with the righteous;* God will not forsake the soul that seeks him. *Mark the perfect man, and behold the upright man, for the end of that man is peace.* God will support persons of this character under all their burdens, dangers and fears; and in due time and manner deliver them. *No temptation shall befall them but what is common to men,* and God *will with the temptation make a way to escape, that they may be able to bear it.* They may be obscured for a time, *persecuted, but not forsaken; cast down, not destroyed. No, their righteousness shall go forth as brightness, and their salvation as a lamp that burneth.* Job was conducted through a scene of sorrows and calamities, that even his three pious and wise friends, thought it would have been his ruin. But God meant not so. He had designs of kindness towards him, and he knew how to deliver the righteous out of temptation, and to save him in it, and under it. All good men may expect the like superintendency of divine providence, and supply of divine grace. If your hearts be upright with God, as Job's was, God will be your defence as he was his. He will restrain your enemies, pardon your infirmities, though it is fit he should shew you them, and humble you for them, and at last be your salvation.

In short, there are many glorious lessons in this book, a scene of providence that one may peruse and contemplate with exceeding great advantage. O learn to understand the use of your Bible, and of the several parts thereof, and I am confident, you will never think meanly of it.

I might illustrate my point by the like reflections on the book of Psalms, and the rest, but have not time. One great advantage of that book is, that it describes the various states, postures and frames of devout souls. It sometimes shows you the good man low and down, full of fears and despondency, lying in sackcloth, and watering his couch with his tears. And then rising out of this state, putting off his sable, and girded with gladness. It is indeed a glorious treasure of devotion, as well as a directory for life. And I am satisfied it would be well worth our while, not only frequently to read it, but to commit as much as we can of it to our memories. This is what many of the primitive christians have done, and others since, with great advantage. If this does not turn to better account than furnishing, I might say debauching your minds with such sorry trash as plays and romances generally, at least, are, I am utterly mistaken. The one is the food, solace, and entertainment of divine minds; what shall I say of the other? but that they are husks for swine to feed upon.

 The book of Solomon's Proverbs and Ecclesiastes have a great deal of excellency in them, and are highly useful. The one is a lively description of the vanity of present enjoyments, and the other affords the most admirable maxims of wisdom. Many of the discourses of the moral philosophers, as Plutarch, Seneca, Epictetus, and Antonine, are justly celebrated in the world. And indeed they want not their excellencies, great excellencies. But here we have not only higher strains of wisdom, but the precepts of it delivered with more certainty and authority. The philosophers were, many of them, wise observers of human nature. They knew its infirmities in some measure, and knew how to prescribe for a cure. But the writers of these divine books were conducted by the author of nature, that perfectly understands man, knows what there is in him; and therefore their maxims are recommended to us, not only by the intrinsic excellency

Y y

of them, but by this diftinguifhing circumftance, that they are all true, infallibly true. And we may be fure, as they are true, fo they are pertinent to the cafes they refer to, and by the bleffing of God fhall be effectual to thofe that receive and apply them.

Let thefe hints recommend the Bible to you, and the feveral parts thereof. If there be fome things in it, we do not well underftand, we fhould not cavil againft the whole on that account, but fay as the philofopher did when he had read the writings of a man of fame, *what I underftand is excellent,* fays he, *and I prefume what I underftand not is fo too.* Certainly this reverence is due to God, whofe book the Bible is, due to infinite wifdom. Acquaint yourfelves with the feveral parts of Scripture, though you fhould be moft converfant in thofe parts that are moft ufeful. Befides the knowledge we fhall thereby gain, we may expect the divine prefence and bleffing with us when thus employed. When we are diligently and ferioufly reading our Bible, we are on holy ground, as I may fay, and confequently, may hope, God will be with us, fhining in upon our minds, drawing our affections to himfelf, fhedding abroad his love in our hearts, pouring out his fpirit upon us, more and more fanctifying us by his word. O endeavour that the *word of God* may *dwell richly in you,* remembering the character of the bleffed man, that *his delight is in the law of the Lord, and in his law does he meditate day and night.*

2 TIM. iii. 16.

All Scripture is given by inspiration of God, and is profitable for doctrine, for reproof, for correction, for instruction in righteousness.

I COME now to the application of the many discourses I have given you, and shall dispatch what I further design in a single short discourse, and so conclude the subject. And here I shall only offer a few practical reflections. As,

I. If the Scripture be given by inspiration of God, it ought certainly to be treated with great esteem and reverence among men. As it is the word of God, indited by the Holy Spirit, a book sent from heaven; it challenges a peculiar regard, and should be distinguished from all human writings. This every one must allow that believes it to be inspired. Let us therefore be careful to treat this holy book in a suitable manner. The apostle expresses his great satisfaction concerning the Thessalonians, that they received the gospel preached to them, *not as the word of men, but as it is in truth, the word of God.* Let it appear that we thus receive the Bible, receive it as a divine revelation, particularly by our reverence of it. If it be asked, how must we shew our reverence? I answer,

1. By a diligent attentive study of it. The ex-

cellency and usefulness of the matter of Scripture demands this of us. But what I now insist upon, is the consideration of the author. It is from God, and therefore a special reverence and esteem is due to it; which we should manifest by our attention thereto, and careful perusal of it.

All writings are commonly received or neglected, according to the qualifications or characters of their authors. Nothing is expected from books published by ignorant, trifling, or mercenary writers, and therefore such are generally despised by men of sense; while the productions of authors of a different character, of better learning, capacity, and more integrity, are proportionably better received and esteemed, and more pains is taken to find out their designs, to take in their schemes, and to understand their arguments and way of reasoning. They are read with application, and not only once, but often, it may be, according to the character of the author, or the opinion of the book itself. And in the writings of those great men, that hold the first rank, every sentence and line, and almost every word, is thought to have its weight, and not to be set down carelessly, without a meaning or necessary use. With what pains and diligence have men weighed the particular words, and even the situation of them, in the composures of Plato, Tully, Homer, Virgil, Horace, Terence, and others. Now if the reputation of wisdom and skill in human books, thus commands our reverence and attention; what is due to the book of God? I am not comparing the contents of these writings, the important design and tendency of them; but merely considering the authors, and I know you will allow me to say, that if we reverence this or that piece of antiquity for the name of its author, no book challenges so much reverence from us as the Bible.

Well then, let us shew our regard to it by the pains we take in it. Many have spent their time, and the greatest part of their lives in criticisms upon some of the heathen authors, settling the reading and marking the beauties thereof. How will this diligence reproach us, if we neglect a book that can claim the only Wise God for its author?

2. We should shew our esteem and reverence for the Bible, by a ready and universal submission to its authority, even in such things as we cannot fully understand, nor are able to account for. We are apt to pay a sort of implicit veneration to the writings of great men. Much more should we do it to the word of God. As he is infinitely wise, holy, just, and good; we may be sure he is neither deceived himself, nor can deceive us; that nothing comes from him that is false, nothing that is weak, nothing that is imperfect; that all he has revealed is true, pertinent, wise, and beneficial; proper to answer the end he had in it. And accordingly we should entertain every part of his revelation with reverence, knowing from whence it proceeds. The want of this principle has ruined the faith and religion of multitudes. They object against this or that in the Bible, because it does not agree with their reason, that is, with their prejudices and fancies; as if infinite wisdom must be measured and governed by our narrow and short views. Thus some find fault with the rites and ceremonies of the Mosaical law. They cannot understand the rationale of them and are ready to call them absurd; thus measuring God by themselves. Others object to the great doctrine of atonement by the sacrifice of the Son of God and saving sinners through his mediation. This they cannot understand and therefore will not believe. Some from the same vanity neglect the sacraments of the New Testament. They cannot see of what advantage it is to

eat a bit of bread and drink a little wine; what this can contribute to the improvement of the mind. And it is well if some do not encourage themselves in gross sins to the like consideration. Surely, say they, God will not damn a man for taking a little pleasure out of the way. What harm can there be in gratifying the inclinations God has given us in instances agreeable thereto? they cannot see any injury to the Supreme Being herein, nor believe he will ever punish offences of this kind so severely as is pretended. But this is not to reverence the Bible and treat it as a revelation from God, but to set up our own foolish fancies in opposition thereto, to make ourselves God's counsellors, and even correctors. And indeed the same principle would carry us to censure any of the works of nature, and find fault with them as not reasonable, not well contrived, not well placed. And thus vain men profanely change place with God, get upon his throne and bring him to the bar. Infinite patience! that bears with such worms, and does not frown them into hell in a moment. If the Scripture is given by inspiration of God, what we have to do, is to make all our reasonings submit to it. Though we do not understand some of its prescriptions, it is enough they are from heaven. That should determine our faith, and silence all cavils. We know not what it is to be creatures till it is thus with us, much less christians.

3. Shew your reverence and esteem of the Bible by a firm adherence to it, and to the religion it prescribes, whatever temptation you may have to the contrary. It is the most valuable treasure God has entrusted us with, and we should resolve by his grace, that no terrors, nor death, shall wrest it out of our hands. The zeal of the primitive christians in this respect, is well known. They would rather submit to any tortures, than give up their Bibles

at the demand of their enemies. And those among them that through fear complied, and would quit their Bibles to save their lives, were looked upon as infamous, and rejected as unworthy of the communion of the christian church. They were called *traditores*, such as delivered up their Bibles, a name of the utmost reproach and scandal among them. Eusebius mentions one Marinus, a military man, who being discovered to be a christian, was ordered to determine in three hours, whether he would relinquish his office, or his profession. In the mean time, Theobectus, bishop of Cæsaria, comes to him and shewed him a sword, the badge of his office, and a Bible, the repository of the christian faith, and bid him chuse which of the two he would have, for he must not keep both; upon which he presently chose the Bible, and was crowned with martyrdom. Should we ever meet with the like trial, we should make the like choice. We do not treat the Bible worthy its original, if it be not dearer to us than our lives. Nor should we part with the religion of the Bible, and give it up in complaisance to the fashions of the age, or humors of those we converse with. The Bible is from heaven: believe it, live by it, whatever measures others are pleased to walk by. Let this prescribe the rules of your conversation, your religious worship, and of all your actions, and be not ashamed of the religion of the Bible, because it may be not agreeable to the customs and modes that may obtain in the world. A christian must herein be resolute. The holy Scriptures are his rule, and the reverence he has for them, must carry him through all discouragements and opposition.

4. Shew your esteem and reverence of the Bible by the manner in which you read it and converse with it. Even an outward reverence is due. People should put their bodies into a decent posture

when they read the word of God, and especially should be careful to possess their minds with reverence and devotion. Consider it as a divine book, that God is speaking to you, and that you are conversing with him in it, and accordingly behave yourselves becoming such a presence, with a due deference and respect to so high an authority. Again,

5. Whenever you mention any part of Scripture, let it be with suitable reverence and esteem. Do not make the Bible a common-place book of jests, as the manner of some is, quoting a text of Scripture to divert their company, which favours not a little of profaneness, and indeed is like Belshazzar's carousing in the consecrating vessels of the temple. Guard against all libertinism of this kind. Remember the Bible is a sacred book, and do not prostitute it to so low a purpose as serving a jest, borrowing its phrases to adorn a piece of wit, or promote mirth and laughter. Farther,

6. Shew your esteem of the Bible, by your delight in it. David was famous for this, as is known to all that know any thing of his character: *O how I love thy law*, says he, *it is my meditation all the day.* And he himself makes it the character of the pious man, that *he delights in the law of the Lord, and therein* doth *he meditate day and night*. And as this is due from us, in consideration that God is the author of this book, so it is due on the account of the excellency and usefulness of it, the tendency it has to improve and enrich the mind. It is observable, that after the just now mentioned character of the good man, That *his delight is in the law of the Lord, &c.* it follows, *He shall be like a tree planted by the rivers of water, that bringeth forth his fruit in season; his leaf also shall not wither, and whatsoever he doth shall prosper*. He is ordinarily the best christian that is most conversant in his Bible, and that takes most pains in the survey of it. He is most

likely to be fruitful, thoroughly furnished to all good works. When the word of God dwells richly in you, you will be able to admonish one another, and to abound in the fruits of righteousness. Once more,

7. Show your esteem of the Bible, by propagating the knowledge of it, and especially in your families and among your children. This has been the way of good people in all ages. *Timothy from a child knew the holy Scriptures*, as the apostle observes in the verse before my text. The Jews were commanded *to teach the words of their law to their children*, to teach them *diligently unto them, and talk of them when they sat in their houses, when they walked by the way, when they lay down, and when they rose up.* And however defective they were in many other things, they expressed an extraordinary zeal in this matter. Their children were trained up in the knowledge of their law, even from their infancy; and were so expert therein, that Josephus tells us, they knew every thing in it as fully as their own names. And the like care was shewn by the primitive christians. Nor indeed can it be said, that we treat the Bible as the word of God, and pay a veneration to it as such, if we neglect to teach it to our children. The humor of the age, as it runs counter to almost every thing that favors of true religion, so it has given an odd turn to the education of young persons. One of the early fathers of the church gives directions in one of his epistles for the education of a young lady of a noble christian family, he advises, that as soon as she was capable she should learn the Psalms, Proverbs and Ecclesiastes; next he taught the four gospels, to have them always in her hands; then get the Acts and Epistles by heart, and after that pass to the reading of the Prophets. How little there is of this in the present discipline of most families, I am ashamed to say. Music, dancing,

play-books, and some light and vain accomplishments, are the main things attended to now in education; which no doubt is one great cause of that degeneracy we so much complain of in the profession of the christian religion. Certainly, we should either disown this book or make another use of it than commonly we do.

But I must not enlarge farther on this point. We should treat the Bible with reverence, and shew our regard to it in the ways I have mentioned. This is my first reflection.

II. Is the *Scripture given by inspiration of God, and profitable* to the church, as you have heard; what reason have we to be thankful for so great a favor and privilege as the holy Bible, and that we have it in our possession. I shall briefly mention a few circumstances, as so many motives to gratitude to the good providence of God on the account of this enjoyment.

You should be thankful not only that you have a divine revelation, but have it entire. It is accounted among the distinguishing privileges of the Jews, that they had *the oracles of God committed* to them. How much greater must our advantages be who have not only their Scripture, but a great addition thereto; have a fuller and clearer light, have the darkness and difficulties of that dispensation they were under removed, and enjoy the entire system of divine doctrines and laws. Certainly if they were so highly favored, the members of the christian church are much more favored; and consequently, under greater engagements to gratitude and adoration. We should be thankful that this glorious book has been preserved and brought down to us safe and uncorrupt. I before took notice of the rage of enemies against it, and what attempts have been made to destroy it, by Antiochus Epiphanes under the Old Testament, by Dioclesian, and Julian, persecuting heathen emperors afterwards. And yet God has watched over this invaluable treasure, and lodged it safe in our hands. O rejoice in his providence, and give him the glory of his own work.

Again, we should be thankful that we have it in our own tongue: a privilege, you know, our forefathers did not enjoy. Some that pretended to be the keepers of this treasure, locked it up from the people, and took away the key of knowledge. This glorious light was by this means put under a bushel. Whereas now it shines among us in all its lustre. The heavenly manna falls about our tent door, and how much are we indebted to God for this. The churches of Germany in the beginning of the reformation had an anniversary thanksgiving, which they called, *the feast of the translation of the Bible*. We should be often devoutly acknowledging the goodness of God herein, and celebrating the bounty of his providence in this instance of it.

I might add, that we have reason to be thankful we have the Bible not only translated, but printed. About three hundred years ago, when printing was first found out, a copy thereof, tolerably written in vellum, would cost at least a hundred pounds sterling, whereas by the invention of printing, the Scriptures are put into every one's hand; the poorest christian needs not want a Bible, if he has but an heart to make use of it.

Again, we should be thankful that we have so many helps to understand the Bible; as by constant ministry of the word, a variety of useful commentaries, and other good books written upon the Scripture and the particular doctrines thereof.

Once more, we ought to consider, that the providence of God in all these instances, has distinguished us from others. To us are *committed the oracles of God*. These are the peculiar glory of the christian church. *He hath shewn his word unto Jacob; his statutes and his judgments unto Israel; he hath not dealt so with any nation; as for his judgments they have not known them.* This may be said of us christians, we have the Bible, which the greatest part of the world are utter strangers to. Let us mind the admonition of the Psalmist hereupon, *Praise ye the Lord*, says he. Surely we ought to praise him on this account, to speak and live his praises. I may add, if we do not praise him in higher strains, and live in a better manner than those that know not God, than the unhappy *people that sit in darkness, and in the region and shadow of death*, great will be our guilt, and great our condemnation.

III. If the Bible be the word of God, and *all Scripture is given by divine inspiration*, how dangerous must it be to reject it? it is not only great folly, as it deprives us of the light, instruction, and comfort of the Scripture, and all the glorious advantages of so excellent a revelation; but it is a flagrant instance of presumption and sin, a high contempt of the goodness of God, and of his wisdom and authority. On which account the case of our deists must be exceedingly deplorable. Indeed they seem to put themselves out of the way of salvation. *If they hear not Moses and the prophets*, says the parable, *neither will they be persuaded though one rose from the dead*: Intimating, that such as will not receive the instruction the Scripture affords, and comply with the way of salvation therein proposed, will yield to no other means of conviction, though never so sensible and glaring, and consequently must remain in their obstinacy, and perish in their sin. Natural reason, the light and conduct of conscience, and any other methods these persons may pretend to value and prefer, will, I am afraid, be found insufficient. *If they will not believe Moses and the prophets,* Christ and his apostles; it would seem there is no help for them.

And there is this aggravation in the unbelief of our modern deists, who live in a christian nation, which the mere negative faith of the heathens has not; that the one never had the Bible laid before them: the other reject it, and all the strong evidence with which it comes attested, and with which it offers itself unto them. I leave them to the righteous judgment of God. But to me their case appears exceedingly hazardous; and, it may be, their guilt approaches the nearest to the sin against the Holy Ghost of any, men now adays are capable of committing. O let us not *refuse him that speaketh from heaven. If he that despised Moses's law, died without mercy, under two or three witnesses: of how much sorer punishment shall he be thought worthy, who hath trodden under foot the Son of God, counted the blood of the covenant an unholy thing, and done despite unto the spirit of grace. If the word spoken by angels was stedfast, and every transgression and disobedience received a just recompence of reward, how shall we escape if we neglect so great salvation; which at first began to be spoken by the Lord, and was confirmed to us by them that heard him, God also bearing them witness with signs and wonders, and with divers miracles and gifts of the Holy Ghost.* To have the Bible among us, and yet contemn and despise it, is so great a sin, that, I think, I may say, how strange soever the expression may look, a wise man would rather choose to be annihilated, than live and die under the guilt of it. Hereupon I add,

IV. As the Scripture is the word of God, a revelation from heaven, and of such eminent use to the church, as you have heard, let us endeavor to make a right use of it; to read it, study it, and converse with it, in a suitable serious manner. And here several directions might be offered. But I shall only stay to mention a few very briefly: and indeed it is less necessary to enlarge, it being a subject I have often touched upon and spoke to.

Endeavour to understand the holy Scripture. It is to no purpose that *God has wrote to us the great things of his law*, if they have been and are, *strange things* to us. Ignorance will seal up the Bible from us as effectually, as if it was in an unknown Tongue. Take care therefore to understand your Bibles. To which purpose sermons and commentaries are useful, a diligent perusal of the Bible, a comparing one Scripture with another is useful, the laying aside prejudices, and preconceived opinions, being willing any thing should be true, and receiving every thing as true, that you have reason to think is taught there; this is useful and necessary. Prayer and dependence on God, and his Spirit for illumination is also highly useful; in the use of these and such like means, study the Bible; often put the question to yourselves, that Philip did to the Ethiopian Eunuch, *Understandest thou what thou readest?* Acts viii. 30. and never think you read to purpose, unless in some measure you understand what you read.

Read it with faith. *The word preached*, says the apostle, *did not profit them, not being mixed with faith in them that heard it*, Heb. iv. 2. Unbelief will strip the word of all its power and efficacy, and leave it a dead letter, and altogether useless. The apostle rejoices in behalf of the Thessalonians, when he observed they *mixed the word with faith*. *For this cause*, says he, in the place I have already cited, *we thank God without ceasing, because when ye received the word of God which ye heard of us, ye received it not as the word of men, but as it is in truth, the word of God, which effectually worketh also in you that believe.* It works effectually in them that believe, and in them only. O endeavor for faith, a divine faith. Receive the Scripture as the word of God; give a firm assent to it; look upon its rules as divine, its promises and threatnings as faithful and true; and entertain it with the same regard, as if God manifested himself in a visible manner, or spake to you with an audible voice. And remember that your faith, if it be of the right kind, will always produce obedience. He that believes the wages of sin is death, will be afraid of sin, and if he is not, it is a sufficient argument he doth not believe. I may apply here what is said of the servants of Pharaoh, when the plague of hail was threatned, *That those of them who feared the word of the Lord, made his servants and his cattle flee into the houses; but he that regarded not the word of the Lord, left his servants and cattle in the field.* If we regard and believe the word of God, we shall comply with its advice, avoid the paths it marks out as leading to destruction; attend to the duties it prescribes, and walk in the way it directs to, as the way of life and salvation. And if we do not do this, it is certain we do not believe. And consequently, like Pharaoh's servants shall fall under the judgment God has threatened. O beg for faith, and that God would increase your faith. Look upon every thing in the Bible as true, certain and infallible, being assured, that not one iota thereof shall fall to the ground till all be fulfilled. If we did this it would have a glorious effect upon us. What manner of persons should we then be in all holy conversation and Godliness.

Read and study with humility, as modest learners, prepare to receive all the instruction there offered. Have a care of a proud, carping, cavilling humor; and if you meet with any thing that seems to you uncouth, do not censure and despise it, because you do not understand it. Instead of that, maintain a reverence of God upon your minds, and wait for his illumination, praying with David, *Open thou mine eyes, that I may behold wondrous things out of thy law,* Pfal. cxix. 18. Nothing is more neceſſary than this. *He reſiſts the proud, but gives grace, yea more grace, to the humble. The meek will he guide in judgment, the meek will he teach his way.*

And then apply what you read; bring it home to yourſelves, compare yourſelves with the rules of the word, and endeavor to conform yourſelves thereto. The Scripture is profitable for correction, correct yourſelves by it; for inſtance, ſuch Scriptures as concern the government of the tongue, the thoughts, deſires and affections; ſuch Scriptures as preſcribe to you in your reſpective relations; and for the management of your callings and converſe. Your doctrines whether ſecret, private, or public; lay them before you, meaſure, and correct yourſelves by them. And I am ſatisfied it would be well worth while to have a liſt of ſuch Scriptures drawn up by you for conſtant uſe.

Laſtly, beg the aſſiſtance of God's holy Spirit in order to the ſtudying and improving your Bibles. The Bible is the book of the Spirit, over which he preſides, and which he teaches. Many have thought they have got the beſt of their knowledge of religion and of the Scriptures upon their knees. And I do not think there is any enthuſiaſm in that method of ſtudy, accompanied with the uſe of other proper means. But I leave theſe things to your ſerious retired thoughts, without further enlargment: and leave you to the divine conduct and bleſſing.

FINIS.

SUBSCRIBERS' NAMES.

A.
DAVID ABEEL, New-Brunswick.
Peter Addis, Middlesex.
Enoha Ayers, Bernardstown.
John Ayers, Roxbury.

B.
Rev. Isaac Blauvelt, New-Rochelle.
John Bray, New-Brunswick.
William Brackstone, do.
John A. Boyd, Princeton.
Jacob Bogart, Somerset, 2 Copies.
Daniel Brinsley, do.
Evert Brokaw, do.
George Boyce, Jun. Middlesex.
Isaac Brokaw, do.
Mary Boyce, do.
Cornelius Barrickloe, do.
Jane Boyce, do.
Nathaniel Ballard, Hillsborough.
James Bergen, Ricefield.
John Baird, Griggstown.
John Barcalo, Cross-Roads.
David Brokaw, Millstone.
———— Bailey, Flemingtown, 10 Copies.
Thomas Blauvelt, Clarkstown.
Ellenor Blauvelt. do.
John J. Blauvelt, do.
Isaac Blauvelt, do.

C.
Rev. Henry Cook, Woodbridge.
Rev. John Corneliuson, Bergen.
Rev. Ira Condict, New-Brunswick.
John Clark, do.
Benjamin Cook, do.
James Crommelin, do.
Francis Covenhoven, do.
James Cooper, do. 10 Copies.
George Clark, do.
Abijah Coon, do.

SUBSCRIBERS' NAMES.

Jonathan Combs, Jun. North-Brunswick.
Lewis Craig, Monmouth.
Harmanus Cortelyou, Middlesex.
David Coriell, Jun. do.
Abraham Coriell, do.
David Coriell, Sen. do.
Eliza Culberston, do.
Henry Cock, do.
Tunis Covert, Somerset.
Elitha Coriell, do.
Peter Covenhoven, Millstone.
Cornelius Clawson, do.
Cornelius Covenhoven, do.
John Cortelyou, Ten Mile Run.
Moses I. Cantine, Princeton.
David Comfort, do.
Israel Crane, do.
Conant Cone, do.
Wm. H. Cunningham, do.
John Covert, Essex.
Gersham Cock, Hillsborough.
Edward Cock do.
Jonathan Conkling, Roxbury.
Samuel Harker Caldwell, do.
Henry Canada, Sourland.

D.

Rev. John Duryea, Raritan, 10 Copies.
John Dey, Middlesex.
Samuel Drake, do.
John Deare, do.
Peter Ditmas, Millstone.
Henry Disbrow, do.
George Dunn, do.
Abraham Ditmars, do.
George Duryea, Bushwick, Long-Island.
Nicholas Dubois, Hillsborough.
William P. Deare, New-Brunswick.
Isaac Davis, Somerset.
William Daily, do.
Peter B. Dumont, do.
Peter A. Dumont, do.
Jeremiah Drake, Roxbury.
Nehemiah Dye, Cranberry.
Peter Dereemer, Spotswood.

SUBSCRIBERS' NAMES.

Robert Dayton, Bernardstown.
Insley Daglish,   do.
Peter Davidson,   do.

E.

Luke Edgerton, Amwell, 20 Copies.
Wilhelmus Eltinge, Princeton.
Cornelius Ervine, Middlebrook.
John Earhart, Spotswood.

F.

Rev. Robert Finley, Princeton.
Rev. Samuel Ford, Roxbury.
Sarah Fulkerson,   do.
Jehiel Freeman, New-Brunswick.
William Forman,   do.
Nathaniel Fitz,   do.
Francis Fort, Somerset.
Richard Field, Jun. do.
Frederick Frelinghuysen, Millstone.
John Frelinghuysen,   do.
Nathaniel Foster, Six Mile Run.
Robert M. Forsyth, Princeton.
William Flagg, Hillsborugh.
Dennis Field, Middlesex.
Mary Ferrell, Monmouth.

G.

Rev. Thomas Grant, Amwell.
Ebenezer Grant,   do.
Peter Gerretsen, New-Brunswick.
John Gulick, South Amboy.
Joachim Griggs, Flemington.
Samuel Griggs,   do.
James Griggs,   do.

H.

John Hill, New-Brunswick.
Luke Hassert,   do.
Lewis Hardenbergh,   do.
Robert Hude,   do.
Jacob R. Hardenbergh, do.
Aaron Hassert,   do.
Aaron Hagaman, Somerset.
Simon Hagaman,   do.
Christopher Hoagland, do.
George Hall,   do.
Henry E. Hall,   do.

SUBSCRIBERS' NAMES.

John Hamilton, Elizabeth-Town.
Albert Hoagland, Nine Mile Run.
John H. Hobart, Princeton.
Benjamin B. Hopkins, do.
James Hamilton, do.
John Hutchins, Middlesex.
Richard Holtom, do.
Harmaunus M. Hoagland, Hillsborough.
John Hatt, do.
Albert Hoagland, do.
Joseph Hedges, Roxbury.
Trustrum Hull, do.
Jared Haines, do.
Elias Howell, do.
Elijah Horton, do.
John N. Hight, Penns-Neck.
Susannah Hight, do.
Everit Hogenkamp, Clarkstown.

I.

Robert Jackson, Princeton.
John Johnson, do.
Adam Jobs, Somerset.
Barent Johnson, Middlesex.
Peter Lott Jaques, do.

L.

Rev. Nicholas Lansing, Orange Town.
Henry Lupp, New-Brunswick.
William Lupp, do.
Ephraim Lorce, do.
Matthew Lane, Bedminster.
Levi Lennex, Essex.
John Lyall, Princeton.
James Lewis, Mendham.
Joseph Lewis, Morristown.
Alexander Low, Monmouth.
Thomas Lowry, Alexandria.

M.

Rev. Walter Monteath, New-Brunswick.
Robert M'Kune, do.
Samuel Munday, Middlesex.
Peter Marselies, Sen. do.
Bartholomew Magrath, New-Brunswick.
George M'Donald, Millstone.

Thomas Macomb, Princeton.
French F. M'Mullen, do.
Aaron Mattison, do.
Phineas Manning, Piscataway.
William Manning, do.
John Miner, Hillsborough.
Cornelius Masilaer, Hunterdon.
Andrew Mershon, Millstone.
Hugh Manyham, Spotswood.

N.

John Neilson, New-Brunswick, 2 Copies.
Garret Nevius, do.
Peter P. Nevius, Middlebush.
David Nevius, do.
Rouliff Nasious, Somerset.

P.

Thomas Paul, New-Brunswick.
John Plum, do.
Peter Probasco, Millstone.
John Perlee, Hillsborough.
John Pool, Jun. Raritan Landing.
John Pittenger, Somerset.
John Pittenger, Jun. Hunterdon.
Jonas Phillips, Morristown.
Francis Peppard, Bernardstown.
John Perine, Monmouth.
Henry Perine, do.
David Pie, Clarkstown.
Daniel Perrine, Middlesex.

Q.

Abraham Quick, Somerset.
Peter Quick, do.
Peter Quick, South Branch.

R.

John Ryckman, New-Brunswick.
Robert Russel, Princeton.
Cornelius Rappleyea, Somerset.
Silas Reeves, Roxbury.
Matthew Rue, Cranberry, 10 Copies.
Israel Richy, Bernardstown.
Jacob Richy, do.
Joseph Roy, do.
John Reading, Flemington.

S.

Rev. Peter Studdiford, Readington.
Moses Scott, New-Brunswick, 6 Copies.
Charles Smith, do.
Gabriel Sylcock, do.
Joseph Sylcock, do.
Abraham Schuyler, do.
Dominicus Stryker, Somerset.
John Christion Stineover, do.
Isaac Slover, do.
John Simonson, Jun. do. 2 copies.
Christopher Stryker, do.
Cornelius Simonson, do.
John Simonson, do.
John Stryker, Middlesex.
Joseph Sparling do.
Jacob Senn, Morris County.
Abraham T. Schenck, Morristown.
Peter I. Stryker, Millstone.
Peter Stryker, Jun. do.
Abraham Stryker, do.
Peter P. Stryker, do.
John Stryker, do.
Garret Schenck, Middlebush.
Cornelius Stoothoff, do.
John Stoothoff, do.
John Spader, do.
David Smally, do.
Benjamin Sulard, do.
Peter Stoothoff, Six mile Run.
Ryke Suydam, do.
Joseph Warren Scott, Princeton.
Thomas Stockton, do.
Samuel Stout, Jun. do.
Peter Suydam, Hillsborough.
Rem Stryker, do.
Bergun Spader, do.
Silas Stilwell, do.
Adam Smith, do.
Jonathan Sharp, Quibble Town.
David Sweezy, Roxbury.
James Skinner, do.
Benjamin Skilman, Griggs Town.
Thomas Skilman, Sourland.

Joseph Stryker, Roxbury.
John Slaback, Penns-Neck.
Peter Schamp, Hunterdon.
Samuel Stout, Hopewell.
Joseph Scudder, Monmouth.
Jasper Smith, Flemington, 10 Copies.
Samuel Stewart, do.

T.

Rensselaer Ten Brook, New-Brunswick.
Peter Thompson, do.
William Ten Brook, do.
Henry Traphagen do.
Jacob Tallman, do.
Andrew Ten Eyck, North-Branch.
Garret Terhune, Middlesex.
Cvrenius Thompson, Millstone.
Willet Taylor, Raritan.
John Ten Eyck, Sen. do.

V.

Rev. John M. Van Harlingen, Millstone.
John Van Doren, do.
Peter Van Doren, do.
Cornelius Van Liew, Somerset.
Frederick Van Liew, do.
Peter Voorhees, do.
Andrew Van Middlesworth, do.
Abraham G. Van Neste, do.
Lowrance Van Derveer, do.
John Ver Meule, do.
Frederick Ver Meule, do.
Abraham Van Pelt, do.
Cornelius Van Compe, do.
Cornelius Ver Meule, Sen. do.
James Voorhees, New-Brunswick.
Nicholas Van Brunt, do.
Richard Van Arsdalen, do.
David Voorhees, do.
Cornelius Vanderbilt, do.
Denice Van Liew, Middlebush.
Garret Voorhees, do.
Jaques Voorhees, do.
Abraham L. Voorhees, do.
Philip I. Van Arsdalen, Bedminster.
Abraham Van Neste, do.

Aaron Van Doren, Bedminster.
James Van Derveer, do.
John Van Middlesworth, Hillsborough.
Isaac Voorhees, do.
Peter Vroom, do.
Garret Voorhees, do.
Peter Vounck, Middlesex.
Albert Voorhees, do.
John Voorhees, Readington.
Peter D. Vroom, Raritan.
John Van Middlesworth, do.
Rynear Veghte, do.
Joseph Van Doren, do. 4 Copies.

W.

Rev. John Woodhull, Monmouth, 2 Copies.
George Spafford Woodhull, do.
Willett Warne, New-Brunswick.
Christian De. Wint do.
John H. Williams do.
Daniel Willis, Elizabeth-Town.
John Williamson, Middlesex.
Daniel Whitehead, do.
John Whitenaght, Millstone.
Joseph Williams, do.
Peter Wyckoff, do.
Isaac Williamson, do.
Matthew Wallace, Princeton.
Thomas Wiggins, do.
John Wyckoff, Middlebush.
John Wortman, Bedminster.
William Wallace, Raritan
Mindert Wilson, Hillsborough.
Cornelius Williamson, do.
Nicholas Williamson, do.
Jacob Wyckoff, Somerset.

www.ingramcontent.com/pod-product-compliance
Lightning Source LLC
Chambersburg PA
CBHW030409230426
43664CB00007BB/805